Grade 7

Differentiated Instruction

Contents

Description of Contents ix

Student Worksheets

Module 1   Adding and Subtracting Integers

Lesson 1-1

Practice and Problem Solving: A/B 1

Practice and Problem Solving: C 2

Practice and Problem Solving: D 3

Reteach 4

Reading Strategies 5

Success for English Learners 6

Lesson 1-2

Practice and Problem Solving: A/B 7

Practice and Problem Solving: C 8

Practice and Problem Solving: D 9

Reteach 10

Reading Strategies 11

Success for English Learners 12

Lesson 1-3

Practice and Problem Solving: A/B 13

Practice and Problem Solving: C 14

Practice and Problem Solving: D 15

Reteach 16

Reading Strategies 17

Success for English Learners 18

Lesson 1-4

Practice and Problem Solving: A/B 19

Practice and Problem Solving: C 20

Practice and Problem Solving: D 21

Reteach 22

Reading Strategies 23

Success for English Learners 24

Module 1 Challenge 25

Module 2   Multiplying and Dividing Integers

Lesson 2-1

Practice and Problem Solving: A/B 26

Practice and Problem Solving: C 27

Practice and Problem Solving: D 28

Reteach 29

Reading Strategies 30

Success for English Learners 31

Lesson 2-2

Practice and Problem Solving: A/B 32

Practice and Problem Solving: C 33

Practice and Problem Solving: D 34

Reteach 35

Reading Strategies 36

Success for English Learners 37

Lesson 2-3

Practice and Problem Solving: A/B 38

Practice and Problem Solving: C 39

Practice and Problem Solving: D 40

Reteach 41

Reading Strategies 42

Success for English Learners 43

Module 2 Challenge 44

Module 3   Rational Numbers

Lesson 3-1

Practice and Problem Solving: A/B 45

Practice and Problem Solving: C 46

Practice and Problem Solving: D 47

Reteach 48

Reading Strategies 49

Success for English Learners 50

Lesson 3-2

Practice and Problem Solving: A/B 51

Practice and Problem Solving: C 52

Practice and Problem Solving: D 53

Reteach...54

Reading Strategies 55

Success for English Learners 56

Lesson 3-3

Practice and Problem Solving: A/B 57

Practice and Problem Solving: C 58

Practice and Problem Solving: D 59

Reteach...60

Reading Strategies 61

Success for English Learners 62

Lesson 3-4

Practice and Problem Solving: A/B 63

Practice and Problem Solving: C 64

Practice and Problem Solving: D 65

Reteach...66

Reading Strategies 67

Success for English Learners 68

Lesson 3-5

Practice and Problem Solving: A/B 69

Practice and Problem Solving: C 70

Practice and Problem Solving: D 71

Reteach...72

Reading Strategies 73

Success for English Learners 74

Lesson 3-6

Practice and Problem Solving: A/B 75

Practice and Problem Solving: C 76

Practice and Problem Solving: D 77

Reteach...78

Reading Strategies 79

Success for English Learners 80

Module 3 Challenge 81

Module 4   Rates and Proportionality

Lesson 4-1

Practice and Problem Solving: A/B.......... 82

Practice and Problem Solving: C............ 83

Practice and Problem Solving: D............ 84

Reteach 85

Reading Strategies 86

Success for English Learners................. 87

Lesson 4-2

Practice and Problem Solving: A/B.......... 88

Practice and Problem Solving: C............ 89

Practice and Problem Solving: D............ 90

Reteach 91

Reading Strategies 92

Success for English Learners................. 93

Lesson 4-3

Practice and Problem Solving: A/B.......... 94

Practice and Problem Solving: C............ 95

Practice and Problem Solving: D............ 96

Reteach 97

Reading Strategies 98

Success for English Learners................. 99

Module 4 Challenge 100

Module 5   Proportions and Percents

Lesson 5-1

Practice and Problem Solving: A/B........ 101

Practice and Problem Solving: C........... 102

Practice and Problem Solving: D.......... 103

Reteach 104

Reading Strategies 105

Success for English Learners............... 106

Lesson 5-2

Practice and Problem Solving: A/B........ 107

Practice and Problem Solving: C........... 108

Practice and Problem Solving: D.......... 109

Reteach 110

Reading Strategies 111

Success for English Learners............... 112

Lesson 5-3

Practice and Problem Solving: A/B 113

Practice and Problem Solving: C 114

Practice and Problem Solving: D 115

Reteach 116

Reading Strategies 117

Success for English Learners 118

Module 5 Challenge 119

Module 6   Expressions and Equations

Lesson 6-1

Practice and Problem Solving: A/B 120

Practice and Problem Solving: C 121

Practice and Problem Solving: D 122

Reteach 123

Reading Strategies 124

Success for English Learners 125

Lesson 6-2

Practice and Problem Solving: A/B 126

Practice and Problem Solving: C 127

Practice and Problem Solving: D 128

Reteach 129

Reading Strategies 130

Success for English Learners 131

Lesson 6-3

Practice and Problem Solving: A/B 132

Practice and Problem Solving: C 133

Practice and Problem Solving: D 134

Reteach 135

Reading Strategies 136

Success for English Learners 137

Lesson 6-4

Practice and Problem Solving: A/B 138

Practice and Problem Solving: C 139

Practice and Problem Solving: D 140

Reteach 141

Reading Strategies 142

Success for English Learners 143

Module 6 Challenge 144

Module 7   Inequalities

Lesson 7-1

Practice and Problem Solving: A/B 145

Practice and Problem Solving: C 146

Practice and Problem Solving: D 147

Reteach 148

Reading Strategies 149

Success for English Learners 150

Lesson 7-2

Practice and Problem Solving: A/B 151

Practice and Problem Solving: C 152

Practice and Problem Solving: D 153

Reteach 154

Reading Strategies 155

Success for English Learners 156

Lesson 7-3

Practice and Problem Solving: A/B 157

Practice and Problem Solving: C 158

Practice and Problem Solving: D 159

Reteach 160

Reading Strategies 161

Success for English Learners 162

Module 7 Challenge 163

Module 8   Modeling Geometric Figures

Lesson 8-1

Practice and Problem Solving: A/B 164

Practice and Problem Solving: C 165

Practice and Problem Solving: D 166

Reteach 167

Reading Strategies 168

Success for English Learners 169

Lesson 8-2

Practice and Problem Solving: A/B 170

Practice and Problem Solving: C 171

Practice and Problem Solving: D 172

Reteach 173

Reading Strategies 174

Success for English Learners 175

Lesson 8-3

Practice and Problem Solving: A/B 176
Practice and Problem Solving: C 177
Practice and Problem Solving: D 178
Reteach 179
Reading Strategies 180
Success for English Learners 181

Lesson 8-4

Practice and Problem Solving: A/B 182
Practice and Problem Solving: C 183
Practice and Problem Solving: D 184
Reteach 185
Reading Strategies 186
Success for English Learners 187

Module 8 Challenge 188

Module 9   Circumference, Area, and Volume

Lesson 9-1

Practice and Problem Solving: A/B 189
Practice and Problem Solving: C 190
Practice and Problem Solving: D 191
Reteach 192
Reading Strategies 193
Success for English Learners 194

Lesson 9-2

Practice and Problem Solving: A/B 195
Practice and Problem Solving: C 196
Practice and Problem Solving: D 197
Reteach 198
Reading Strategies 199
Success for English Learners 200

Lesson 9-3

Practice and Problem Solving: A/B 201
Practice and Problem Solving: C 202
Practice and Problem Solving: D 203
Reteach 204
Reading Strategies 205
Success for English Learners 206

Lesson 9-4

Practice and Problem Solving: A/B 207
Practice and Problem Solving: C 208
Practice and Problem Solving: D 209
Reteach 210
Reading Strategies 211
Success for English Learners 212

Lesson 9-5

Practice and Problem Solving: A/B 213
Practice and Problem Solving: C 214
Practice and Problem Solving: D 215
Reteach 216
Reading Strategies 217
Success for English Learners 218

Module 9 Challenge 219

Module 10   Random Samples and Populations

Lesson 10-1

Practice and Problem Solving: A/B 220
Practice and Problem Solving: C 221
Practice and Problem Solving: D 222
Reteach 223
Reading Strategies 224
Success for English Learners 225

Lesson 10-2

Practice and Problem Solving: A/B 226
Practice and Problem Solving: C 227
Practice and Problem Solving: D 228
Reteach 229
Reading Strategies 230
Success for English Learners 231

Lesson 10-3

Practice and Problem Solving: A/B 232
Practice and Problem Solving: C 233
Practice and Problem Solving: D 234
Reteach 235
Reading Strategies 236
Success for English Learners 237

Module 10 Challenge 238

Module 11 Analyzing and Comparing Data

Lesson 11-1
Practice and Problem Solving: A/B 239
Practice and Problem Solving: C 240
Practice and Problem Solving: D 241
Reteach..242
Reading Strategies 243
Success for English Learners 244

Lesson 11-2
Practice and Problem Solving: A/B 245
Practice and Problem Solving: C 246
Practice and Problem Solving: D 247
Reteach..248
Reading Strategies 249
Success for English Learners 250

Lesson 11-3
Practice and Problem Solving: A/B 251
Practice and Problem Solving: C 252
Practice and Problem Solving: D 253
Reteach..254
Reading Strategies 255
Success for English Learners 256

Module 11 Challenge 257

Module 12 Experimental Probability

Lesson 12-1
Practice and Problem Solving: A/B 258
Practice and Problem Solving: C 259
Practice and Problem Solving: D 260
Reteach..261
Reading Strategies 262
Success for English Learners 263

Lesson 12-2
Practice and Problem Solving: A/B 264
Practice and Problem Solving: C 265
Practice and Problem Solving: D 266
Reteach..267
Reading Strategies 268
Success for English Learners 269

Lesson 12-3
Practice and Problem Solving: A/B 270
Practice and Problem Solving: C 271
Practice and Problem Solving: D 272
Reteach 273
Reading Strategies 274
Success for English Learners 275

Lesson 12-4
Practice and Problem Solving: A/B 276
Practice and Problem Solving: C 277
Practice and Problem Solving: D 278
Reteach 279
Reading Strategies 280
Success for English Learners 281

Module 12 Challenge 282

Module 13 Theoretical Probability and Simulations

Lesson 13-1
Practice and Problem Solving: A/B 283
Practice and Problem Solving: C 284
Practice and Problem Solving: D 285
Reteach 286
Reading Strategies 287
Success for English Learners 288

Lesson 13-2
Practice and Problem Solving: A/B 289
Practice and Problem Solving: C 290
Practice and Problem Solving: D 291
Reteach 292
Reading Strategies 293
Success for English Learners 294

Lesson 13-3
Practice and Problem Solving: A/B 295
Practice and Problem Solving: C 296
Practice and Problem Solving: D 297
Reteach 298
Reading Strategies 299
Success for English Learners 300

Lesson 13-4

Practice and Problem Solving: A/B 301

Practice and Problem Solving: C 302

Practice and Problem Solving: D 303

Reteach 304

Reading Strategies 305

Success for English Learners 306

Module 13 Challenge 307

Answers

Module 1 308

Module 2 313

Module 3 316

Module 4 326

Module 5 329

Module 6 334

Module 7 338

Module 8 342

Module 9 345

Module 10 351

Module 11 355

Module 12 358

Module 13 362

Description of Contents

Using the Differentiated Instruction Worksheets	Integrating Language Arts
Practice and Problem Solving: A/B, C, D There are three worksheets for every lesson. All of these reinforce and practice the content of the lesson. Level A/B (slightly below/on level students) Level C (above level students) Level D (considerably below level students who require modified worksheets)	The *Differentiated Instruction* worksheets help students become successful learners by integrating the literacy grade-level expectations. The worksheets provide opportunities for students to: • demonstrate independence as they become self-directed learners. • show their mastery of content through writing. • justify and defend their reasoning by using relevant evidence. • view critically and constructively the reasoning of others. • use technology appropriately.
Reteach (one worksheet per lesson) Provides an alternate way to teach or review the main concepts of the lesson, and for students to have further practice at a basic level.	**LACC.68.RST.1.3** Follow precisely a multistep procedure…
Reading Strategies (one worksheet per lesson) Provides tools to help students master the math vocabulary or symbols, and comprehend word problems.	**LACC.68.RST.2.4** Determine the meaning of symbols, key terms… **LACC.68.RST.3.7** Integrate quantitative or technical information…
Success for English Learners (one worksheet per lesson) Provides teaching strategies for differentiated instruction and alternate practice. The worksheets use a visual approach with fewer words, making them ideal for English language learners as well as other students who are having difficulties with the lesson concepts.	**LACC.68.WHST.1.1** Write arguments focused on discipline-specific content…
Challenge (one worksheet per module) Provides extra non-routine problem solving opportunities, enhances critical thinking skills, and requires students to apply the math process skills.	**LACC.68.WHST.2.4** Produce clear and coherent writing…

Adding Integers with the Same Sign

Practice and Problem Solving: A/B

Find each sum. White counters are positive. Black counters are negative.

1. −5 + (−3)

   ● ● ● ● ●
   ● ● ●

   a. How many counters are there? _____

   b. Do the counters represent positive

      or negative integers? _____

   c. −5 + (−3) = _____

2. −4 + (−7)

   ● ● ● ●
   ● ● ● ● ● ● ●

   a. How many counters are there? _____

   b. Do the counters represent positive

      or negative integers? _____

   c. −4 + (−7) = _____

Model each addition problem on the number line to find each sum.

3. −4 + (−2) = _____

   ←+—+—+—+—+—+—+—+—+→
   −8 −7 −6 −5 −4 −3 −2 −1 0

4. −5 + (−5) = _____

   ←+—+—+—+—+—+—+—+—+→
   −20   −16   −12   −8   −4

5. −3 + (−6) = _____

   ←+—+—+—+—+—+—+—+—+→
   −11 −10 −9 −8 −7 −6 −5 −4 −3

6. −7 + (−5) = _____

   ←+—+—+—+—+—+—+—+—+—+→
   −13 −12 −11 −10 −9 −8 −7 −6 −5

Find each sum.

7. −7 + (−1) = _____

8. −5 + (−4) = _____

9. −36 + (−17) = _____

10. −51 + (−42) = _____

11. 98 + 126 = _____

12. −20 + (−75) = _____

13. −350 + (−250) = _____

14. −110 + (−1200) = _____

Solve.

15. A construction crew is digging a hole. On the first day, they dug a hole
    3 feet deep. On the second day, they dug 2 more feet. On the third day,
    they dug 4 more feet. Write a sum of negative numbers to represent
    this situation. Find the total sum and explain how it is related to the problem.

_____

LESSON
1-1

Adding Integers with the Same Sign
Practice and Problem Solving: C

Solve.

1. A grocery sells green apples and red apples. On Monday, the store put 500 of each kind of apple on display. That day, the store sold 42 red apples and 57 green apples. On Tuesday, the store sold 87 red apples and 75 green apples. On Wednesday, the store sold 29 red apples and 38 green apples.

   a. Write an addition expression using negative integers to show the number of red apples the store sold.

   _____

   b. Write an addition expression using negative integers to show the number of green apples the store sold.

   _____

   c. Did the store have more red apples or green apples left over? Explain.

   _____

   _____

2. A hotel has 18 floors. The hotel owner believes the number 13 is unlucky. The first 12 floors are numbered from 1 to 12. Floor 13 is numbered 14, and the remaining floors are numbered from 15 to 19. The hotel manager starts on the top floor of the apartment building. He rides the elevator two floors down. The doors open and a hotel guest gets in. They ride the elevator three floors down. The hotel guest gets off the elevator. The hotel manager rides the elevator the remaining floors down to the first floor.

   a. Write an addition expression using negative integers to show the number of floors the hotel manager rode down in the elevator.

   _____

   b. On what floor did the hotel guest get off the elevator? Explain.

   _____

   _____

LESSON 1-1 Adding Integers with the Same Sign
Practice and Problem Solving: D

Find each sum. White counters are positive. Black counters are negative. The first one is done for you.

1. 5 + 2 =

   a. How many counters are there? __7__

   b. Do the counters represent positive

   or negative numbers? __positive__

   c. 5 + 2 = ____+7____

2. −4 + (−6) =

   a. How many counters are there? _____

   b. Do the counters represent positive

   or negative numbers? _____

   c. −4 + (−6) = _____

Model each addition problem on the number line to find each sum. The first one is done for you.

3. −3 + (−2) = __−5__

   −7 −6 −5 −4 −3 −2 −1

4. −5 + (−1) = _____

   −7 −6 −5 −4 −3 −2 −1

5. −4 + (−3) = _____

   −7 −6 −5 −4 −3 −2 −1

6. −1 + (−6) = _____

   −7 −6 −5 −4 −3 −2 −1

Find each sum. The first one is done for you.

7. −3 + (−1) = __−4__

8. −6 + (−2) = _____

9. −12 + (−7) = _____

10. −20 + (−15) = _____

Solve.

11. The table shows how much money Hannah withdrew in 3 days.

Day	Day 1	Day 2	Day 3
Dollars	−5	−1	−2

Find the total amount Hannah withdrew. _____

LESSON 1-1

Adding Integers with the Same Sign
Reteach

How do you add integers with the same sign?

Add $4 + 5$.

Step 1 Check the signs. Are the integers both positive or negative?

4 and 5 are both positive.

Step 2 Add the integers.

$4 + 5 = 9$

Step 3 Write the sum as a positive number.

$4 + 5 = 9$

Add $-3 + (-4)$.

Step 1 Check the signs. Are the integers both positive or negative?

-3 and -4 are both negative.

Step 2 Ignore the negative signs for now. Add the integers.

$3 + 4 = 7$

Step 3 Write the sum as a negative number.

$-3 + (-4) = -7$

Find each sum.

1. $3 + 6$

   a. Are the integers both positive or negative? _____

   b. Add the integers. _____

   c. Write the sum. $3 + 6 =$ _____

2. $-7 + (-1)$

   a. Are the integers both positive or negative? _____

   b. Add the integers. _____

   c. Write the sum. $-7 + (-1) =$ _____

3. $-5 + (-2)$

   a. Are the integers both positive or negative? _____

   b. Add the integers. _____

   c. Write the sum. $-5 + (-2) =$ _____

4. $6 + 4$

   a. Are the integers both positive or negative? _____

   b. Add the integers. _____

   c. Write the sum. $6 + 4 =$ _____

Find each sum.

5. $-10 + (-3) =$ _____

6. $-4 + (-12) =$ _____

7. $22 + 15 =$ _____

8. $-10 + (-31) =$ _____

9. $-18 + (-6) =$ _____

10. $35 + 17 =$ _____

LESSON 1-1

Adding Integers with the Same Sign

Reading Strategies: Use a Model

Sarah withdraws the following amounts from her bank account in 4 days.

Day	1	2	3	4
Withdrawal	−3	−5	−4	−1

Write a sum of negative integers to represent this situation.
Find the sum and explain how it is related to the problem.

You can use counters to model this problem.

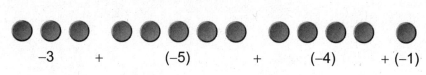

KEY
◯ = 1
⬤ = −1

−3   +   (−5)   +   (−4)   + (−1)

To represent this situation, write: −3 + (−5) + (−4) + (−1)

The total number of counters is 13.

Since the counters are negative, the sum is −13.

Over the four days, Sarah withdrew a total of $13 from her bank account.

Answer each question.

1. What does each counter represent?

   _____

2. How do the counters help you represent the information in the table?

   _____

   _____

3. How do the counters help you find the sum?

   _____

   _____

4. Write an equation to show the total amount Sarah withdrew from her bank account.

   _____

Name _____ Date _____ Class_____

 LESSON 1-1

Adding Integers with the Same Sign
Success for English Learners

Problem 1

7 + 5

Use counters.

KEY
○ = 1
● = −1

7 + 5 = 12

Problem 2

−5 + (−4)

Use a number line.

Start at − 5.

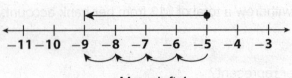

Move left 4.

1. What kind of counters are used in Problem 1, positive or negative?

_____

2. Why do you move left in Problem 2?

_____

3. Write a word problem about adding integers with the same sign.

_____

_____

LESSON 1-2

Adding Integers with Different Signs

Practice and Problem Solving: A/B

Show the addition on the number line. Find the sum.

1. 2 + (−3) _____

2. −3 + 4 _____

Find each sum.

3. − 4 + 9	4. 7 + (−8)	5. −2 + 1	6. 6 + (−9)
_____	_____	_____	_____
7. 5 + (−7)	8. 9 + (−5)	9. (−1) + 9	10. 9 + (−7)
_____	_____	_____	_____
11. 50 + (−7)	12. 27 + (−6)	13. 1 + (−30)	14. 15 + (−25)
_____	_____	_____	_____

Solve.

15. The temperature outside dropped 13°F in 7 hours. The final temperature was −2°F. What was the starting temperature?

_____

16. A football team gains 8 yards in one play, then loses 5 yards in the next. What is the team's total yardage for the two plays?

_____

17. Matt is playing a game. He gains 7 points, loses 10 points, gains 2 points, and then loses 8 points. What is his final score?

_____

18. A stock gained 2 points on Monday, lost 5 points on Tuesday, lost 1 point on Wednesday, gained 4 points on Thursday, and lost 6 points on Friday.

    a. Was the net change for the week positive or negative? _____

    b. How much was the gain or loss? _____

LESSON 1-2	**Adding Integers with Different Signs**

Practice and Problem Solving: C

Tell whether each sum will be positive or negative. Then find each sum.

1. $-3 + (-7)$ 2. $14 + (-9)$ 3. $-12 + 5$ 4. $-3 + 8$

_____   _____   _____   _____

5. $11 + (-5)$ 6. $7 + 8$ 7. $-8 + 7$ 8. $-2 + 3$

_____   _____   _____   _____

9. If two integers have the same sign, what is the sign of their sum?

_____

10. When adding two integers with different signs, how do you find the sign?

_____

Evaluate $a + b$ for the given values.

11. $a = 9, b = -24$ 12. $a = -17, b = -7$ 13. $a = 32, b = -19$

_____   _____   _____

14. $a = -15, b = -15$ 15. $a = -20, b = 20$ 16. $a = -30, b = 12$

_____   _____   _____

Solve.

17. The high temperature for the day dropped 7°F between Monday and Tuesday, rose 9°F on Wednesday, dropped 2°F on Thursday, and dropped 5°F on Friday. What was the total change in the daily high temperature from Monday to Friday?

_____

18. Karen deposited $25 in the bank on Monday, $50 on Wednesday and $15 on Friday. On Saturday, she took out $40. Karen's original balance was $100. What is her balance now?

_____

19. Lance and Rita were tied in a game. Then Lance got these scores: 19, −7, 3, −11, 5. Rita got these scores: 25, −9, 5, −9, 8. Who had the higher score? How much higher was that higher score?

_____

LESSON
1-2

Adding Integers with Different Signs

Practice and Problem Solving: D

Show the addition on the number line. Then write the sum. The first one is done for you.

1. $2 + (-3)$

2. $-3 + (-4)$

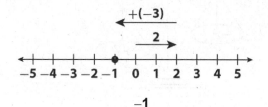

$-5\ -4\ -3\ -2\ -1\ \ 0\ \ 1\ \ 2\ \ 3\ \ 4\ \ 5$

_____ -1 _____

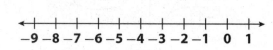

$-9\ -8\ -7\ -6\ -5\ -4\ -3\ -2\ -1\ \ 0\ \ 1$

_____

Find each sum. The first one is done for you.

3. $4 + (-9)$

_____ -5 _____

4. $7 + (-8)$

_____

5. $-2 + 1$

_____

6. $5 + 7$

_____

7. $9 + (-5)$

_____

8. $-1 + 9$

_____

9. $2 + (-7)$

_____

10. $-6 + (-4)$

_____

11. $-15 + 9$

_____

Solve. The first one is done for you.

12. The temperature dropped 12°F in 8 hours. If the final temperature was
    −7°F, what was the starting temperature?

    ____ 5°F _____

13. At 3 P.M., the temperature was 9°F. By 11 P.M., it had dropped 31°F.
    What was the temperature at 11 P.M.?

    _____

14. A submarine submerged at a depth of −40 feet dives 57 feet more.
    What is the new depth of the submarine?

    _____

15. An airplane cruising at 20,000 feet drops 2,500 feet in altitude. What is
    the airplane's new altitude?

    _____

LESSON 1-2

Adding Integers with Different Signs
Reteach

This balance scale "weighs" positive and negative numbers. Negative numbers go on the left of the balance, and positive numbers go on the right.

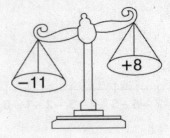

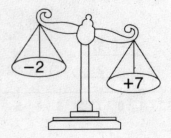

Find −11 + 8.
The scale will tip to the left side because the sum of −11 and +8 is negative.
−11 + 8 = −3

Find −2 + 7.
The scale will tip to the right side because the sum of −2 and +7 is positive.
−2 + 7 = 5

Find 3 + (−9).

1. Should you add or subtract 3 and 9? Why?

   _____

2. Is the sum positive or negative? _____

   3 + (−9) = −6

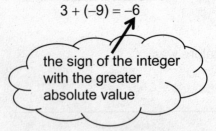

the sign of the integer with the greater absolute value

Find the sum.

3. 7 + (−3) = _____

4. −2 + (−3) = _____

5. −5 + 4 = _____

6. −3 + (−1) = _____

7. −7 + 9 = _____

8. 4 + (−9) = _____

9. 16 + (−7) = _____

10. −21 + 11 = _____

11. −12 + (−4) = _____

12. When adding 3 and −9, how do you know that the sum is negative?

    _____

LESSON 1-2

Adding Integers with Different Signs

Reading Strategies: Use Graphic Aids

Randy's football team had the ball on its own zero yard line. On their first play they gained 6 yards. On the second play they lost 4 yards. On what yard line is the ball now?

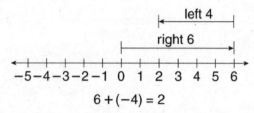

$$6 + (-4) = 2$$

Use the number line to help you answer the questions.

1. On which number do you begin? _____

2. In which direction do you move first? How many places do you move?

   _____

3. In which direction do you move next? How many places do you move?

   _____

4. At which number do you end up? _____

The temperature was zero degrees. Two hours later, the temperature went down 5 degrees. Then, the temperature went down another 3 degrees. What was the final temperature?

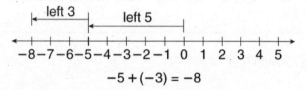

$$-5 + (-3) = -8$$

Use the number line to help you answer the questions.

5. On which number do you begin? _____

6. In which direction do you move first? How many spaces?

   _____

7. In which direction do you move next? How many spaces?

   _____

8. At which number do you end up? _____

Adding Integers with Different Signs

LESSON 1-2

Success for English Learners

Problem 1

$6 + (-5)$

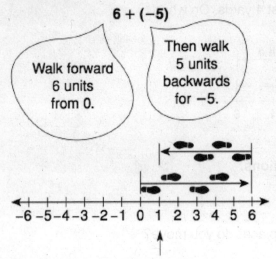

Walk forward 6 units from 0.

Then walk 5 units backwards for −5.

You stop at 1. This is the sum.

Problem 2

$-7 + (4)$

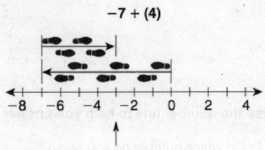

You stop at −3. This is the sum.

1. The sum of $x + y$ is to the left of x on a number line. Is y a positive number or a negative number?

   _____

2. Based on Problems 1 and 2, does the addition of integers always mean the sum is positive? Explain.

   _____

   _____

3. Is the sum of $3 + (-9)$ positive or negative?

   _____

4. Is the sum of $13 + (-11)$ positive or negative?

   _____

LESSON
1-3

Subtracting Integers
Practice and Problem Solving: A/B

Show the subtraction on the number line. Find the difference.

1. $-2 - 3$

$$-6\ -5\ -4\ -3\ -2\ -1\ \ 0\ \ 1\ \ 2$$

_____

2. $5 - (-1)$

$$-1\ \ 0\ \ 1\ \ 2\ \ 3\ \ 4\ \ 5\ \ 6\ \ 7$$

_____

Find the difference.

3. $-6 - 4$

_____

4. $-7 - (-12)$

_____

5. $12 - 16$

_____

6. $5 - (-19)$

_____

7. $-18 - (-18)$

_____

8. $23 - (-23)$

_____

9. $-10 - (-9)$

_____

10. $29 - (-13)$

_____

11. $9 - 15$

_____

12. $-12 - 14$

_____

13. $22 - (-8)$

_____

14. $-16 - (-11)$

_____

Solve.

15. Monday's high temperature was 6°C. The low temperature was –3°C. What was the difference between the high and low temperatures?

_____

16. The temperature in Minneapolis changed from –7°F at 6 A.M. to 7°F at noon. How much did the temperature increase?

_____

17. Friday's high temperature was –1°C. The low temperature was –5°C. What was the difference between the high and low temperatures?

_____

18. The temperature changed from 5°C at 6 P.M. to –2°C at midnight. How much did the temperature decrease?

_____

19. The daytime high temperature on the moon can reach 130°C. The nighttime low temperature can get as low as –110°C. What is the difference between the high and low temperature?

_____

LESSON
1-3

Subtracting Integers

Practice and Problem Solving: C

For each set of values find *x* – *y*. Answer the questions that follow.

1. *x* = 14, *y* = –2

2. *x* = –11, *y* = 11

3. *x* = –8, *y* = –15

_____

_____

_____

4. *x* = –9, *y* = –9

5. *x* = 9, *y* = –20

6. *x* = 0, *y* = –9

_____

_____

_____

7. *x* = 9, *y* = 11

8. *x* = –1, *y* = –1

9. *x* = –5, *y* = 5

_____

_____

_____

10. If *x* and *y* are both positive, when is *x* – *y* negative? _____

11. If *x* and *y* are both negative, when is *x* – *y* positive? _____

Solve.

12. The temperature changed from 7°F at 6 P.M. to –5°F at midnight. What was the difference between the high and low temperatures? What was the average change in temperature per hour?

_____

13. The lowest point in the Pacific Ocean is about –11,000 meters. The lowest point in the Atlantic Ocean is about –8,600 meters. Which ocean has the lower point? How much lower?

_____

14. At 11,560 feet above sea level, Climax, Colorado, is the highest town in the United States. The lowest town is Calipatria, California, at 185 feet below sea level. Express both of these distances as integers and tell which is closer to sea level. How much closer to sea level is the town that is closer?

_____

Use the table for 15–16.

Temperatures at a Ski Resort

Day	High	Low
Saturday	8°F	–3°F
Sunday	6°F	–2°F

15. On which day was the difference in temperature greater? _____

16. How much greater was the difference one day than the other? _____

LESSON 1-3

Subtracting Integers

Practice and Problem Solving: D

Show the subtraction on the number line. Then write the difference. The first one is done for you.

1. 3 – 8

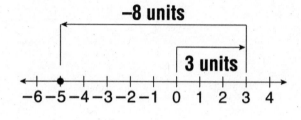

–8 units

3 units

–6 –5 –4 –3 –2 –1 0 1 2 3 4

_____**–5**_____

2. –5 – (–1)

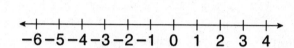

–6 –5 –4 –3 –2 –1 0 1 2 3 4

_____

Find each difference. The first one is done for you.

3. –3 – 4	4. –7 – (–2)	5. 12 – 6
_____**–7**_____	_____	_____
6. –8 – 8	7. –5 – (–5)	8. –1 – (–2)
_____	_____	_____
9. 8 – 1	10. 7 – (–9)	11. –3 – 8
_____	_____	_____

Solve. The first one is done for you.

12. The daytime temperature on the planet Mercury can reach 430°C. The nighttime temperature can drop to –180°C. What is the difference between these temperatures?

_____**610°C**_____

13. An ice cream company made a profit of $24,000 in 2011. The same company had a loss of $11,000 in 2012. What is the difference between the company's financial results for 2011 and 2012?

_____

14. The high temperature on Saturday day was 6°F. The low temperature was –3°F. What was the difference between the high and low temperatures for the day?

_____

**LESSON
1-3**

Subtracting Integers
Reteach

The total value of the three cards shown is –6.

$$3 + (-4) + (-5) = -6$$

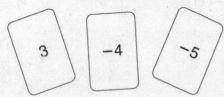

What if you take away the 3 card?

Cards –4 and –5 are left. The new value is –9.

$$-6 + -(3) = -9$$

What if you take away the –4 card?

Cards 3 and –5 are left. The new value is –2.

$$-6 - (-4) = -2$$

Answer each question.

1. Suppose you have the cards shown.
   The total value of the cards is 12.

   a. What if you take away the 7 card? $12 - 7 =$ _____

   b. What if you take away the 13 card? $12 - 13 =$ _____

   c. What if you take away the –8 card? $12 - (-8) =$ _____

2. Subtract. $-4 - (-2)$.

   a. $-4 < -2$. Will the answer be positive or negative? _____

   b. $|4| - |2| =$ _____

   c. $-4 - (-2) =$ _____

Find the difference.

3. $31 - (-9) =$ _____   4. $15 - 18 =$ _____   5. $-9 - 17 =$ _____

6. $-8 - (-8) =$ _____   7. $29 - (-2) =$ _____   8. $13 - 18 =$ _____

LESSON
1-3
Subtracting Integers
Reading Strategies: Use Graphic Aids

Brett borrowed $7 from his father to buy a cap. He paid back $3.
How much money does Brett have now?

A number line can help you picture this situation.

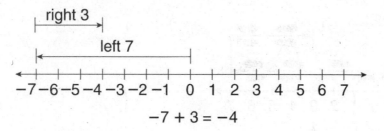

$$-7 + 3 = -4$$

1. Beginning at 0, in which direction will you move first? _____

2. How many places? _____

3. In which direction do you move next? _____

4. How many places? _____

5. On what number do you end? _____

Brett does not have any more money. He owes his dad $4. He has negative $4.

Sally and her friends made up a game with points. You can either win or lose up to ten points on each round of the game. After the first round, Sally's team had 2 points. In the second round, they lost 6 points. By how many points was Sally's team down after the second round?

The number line will help you picture the problem.

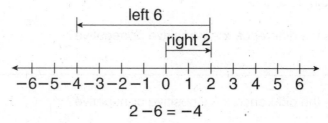

$$2 - 6 = -4$$

6. Beginning at 0, in which direction will you move first? How many places?

_____

7. Which direction will you move next? How many places?

_____

8. On what number do you end? _____

LESSON 1-3

Subtracting Integers

Success for English Learners

Problem 1

What is the difference?

$$7 - 4$$

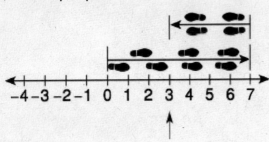

You stop at 3. This is the difference.

Problem 2

What is the difference?

$$-8 - (-2)$$

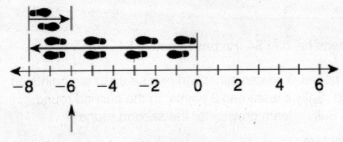

You stop at –6. This is the difference.

1. If $x > 0$ and $x > y$, is the difference $x - y$ positive or negative?

_____

2. If $x > 0$ and $y > x$, is the difference $x - y$ positive or negative?

_____

LESSON 1-4 Applying Addition and Subtraction of Integers
Practice and Problem Solving: A/B

Write an expression to represent the situation. Then solve by finding the value of the expression.

1. Owen is fishing from a dock. He starts with the bait 2 feet below the surface of the water. He reels out the bait 19 feet, then reels it back in 7 feet. What is the final position of the bait relative to the surface of the water?

   _____

2. Rita earned 45 points on a test. She lost 8 points, earned 53 points, then lost 6 more points. What is Rita's final score on the test?

   _____

Find the value of each expression.

3. $-7 + 12 + 15$

4. $-5 - 9 - 13$

5. $40 - 33 + 11$

6. $57 + 63 - 10$

7. $-21 - 17 + 25 + 65$

8. $12 + 19 + 5 - 2$

Compare the expressions. Write <, > or =.

9. $-15 + 3 - 7$ ◯ $-9 - 1 + 16$

10. $31 - 4 + 6$ ◯ $-17 + 22 - 5$

Solve.

11. Anna and Maya are competing in a dance tournament where dance moves are worth a certain number of points. If a dance move is done correctly, the dancer earns points. If a dance move is done incorrectly, the dancer loses points. Anna currently has 225 points.

    a. Before her dance routine ends, Anna earns 75 points and loses 30 points. Write and solve an expression to find Anna's final score.

    _____

    b. Maya's final score is 298. Which dancer has the greater final score?

    _____

Applying Addition and Subtraction of Integers

LESSON 1-4

Practice and Problem Solving: C

Write an expression to represent the situation. Then solve by finding the value of the expression.

1. Jana is doing an experiment. She is on a dock that is 10 feet above the surface of the water. Jana drops the weighted end of a fishing line 35 feet below the surface of the water. She reels out the line 29 feet, and then reels it back in 7 feet. What is the final distance between Jana and the end of the fishing line?

   _____

2. Kirsten and Gigi are riding in hot air balloons. They start 500 feet above the ground. Kirsten's balloon rises 225 feet, falls 105 feet, and then rises 445 feet. Every time Kirsten's balloon travels up or down, Gigi's balloon travels 15 feet farther in the same direction. Then both balloons stop moving so a photographer on the ground can take a picture.

   a. Find Kirsten's final position relative to the ground.

   _____

   b. Is Kirsten or Gigi closer to the ground when the photographer takes the picture?

   _____

3. In a ring-toss game, players get points for the number of rings they can toss and land on a colored stake. They earn 20 points for landing on a red stake and 30 points for landing on a blue stake. They lose 10 points each time they miss. The table shows the number of rings tossed by David and Jon during the game.

   a. Write and evaluate an expression that represents David's total score.

Player	Red	Blue	Miss
David	2	3	3
Jon	3	2	2

   b. Who scored more points during the game?

   _____

LESSON 1-4 Applying Addition and Subtraction of Integers
Practice and Problem Solving: D

Write an expression to represent the situation. Then solve by finding the value of the expression. The first one is done for you.

1. Jeremy is fishing from a dock. He starts with the bait 2 feet below the surface of the water. He lowers the bait 9 feet, then raises it 3 feet. What is the final position of the bait relative to the surface of the water?

   $-2 - 9 + 3 = -8$; 8 feet below the surface of the water

2. Rita earned 20 points on a quiz. She lost 5 points for poor penmanship, then earned 10 points of extra credit. What is Rita's final score on the quiz?

   _____

Find the value of each expression. The first one is done for you.

3. $-7 + 1 + 5$

   _____-1_____

4. $-5 - 9 - 10$

   _____

5. $40 - 30 + 10$

   _____

6. $2 + 8 - 19$

   _____

7. $-12 + 14 + 6$

   _____

8. $50 + 60 - 10$

   _____

Compare the expressions. Write <, >, or =.

9. $-20 + 5 - 10$ $\bigcirc$ $-10 - 11 + 30$

10. $-10 + 40 - 5$ $\bigcirc$ $25 - 15 + 3$

Solve.

11. Angela is competing in a dance competition. If a dance move is done correctly, the dancer earns points. If a dance move is done incorrectly, the dancer loses points. Angela currently has 200 points. Angela then loses 30 points and earns 70 points. Write and evaluate an expression to find Angela's final score.

    _____

LESSON 1-4

Applying Addition and Subtraction of Integers
Reteach

How do you find the value of expressions involving addition and subtraction of integers?

Find the value of $17 - 40 + 5$.

$(17 + 5) - 40$	Regroup the integers with the same sign.
$22 - 40$	Add inside the parentheses.
$22 - 40 = -18$	Subtract.

So, $17 - 40 + 5 = -18$.

Find the value of each expression.

1. $10 - 19 + 5$

    a. Regroup the integers.

    _____

    b. Add and subtract.

    _____

    c. Write the sum. $10 - 19 + 5 =$ _____

2. $-15 + 14 - 3$

    a. Regroup the integers.

    _____

    b. Add and subtract.

    _____

    c. Write the sum. $-15 + 14 - 3 =$ _____

3. $-80 + 10 - 6$

    a. Regroup the integers.

    _____

    b. Add and subtract.

    _____

    c. Write the sum. $-80 + 10 - 6 =$ _____

4. $7 - 21 + 13$

    a. Regroup the integers.

    _____

    b. Add and subtract.

    _____

    c. Write the sum. $7 - 21 + 13 =$ _____

5. $-5 + 13 - 6 + 2$

    a. Regroup the integers.

    _____

    b. Add and subtract.

    _____

    c. Write the sum. $-5 + 13 - 6 + 2 =$ ___

6. $18 - 4 + 6 - 30$

    a. Regroup the integers.

    _____

    b. Add and subtract.

    _____

    c. Write the sum. $18 - 4 + 6 - 30 =$ ___

Name _____ Date _____ Class _____

 LESSON 1-4

Applying Addition and Subtraction of Integers
Reading Strategies: Analyze Information

Read the problem below.

> Angelo is riding in a hot air balloon. The balloon begins at 700 feet above the ground. It drops 200 feet, rises 500 feet, and then drops 100 feet. Write and evaluate an expression to find Angelo's position relative to the ground.

To solve this problem, look at the meanings of words to help you:

- decide what integer starts the expression.
- decide when to add.
- decide when to subtract.

Answer each question.

1. What integer starts the expression? What word tells you if it is positive or negative?

   _____

2. When do you add? What word tells you when to add?

   _____

3. When do you subtract? What word tells you when to subtract?

   _____

4. Write and find the value of the expression to solve the problem.

   _____

5. Where is Angelo's hot air balloon in relation to the ground?

   _____

6. Is Angelo higher or lower than where he started? Explain.

   _____

   _____

   _____

Applying Addition and Subtraction of Integers

LESSON 1-4

Success for English Learners

Problem

Casey starts with $180 in her bank account. She withdraws $90, and then she deposits $50. Mitchell starts with $120 in his bank account. He deposits $75, and then he withdraws $45. Who has more money in the bank at the end?

Draw a diagram and evaluate.

Casey

STARTS	WITHDRAWS	DEPOSITS	
$180	−$90	+$50	= $140

Mitchell

STARTS	DEPOSITS	WITHDRAWS	
$120	+$75	−$45	= $150

Now, compare.

Casey		**Mitchell**
$140	<	$150

At the end, Mitchell has more money in his account.

1. Why do you subtract when money is withdrawn?

   _____

2. Why do you add when money is deposited?

   _____

3. Write a word problem adding and subtracting integers. Solve.

   _____

   _____

   _____

Adding and Subtracting Integers
Challenge

Maria wants to compare the difficulty of different bicycle paths in her town. She recorded the elevation of the trail at each mile marker. She also calculated the difference in the elevation at each mile marker with the elevation at the previous mile marker. The difficulty score she assigned to each trail is the sum of these differences.

Trail	Elevation (ft)					
	Start	Mile 1	Mile 2	Mile 3	Mile 4	Mile 5
Easy Rider	1	–2	10	–1	120	–5
Breakneck	–2	100	–2	150	–8	250
Lake Shore	–10	0	6	55	–1	60
Mountain View	40	–2	120	35	200	180

For example, to find the difficulty of the Easy Rider trail, Maria first calculated the differences in elevation at each mile marker.

	Mile 1	Mile 2	Mile 3	Mile 4	Mile 5
Difference in Elevation	–2 – 1 = –3	10 – (–2) = 12	–1 – 10 = –11	120 – (–1) =121	–5 – 120 = –125

The difficulty score of the Easy Rider is the sum of these differences.

$$-3 + 12 + (-11) + 121 + (-125) = -6$$

1. Which trail has the highest difficulty rating? Show your work in a table.

_____

Solve.

2. –3 ☐ 5 ☐ –4 ☐ –10 ☐ 18

   Each of the boxes in the expression above can be filled with + or – .

   What is the greatest possible value of the expression? Explain.

_____

LESSON 2-1

Multiplying Integers
Practice and Problem Solving: A/B

Find each product.

1. 4(−20)

_____

2. −6(12)

_____

3. (−8)(−5)

_____

4. (13)(−3)

_____

5. (−10)(0)

_____

6. (−5)(16)

_____

7. (−9)(−21)

_____

8. 11(−1)

_____

9. 18(−4)

_____

10. 10(8)

_____

11. 9(−6)

_____

12. −7(−7)

_____

Write a mathematical expression to represent each situation. Then find the value of the expression to solve the problem.

13. You play a game where you score −6 points on the first turn and on each of the next 3 turns. What is your score after those 4 turns?

_____

14. The outdoor temperature declines 3 degrees each hour for 5 hours. What is the change in temperature at the end of those 5 hours?

_____

15. You have $200 in a savings account. Each week for 8 weeks, you take out $18 for spending money. How much money is in your account at the end of 8 weeks?

_____

16. The outdoor temperature was 8 degrees at midnight. The temperature declined 5 degrees during each of the next 3 hours. What was the temperature at 3 A.M.?

_____

17. The price of a stock was $325 a share. The price of the stock went down $25 each week for 6 weeks. What was the price of that stock at the end of 6 weeks?

_____

LESSON 2-1

Multiplying Integers

Practice and Problem Solving: C

Find each product.

1. (−14)(7)

_____

2. (−24)(−5)

_____

3. 12(−12)

_____

4. 15(−9)(−1)

_____

5. 2(−3)(4)

_____

6. −3(−6)(−2)

_____

7. 40(−78)(0)

_____

8. −6(−60)(−4)

_____

9. −24(7)(−7)

_____

Write a mathematical expression to represent each situation. Then find the value of the expression to solve the problem.

10. A football team loses 4 yards on each of three plays. Then they complete a pass for 9 yards. What is the change in yardage after those four plays?

_____

11. You have $220 in your savings account. You take $35 from your account each week for four weeks. How much is left in your account at the end of the four weeks?

_____

12. A submarine is at −125 feet in the ocean. The submarine makes three dives of 50 feet each. At what level is the submarine after the three dives?

_____

Find each product. Use a pattern to complete the sentences.

13. −1(−1) _____

14. −1(−1)(−1) _____

15. −1(−1)(−1)(−1) _____

16. −1(−1) (−1)(−1)(−1) _____

17. −1(−1)(−1)(−1)(−1)(−1) _____

18. When multiplying integers, if there is an odd number of negative

factors, then the product is _____.

If there is an even number of negative factors, then the product is

_____.

LESSON 2-1

Multiplying Integers

Practice and Problem Solving: D

Find each product. The first one is done for you.

1. 3(–2)

   _____ **–6** _____

2. 5(0)

   _____

3. (–1)(–8)

   _____

4. (–4)(7)

   _____

5. (–3)(–4)

   _____

6. (6)(–6)

   _____

7. 10(–5)

   _____

8. –2(9)

   _____

9. 7(–10)

   _____

10. –1(–1)

    _____

11. 2(–6)

    _____

12. –2(–2)

    _____

Write a mathematical expression to represent each situation. Then find the value of the expression to solve the problem. The first one is done for you.

13. You play a game where you score –3 points on the first 5 turns. What is your score after those 5 turns?

    5(–3) = –15; –15 points _____

14. The outdoor temperature gets 1 degree colder each hour for 3 hours. What is the change in temperature at the end of those 3 hours?

    _____

15. A football team loses 4 yards on each of 2 plays. What is the change in yardage after those 2 plays?

    _____

16. You take $9 out of your savings account each week for 7 weeks. At the end of 7 weeks, what is the change in the amount in your savings account?

    _____

17. The price of a stock went down $5 each week for 5 weeks. What was the change in the price of that stock at the end of 5 weeks?

    _____

LESSON 2-1

Multiplying Integers
Reteach

You can use patterns to learn about multiplying integers.

$6(2) = 12$

$6(1) = 6$ -6

$6(0) = 0$ -6

$6(-1) = -6$ -6

$6(-2) = -12$ -6

Each product is 6 less than the previous product.

The product of two positive integers is positive.

The product of a positive integer and a negative integer is negative.

Here is another pattern.

$-6(2) = -12$

$-6(1) = -6$ $+6$

$-6(0) = 0$ $+6$

$-6(-1) = 6$ $+6$

$-6(-2) = 12$ $+6$

Each product is 6 more than the previous product.

The product of a negative integer and a positive integer is negative.

The product of two negative integers is positive.

Find each product.

1. $1(-2)$

   Think: $1 \times 2 = 2$. A negative and a positive integer have a negative product.

   _____

2. $-6(-3)$

   Think: $6 \times 3 = 18$. Two negative integers have a positive product.

   _____

3. $(5)(-1)$

   _____

4. $(-9)(-6)$

   _____

5. $11(4)$

   _____

Write a mathematical expression to represent each situation.
Then find the value of the expression to solve the problem.

6. You are playing a game. You start at 0. Then you score −8 points on each of 4 turns. What is your score after those 4 turns?

   _____

7. A mountaineer descends a mountain for 5 hours. On average, she climbs down 500 feet each hour. What is her change in elevation after 5 hours?

   _____

LESSON 2-1

Multiplying Integers
Reading Strategies: Use Graphic Aids

The opposite of 6 is –6.

Losing points is the opposite of gaining points.

Losing 6 points is the opposite of gaining 6 points.

Answer each question.

1. What is the opposite of losing 10 points? _____

2. What is the opposite of gaining 17 points? _____

You start a game with a score of 0. You lose 4 points on each of the first three turns. How many points will you lose in all on those three turns? What will your score be after the third turn?

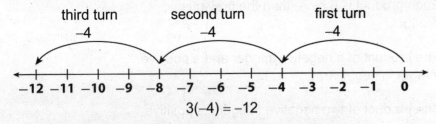

$$3(-4) = -12$$

Use the number line to help you answer the questions.

3. Starting at zero, which direction do you move first? _____

4. How many places do you move? _____

5. Which direction do you move next? _____

6. How many places do you move? _____

7. Which direction do you move next? _____

8. How many places do you move? _____

9. How did your score change from the beginning of the game to the end of the third move?

_____

10. What was your score at the end of the third move? _____

11. Suppose you lose another 4 points on your next move.
What would your score be at the end of that move?

_____

LESSON 2-1
Multiplying Integers
Success for English Learners

Problem 1

Multiply: -8×5.

Use the absolute values of the numbers.

$|-8| = 8 \qquad |5| = 5$

Think about multiplying integers.

Since $8 \times 5 = 40$, $(-8)(5) = -40$

$(1)(-1) = -1 \qquad (-1)(1) = -1$
Multiply numbers with *different* signs, and get a *negative* product.

Problem 2

Multiply: -6×-4.

Use the absolute values of the numbers.

$|-6| = 6 \qquad |-4| = 4$

Think about multiplying integers.

Since, $6 \times 4 = 24$, $(-6)(-4) = 24$

$(1)(1) = 1 \qquad (-1)(-1) = 1$
Multiply numbers with *the same* sign, and get a *positive* product.

You have money in a bank account. You take out $20 each week for three weeks. After the three weeks, what is the change in the amount of money in your account?

1. What integer shows the money you take out each week? _____

2. What integer shows the number of weeks you take money out?

   _____

3. What expression can you use to solve the problem? _____

4. What is the change in your account after three weeks? _____

Answer each question.

5. You know $50 \times 8 = 400$. Explain how that helps you find $(-50)(-8)$.

   _____

   _____

6. Are the products of 4×-8 and -4×8 the same? Explain.

   _____

   _____

   _____

LESSON 2-2

Dividing Integers
Practice and Problem Solving: A/B

Find each quotient.

1. $7\overline{)-84}$

2. $-38 \div -2$

3. $-27\overline{)81}$

4. $-28 \div 7$

5. $-121 \div -11$

6. $-35 \div 4$

Simplify.

7. $(-6 - 4) \div 2$

8. $5(-8) \div 4$

9. $-6(-2) \div 4(-3)$

Write a mathematical expression for each phrase.

10. thirty-two divided by the opposite of 4

11. the quotient of the opposite of 30 and 6, plus the opposite of 8

12. the quotient of 12 and the opposite of 3 plus the product of the opposite of 14 and 4

Solve. Show your work.

13. A high school athletic department bought 40 soccer uniforms at a cost of $3,000. After soccer season, they returned some of the uniforms but only received $40 per uniform. What was the difference between what they paid for each uniform and what they got for each return?

14. A commuter has $245 in his commuter savings account.

   a. This account changes by –$15 each week he buys a ticket. In one time period, the account changed by –$240. For how many weeks did the commuter buy tickets?

   b. How much must he add to his account if he wants to have 20 weeks worth of tickets in his account?

**LESSON
2-2**

Dividing Integers

Practice and Problem Solving: C

Simplify.

1. $-\dfrac{-8}{-2} + (-12)$

2. $\dfrac{6}{-3} - \dfrac{15-7}{-2}$

3. $3 - 2(4-7) \div 9$

_____ _____ _____

The integers from −3 to +3 can be used in the blanks below. Which of these integers produces a positive, even integer for the expression? Show your work for those that do.

4. $-\dfrac{8}{2} + 4 \, (\underline{}) - 2$

5. $\dfrac{(\underline{})}{4} + \dfrac{3}{2}$

_____ _____

6. $\underline{} \div \dfrac{2}{-3}$

7. $\left(\dfrac{-1}{\underline{}}\right) \div -\dfrac{1}{2}$

_____ _____

Solve. Show your work.

8. In a sports competition, Alyssa was penalized −16 points. She received the same number of penalty points in each of 4 events. How many points was she penalized in each event?

_____

9. The surface temperature of a deep, spring-fed lake is 70°F. The lake temperature drops 2°F for each yard below the lake surface until a depth of 6 yards is reached. From 6 yards to 15 yards deep, the temperature is constant. From 15 yards down to the spring source, the temperature *increases* 3°F per *foot* until the spring source is reached at 20 yards below the surface.

a. What is the temperature at 10 yards below the surface?

_____

b. What is the temperature at 50 feet below the surface?

_____

_____

c. Write an expression for finding the lake temperature at the spring source.

_____

**LESSON
2-2**

Dividing Integers

Practice and Problem Solving: D

Find the quotient. The first one is done for you.

1. $-3\overline{)-15}$

    _____5_____

2. $27 \div (-3)$

    _____

3. $\dfrac{28}{-7}$

    _____

Compare the quotients. Write >, <, or =.

4. $-4\overline{)-16}$ ◯ $-16\overline{)-4}$

5. $11 \div 77$ ◯ $77 \div 11$

6. $\dfrac{48}{-6}$ ◯ $\dfrac{-48}{6}$

Write a mathematical expression for the written expression. Then solve. The first one is done for you.

7. the opposite of 45 divided by 5

    $$-45 \div 5 = -9$$

8. fifty-five over negative eleven

    _____

9. negative 38 divided by positive 19

    _____

10. negative four divided by negative two

    _____

Solve. Show your work. The first one is done for you.

11. Four investors lost 24 percent of their combined investment in a company. On average, how much did each investor lose?

    $-24 \div 4 = -6$; On average, each investor lost 6%.

    _____

12. The temperature in a potter's kiln dropped 760 degrees in 4 hours. On average, how much did the temperature drop per hour?

    _____

    _____

13. The value of a car decreased by $5,100 over 3 years. On average, how much did its value decrease each year?

    _____

    _____

Name _____ Date _____ Class_____

Dividing Integers
Reteach

You can use a number line to divide a negative integer by a positive integer.

$-8 \div 4$

Step 1 Draw the number line.

Step 2 Draw an arrow to the left from 0 to the value of the dividend, -8.

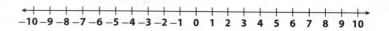

Step 3 Divide the arrow into the same number of small parts as the divisor, 4.

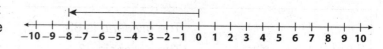

Step 4 How long is each small arrow? When a negative is divided by a positive the quotient is negative, so the sign is negative.

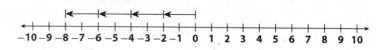 Each arrow is -2.

So, $-8 \div 4 = -2$.

On a number line, in which direction will an arrow that represents the dividend point? What is the sign of the divisor? Of the quotient?

1. $54 \div (-9)$

   Dividend: _____

   Sign of
   Divisor: _____

   Sign of
   Quotient: _____

2. $-4\overline{)-52}$

   Dividend: _____

   Sign of
   Divisor: _____

   Sign of
   Quotient: _____

3. $\dfrac{-39}{3}$

   Dividend: _____

   Sign of
   Divisor: _____

   Sign of
   Quotient: _____

Complete the table.

4.

Divisor	Dividend	Quotient
+	+	
	+	
	−	−
		+

Name _____ Date _____ Class_____

 Dividing Integers

LESSON
2-2

Reading Strategies: Understand Symbols

Different symbols can be used to show division with integers.
Each symbol can also be described with words.

$-8\overline{)-136}$ ←	The *dividend* is −136. The *divisor* is −8. "−8 goes into −136."
$63 \div (-3)$ ←	The *dividend* is 63. The *divisor* is −3. "63 divided by −3."
$\dfrac{-125}{5}$ ←	The *dividend* is −125. The *divisor* is 5. "−125 over 5."

Name the dividend and the divisor. Then find the quotient.

1. The total distance is 3,600 kilometers. The average speed is
   225 kilometers per hour. How long did it take to drive that distance?

   dividend: _____ divisor: _____ quotient: _____

2. The temperature dropped 35 degrees in 7 hours. What was the
   average drop in temperature per hour?

   dividend: _____ divisor: _____ quotient: _____

3. A beverage company produced 1,600 liters of fruit punch, which will be
   bottled in 2-liter bottles. How many bottles can be filled?

   dividend: _____ divisor: _____ quotient: _____

Use words to describe each division problem two ways.

4. $-6\overline{)102}$ _____

   _____

5. $\dfrac{-221}{-17}$ _____

   _____

LESSON 2-2 Dividing Integers
Success for English Learners

Problem 1

Words help you find the dividend, the divisor, and the quotient.
They also tell the sign of the numbers.

"45 *divided by* negative 5 *is* the opposite of 9."

dividend   divisor   quotient

$-5\overline{)45} = -9$

OR $\dfrac{45}{-5} = -9$

OR $45 \div (-5) = -9$

Write a math expression for the words. Then solve.

1. the opposite of 210 over 70 _____

2. negative 4,200 divided by 300 _____

3. negative 50 divided by positive 10 _____

4. 54 divided by 27 _____

Problem 2

Find the sign of the quotient before dividing.

$\dfrac{-720}{-8}$ ⟵ Negative (−) divided by negative (−) gives positive (+).

Negative (−) divided by positive (+) gives negative (−).

Positive (+) divided by negative (−) gives negative (−).

Positive (+) divided by positive (+) gives positive (+).

Write the sign of the quotient, + or −. Then find the quotient.

5. $\dfrac{33}{33}$ 6. $\dfrac{128}{-4}$ 7. $\dfrac{-100}{25}$ 8. $\dfrac{-75}{-15}$

Sign: _____   Sign: _____   Sign: _____   Sign: _____

Quotient: Quotient: Quotient: Quotient:

_____   _____   _____   _____

LESSON 2-3

Applying Integer Operations

Practice and Problem Solving: A/B

Find the value of each expression.

1. $(-3)(-2) + 8$

2. $(-18) \div 3 + (5)(-2)$

3. $7(-3) - 6$

_____

_____

_____

4. $24 \div (-6)(-2) + 7$

5. $4(-8) + 3$

6. $(-9)(0) + (8)(-5)$

_____

_____

_____

Compare. Write <, =, or >.

7. $(-5)(8) + 3$ ◯ $(-6)(7) + 1$

8. $(-8)(-4) + 16 \div (-4)$ ◯ $(-9)(-3) + 15 \div (-3)$

Write an expression to represent each situation. Then find the value of the expression to solve the problem.

9. Dave owns 15 shares of ABC Mining stock. On Monday, the value of each share rose $2, but on Tuesday the value fell $5. What is the change in the value of Dave's shares?

_____

10. To travel the Erie Canal, a boat must go through locks that raise or lower the boat. Traveling east, a boat would have to be lowered 12 feet at Amsterdam, 11 feet at Tribes Hill, and 8 feet at Randall. By how much does the elevation of the boat change between Amsterdam and Randall?

_____

11. The Gazelle football team made 5 plays in a row where they gained 3 yards on each play. Then they had 2 plays in a row where they lost 12 yards on each play. What is the total change in their position from where they started?

_____

12. On Saturday, Mrs. Armour bought 7 pairs of socks for $3 each, and a sweater for her dog for $12. Then she found a $5 bill on the sidewalk. Over the course of Saturday, what was the change in the amount of money Mrs. Armour had?

_____

Name _____ Date _____ Class_____

LESSON 2-3

Applying Integer Operations

Practice and Problem Solving: C

Complete the table to answer 1–4.

	You Own	Company	Monday	Tuesday	Wednesday	Net Gain or Loss
1.	5 shares	ABC	−$2	+$5	−$1	
2.	2 shares	DEF	+$8	−$7	−$10	
3.	8 shares	GHI	−$2	+$9	+$6	
4.	7 shares	JKL	+$5	−$12	+$3	

5. What expression shows your net gain or loss on GHI Company?

_____

6. How much value did you gain or lose overall? _____

Write an expression to represent each situation. Then, find the value of the expression to solve the problem.

7. A submarine cruised below the surface of the water. During a training exercise, it made 4 dives, each time descending 45 feet more. Then it rose 112 feet. What is the change in the submarine's position?

_____

8. A teacher wanted to prevent students from guessing answers on a multiple-choice test. The teacher graded 5 points for a correct answer, 0 points for no answer, and −2 points for a wrong answer. Giselle answered 17 questions correctly, left 3 blank, and had 5 wrong answers. She also got 8 out of 10 possible points for extra credit. What was her final score?

_____

9. Hugh wrote six checks from his account in the following amounts: $20, $20, $12, $20, $12, and $42. He also made a deposit of $57 and was charged a $15 service fee by the bank. What is the change in Hugh's account balance?

_____

10. a. Without finding the product, what is the sign of this product? Explain how you know.

   $(-4)(-1)(-2)(-6)(-3)(-5)(-2)(-2)$

_____

   b. Find the product. _____

Original content Copyright © by Houghton Mifflin Harcourt. Additions and changes to the original content are the responsibility of the instructor.

LESSON
2-3

Applying Integer Operations
Practice and Problem Solving: D

Find the value of each expression. Show your work. The first one is done for you.

1. $15 + (-6)(2)$

   $= 15 + (-12)$ **Multiply**

   $= 3$ **Add.**

2. $(-5)(-3) + 18$

3. $42 \div (-6) + 23$

4. $52 + 45 \div (-9)$

Write an expression to represent each situation. Then find the value of the expression to solve the problem. The first one is done for you.

5. Mr. Carlisle paid his utility bills last weekend. He paid $50 to the phone company, $112 to the power company, and $46 to the water company. After he paid those bills, what was the change in the total amount of money that Mr. Carlisle had?

   $(-50) + (-112) + (-46) = -208$; **He had $208 less.**

6. Over 5 straight plays, a football team gained 8 yards, lost 4 yards, gained 7 yards, gained 3 yards, and lost 11 yards. What is the team's position now compared to their starting position?

7. At the grocery store, Mrs. Knight bought 4 pounds of apples for $2 per pound and 2 heads of lettuce for $1 each. She had a coupon for $3 off the price of the apples. After her purchases, what was the change in the amount of money that Mrs. Knight had?

8. The depth of the water in a water tank changes every time someone in the Harrison family takes a bath or does laundry. A bath lowers the water level by 4 inches. Washing a load of laundry lowers the level by 2 inches. On Monday the Harrisons took 3 baths and washed 4 loads of laundry. By how much did the water level in the water tank change?

LESSON 2-3 Applying Integer Operations
Reteach

To evaluate an expression, follow the order of operations.

1. Multiply and divide in order from left to right.

   $(-5)(6) + 3 + (-20) \div 4 + 12$

   $-30 + 3 + (-20) \div 4 + 12$

   $-30 + 3 + (-20) \div 4 + 12$

   $-30 + 3 + (-5) + 12$

2. Add and subtract in order from left to right.

   $-30 + 3 + (-5) + 12$

   $-27 + (-5) + 12$

   $-32 + 12 = -20$

Name the operation you would do first.

1. $-4 + (3)(-8) + 7$

   _____

2. $-3 + (-8) - 6$

   _____

3. $16 + 72 \div (-8) + 6(-2)$

   _____

4. $17 + 8 + (-16) - 34$

   _____

5. $-8 + 13 + (-24) + 6(-4)$

   _____

6. $12 \div (-3) + 7(-7)$

   _____

7. $(-5)6 + (-12) - 6(9)$

   _____

8. $14 - (-9) - 6 - 5$

   _____

Find the value of each expression.

9. $(-6) + 5(-2) + 15$

   _____

10. $(-8) + (-19) - 4$

   _____

11. $3 + 28 \div (-7) + 5(-6)$

   _____

12. $15 + 32 + (-8) - 6$

   _____

13. $(-5) + 22 + (-7) + 8(-9)$

   _____

14. $21 \div (-7) + 5(-9)$

   _____

Name _____ Date _____ Class_____

LESSON 2-3

Applying Integer Operations
Reading Strategies: Use Context

Someone mentions an amount when describing a mathematical situation.

Should you represent that number with a positive integer or a negative integer?

Use key words to help you decide.

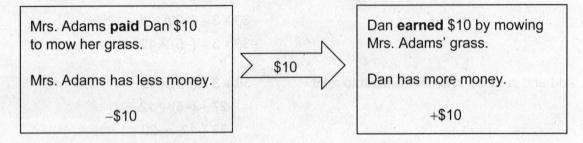

Words That Show Negative Numbers	Words That Show Positive Numbers
He **spent** $20. −20	He **found** $5. +5
They **lost** 8 yards. −8	120 feet **above** sea level. +120
15° **below** zero. −15	They **gained** 38 yards. +38

Write an expression to represent each situation. Underline the words you used to decide whether each number in your expression should be positive or negative. Find the value of the expression to solve the problem.

1. Antoine went to the store. He paid $3 each for 4 pounds of grapefruit. When he got home, his mother gave him $7 for some of the grapefruit. What is the change in the amount of money Antoine has?

   _____

2. Matt went scuba diving. He dove to a depth of 48 feet below the surface. Elena dove one-fourth as deep as Matt. What number describes the depth Elena dove?

   _____

3. The Cougars football team had 3 straight plays where they lost 5 yards on each play. On the fourth play they gained 32 yards. How many yards did they gain or lose for those 4 plays?

   _____

Applying Integer Operations
Success for English Learners

LESSON 2-3

Problem 1

What is the value?

$$(-3)(2) + 4 + (-16) \div 4 + 3$$

1. First, **multiply and divide** from left to right.

   $(\mathbf{-3)(2)} + 4 + \mathbf{(-16)} \div \mathbf{4} + 3$
   $-6 + 4 + (-4) + 3$

2. Then **add and subtract** from left to right.

   $\mathbf{-6 + 4} + (-4) + 3$
   $\mathbf{-2 + (-4)} + 3$
   $\mathbf{-6 + 3 = -3}$

Problem 2

To solve the problem, write a math expression.

> Manny bought 8 gallons of gas. He paid $4 for each gallon. What is the change in the amount of money Manny has?

Manny *paid* $4 for each gallon, so the 4 is negative.

Manny bought 8 gallons. So, multiply by the cost of one gallon by 8.

$$8(-4) = -32$$

Manny has $32 less now.

Find the value.

1. $(-4)(-5) + 19$

   _____

2. $(-9)(4) + 31$

   _____

3. $(-36) \div 9 + 4 + (-2)(-3)$

   _____

4. a. Write a problem that could be shown by this expression.

   $$3(-20) + 5$$

   _____

   _____

   _____

   b. Find the value of the expression to solve the problem.

   _____

Multiplying and Dividing Integers
Challenge

1. Write an expression with integers that uses all four operations, includes at least 5 terms, and that, when simplified, is −17. Use the rules for the order of operations. Show your work.

_____

_____

_____

_____

2. You have two sets of integer cards −15 to 15, and four sets of operation cards (+, −, ×, and ÷). Make up a game that could be played using these cards. Write the rules for your game.

_____

_____

_____

_____

_____

3. Explain to a new student how to simplify the expression below. Show the updated expression after each step you take.

$$(-8) + (-3) + (-4)(7) \div 14 + 9\,(-2)$$

_____

_____

_____

_____

_____

_____

Name _____ Date _____ Class_____

LESSON
3-1

Rational Numbers and Decimals

Practice and Problem Solving: A/B

Write each rational number as a terminating decimal.

1. $\dfrac{19}{20}$

2. $-\dfrac{1}{8}$

3. $\dfrac{17}{5}$

_____   _____   _____

Write each rational number as a repeating decimal.

4. $-\dfrac{7}{9}$

5. $\dfrac{11}{15}$

6. $\dfrac{8}{3}$

_____   _____   _____

Write each mixed number as an improper fraction and as a decimal.
Then tell whether the decimal is terminating or repeating.

7. $3\dfrac{2}{9}$ _____

8. $15\dfrac{1}{20}$ _____

9. $-5\dfrac{3}{10}$ _____

10. In part a and in part b, use each of the digits 2, 3, and 4 exactly once.

    a. Write a mixed number that has a terminating decimal, and write the decimal.

    _____

    b. Write a mixed number that has a repeating decimal, and write the decimal.

    _____

11. The ruler is marked at every $\dfrac{1}{16}$ inch. Do the labeled measurements

    convert to repeating or terminating decimals? _____

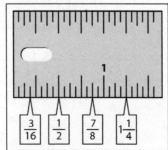

Original content Copyright © by Houghton Mifflin Harcourt. Additions and changes to the original content are the responsibility of the instructor.

45

Rational Numbers and Decimals

LESSON 3-1

Practice and Problem Solving: C

Use the table to answer problems 1 to 4.
The table lists the commuting times for 5 people. Write each ratio in

the form $\dfrac{a}{b}$, and then as a decimal. Tell whether each decimal is a

terminating or a repeating decimal.

1. Beau's time to the sum of Charra's
   and DeLee's times

   _____

2. The product of DeLee's time and
   Beau's time to Adelle's time

   _____

Person	Commuting Time (min.)
Adelle	15
Beau	25
Charra	10
DeLee	8
Emmet	20

3. Write two or three rational numbers with
   Emmet's time in each denominator. Is
   the rational number always a terminating
   decimal? Justify your answer.

   _____

   _____

   _____

4. Use Adelle's time as the denominator of rational numbers. Find a
   numerator that results in a terminating decimal and find a numerator
   that results in a repeating decimal. Explain how to find numerators for
   each type of rational number.

   _____

   _____

5. Is $\dfrac{1.5}{7.5}$ a rational number? If not, explain why. If so, explain why and

   write it as a decimal.

   _____

   _____

LESSON 3-1

Rational Numbers and Decimals

Practice and Problem Solving: D

Write each rational number as a repeating decimal or a terminating decimal. Then tell whether the decimal is terminating or repeating. The first two are done for you.

1. $\dfrac{13}{20}$ __0.65, terminating__

$$20\overline{)13.00}$$
$$\phantom{20\overline{)}}\underline{0.65}$$
$$\phantom{20\overline{)1}}120$$
$$\phantom{20\overline{)1}}\overline{100}$$
$$\phantom{20\overline{)1}}\underline{100}$$
$$\phantom{20\overline{)11}}0$$

2. $4\dfrac{2}{3}$ _____ $4.\overline{6}$, **repeating**

$$4\dfrac{2}{3} = \dfrac{12}{3} + \dfrac{2}{3} = \dfrac{14}{3}$$

$$3\overline{)14.000}$$
$$\phantom{3\overline{)}}\underline{4.666}$$
$$\phantom{3\overline{)1}}12$$
$$\phantom{3\overline{)1}}\overline{20}$$
$$\phantom{3\overline{)1}}\underline{18}$$
$$\phantom{3\overline{)11}}20$$
$$\phantom{3\overline{)11}}\underline{18}$$
$$\phantom{3\overline{)111}}20$$

3. $\dfrac{5}{9}$ _____

4. $3\dfrac{5}{6}$ _____

5. $8\dfrac{3}{4}$ _____

6. $10\dfrac{5}{8}$ _____

The decimal for $\dfrac{5}{16}$ is 0.3125. Use that value to write each decimal.

7. $1\dfrac{5}{16}$

8. $7\dfrac{5}{16}$

9. $26\dfrac{5}{16}$

_____   _____   _____

The decimal for $\dfrac{4}{15}$ is 0.266... or $0.2\overline{6}$. Use that value to write each decimal.

10. $1\dfrac{4}{15}$

11. $17\dfrac{4}{15}$

12. $23\dfrac{4}{15}$

_____   _____   _____

LESSON 3-1

Rational Numbers and Decimals
Reteach

A teacher overheard two students talking about how to write a mixed number as a decimal.

Student 1: I know that $\frac{1}{2}$ is always 0.5, so $6\frac{1}{2}$ is 6.5 and $11\frac{1}{2}$ is 11.5.

I can rewrite any mixed number if the fraction part is $\frac{1}{2}$.

Student 2: You just gave me an idea to separate the whole number part

and the fraction part. For $5\frac{1}{3}$, the fraction part is

$\frac{1}{3} = 0.333...$ or $0.\overline{3}$, so $5\frac{1}{3}$ is 5.333... or $5.\overline{3}$.

I can always find a decimal for the fraction part, and then write the decimal next to the whole number part.

The teacher asked the two students to share their ideas with the class.

For each mixed number, find the decimal for the fraction part. Then write the mixed number as a decimal.

1. $7\frac{3}{4}$

   _____

2. $11\frac{5}{6}$

   _____

3. $12\frac{3}{10}$

   _____

4. $8\frac{5}{18}$

   _____

For each mixed number, use two methods to write it as a decimal. Do you get the same result using each method?

5. $9\frac{2}{9}$

   _____

   _____

6. $21\frac{5}{8}$

   _____

   _____

Rational Numbers and Decimals

Reading Strategies: Understanding Key Phrases

The definition of *rational number* uses two key phrases.

• A rational number is a number that can be written as **a ratio of two integers** a and b... .

• A rational number is a number that **can be** written as a ratio of two integers a and b... .

The phrase **ratio of two integers** means fractions such as $\frac{5}{8}$, $\frac{9}{11}$, or $\frac{-7}{12}$.

Each fraction is a ratio and both the numerator and the denominator in the ratio are integers.

Tell whether or not each numerator and denominator is an integer.

1. $\frac{-3}{5}$ _____

2. $\frac{2}{1.17}$ _____

3. $\frac{1}{\frac{1}{3}}$ _____

4. $\frac{\sqrt{2}}{\sqrt{4}}$ _____

The phrase **can be** means that you have to think about rewriting the fraction.

For example, question 2 shows the fraction $\frac{2}{1.17}$. We can rewrite $\frac{2}{1.17}$ as $\frac{200}{117}$, so $\frac{2}{1.17}$ is a rational number because it *can be* written as a ratio of two integers.

Similarly, $\frac{1}{\frac{1}{3}} = 3$ or $\frac{3}{1}$, so it is a rational number because it *can be* written as a ratio of two integers.

Explain whether or not each fraction *can be* written as a ratio of two integers.

5. $\frac{\sqrt{3}}{\sqrt{6}}$ _____

6. $\frac{\sqrt{2}}{\sqrt{2}}$ _____

7. $\frac{\sqrt{4}}{\sqrt{25}}$ _____

8. $\frac{\sqrt{1}}{2}$ _____

LESSON 3-1

Rational Numbers and Decimals

Success for English Learners

Problem 1

How many digits repeat?

$5\frac{2}{3} = 5.6\underline{6}\underline{6}...$

One digit repeats.

$\frac{7}{33} = 0.\underline{21}\underline{21}21...$

Two digits repeat.

$\frac{11}{333} = 0.\underline{033}\underline{033}\underline{033}...$

Three digits repeat.

Problem 2

How do you show a repeating decimal?

$5\frac{2}{3} = 5.666...$

$\frac{7}{33} = 0.212121...$

$\frac{11}{333} = 0.033033033...$

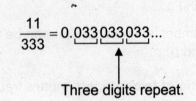

Use three dots "..." to show that there is a pattern.

or

$5\frac{2}{3} = 5.\overline{6}$

$\frac{7}{33} = 0.\overline{21}$

$\frac{11}{333} = 0.\overline{033}$

Use a bar over the digits that repeat.

1. The decimal for $\frac{5,141}{9,999}$ is 0.51415141... .

   How many repeating digits does it have?

   A It has one repeating digit, which is 5.

   B It has two repeating digits, 5 and 1.

   C It has a group of three repeating digits, 141.

   D It has a group of four repeating digits, 5,141.

2. How can you use a bar to show that 0.51415141...
   is a repeating decimal?

   A $0.\overline{5}141$ C $0.\overline{51415}$

   B $0.\overline{5141}$ D $0.5\overline{141}$

3. Use three dots "..." to write a decimal that has two repeating digits.
   Then use a bar to write the same repeating decimal.

   _____

Name _____ Date _____ Class_____

Adding Rational Numbers
Practice and Problem Solving: A/B

Use a number line to find each sum.

1. $-3 + 4$

2. $1 + (-8)$

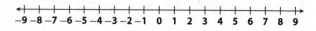

_____   _____

Find each sum without using a number line.

3. $4 + 5$

4. $-3 + \dfrac{1}{2}$

5. $-\dfrac{2}{9} + \dfrac{3}{9}$

_____   _____   _____

6. $-3.5 + (-4.9)$

7. $-2\dfrac{1}{4} + \left(-3\dfrac{1}{4}\right)$

8. $-0.6 + (-2.5)$

_____   _____   _____

9. $-\dfrac{3}{4} + \dfrac{1}{5}$

10. $3 + (-7.5) + 1.2$

11. $-1.32 + 5.02 + (-1.24)$

_____   _____   _____

12. $-3 + (-1.35) + 2.5$

13. $-6.5 + (-0.15) + (-0.2)$

14. $-\dfrac{3}{2} - \dfrac{7}{4} + \dfrac{1}{8}$

_____   _____   _____

Solve.

15. Alex borrowed $12.50 from his friend Danilo. He paid him back $8.75. How much does he still owe?

_____

16. A football team gains 18 yards in one play and then loses 12 yards in the next. What is the team's total yardage?

_____

17. Dee Dee bought an apple for $0.85, a sandwich for $4.50, and a bottle of water for $1.50. How much did Dee Dee spend?

_____

18. Andre went hiking near his house. The first trail he hiked on took him 4.5 miles away from his house. The second trail he hiked took him 2.4 miles closer to his house. The third trail took him 1.7 miles further away from his house. After Andre hiked the three trails, how far from his house was he?

_____

LESSON
3-2
Adding Rational Numbers
Practice and Problem Solving: C

Find each sum.

1. $3\frac{1}{4} + \left(-1\frac{1}{2}\right) + 2\frac{1}{4}$

_____

2. $3\frac{3}{5} + \left(-1\frac{4}{9}\right) + \frac{1}{5}$

_____

3. $-\frac{1}{9} + 8\frac{3}{5} - \frac{1}{15}$

_____

4. $-3.5 + (-4.9) + 0.8$

_____

5. $-\frac{1}{12} + \left(-3\frac{3}{8}\right) + \frac{4}{3}$

_____

6. $-0.25 + (-1.65) + 0.77$

_____

7. $-\frac{3}{4} + \frac{1}{5} + \frac{2}{9}$

_____

8. $0.3 + (-5.5) + 5.2$

_____

9. $-1.091 + 12.12 + (-1.1)$

_____

10. $-3.24 + (-1.55) + 2.512$

_____

11. $-1.27 + (-0.35) + (-0.13)$

_____

12. $-1\frac{1}{2} + \left(-2\frac{12}{23}\right) + 5\frac{7}{46}$

_____

Solve.

13. Marley bought an action figure for $10.99, a board game for $24.95 and a book for $5.99. She paid with a $50 bill. How much change did Marley receive?

_____

14. Tim bought a pen for $2.25, a pencil for $0.59, a notebook for $6.49, and a highlighter for $1.49. He used a coupon that gave him $5.25 off his entire purchase. How much did he spend in total?

_____

15. During the first hour of a snowstorm, $1\frac{1}{2}$ inches of snow fell. In the next hour, $4\frac{3}{8}$ inches fell. In the third hour, the snow stopped and $\frac{7}{8}$ inches of snow melted. How much snow was on the ground at the end of the third hour?

_____

LESSON 3-2

Adding Rational Numbers

Practice and Problem Solving: D

Use a number line to find each sum. The first one is done for you.

1. $2 + 3$

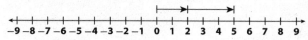

_____ **5** _____

2. $-2 + 1$

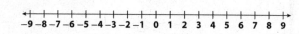

_____

3. $-5 + (-3)$

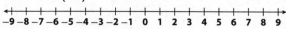

_____

4. $-2 + 5$

+—+
−9 −8 −7 −6 −5 −4 −3 −2 −1 0 1 2 3 4 5 6 7 8 9

_____

5. $1 + 7$

+—+
−9 −8 −7 −6 −5 −4 −3 −2 −1 0 1 2 3 4 5 6 7 8 9

_____

6. $-8 + 2$

+—+
−9 −8 −7 −6 −5 −4 −3 −2 −1 0 1 2 3 4 5 6 7 8 9

_____

7. $1 + (-0.5)$

+—+
−9 −8 −7 −6 −5 −4 −3 −2 −1 0 1 2 3 4 5 6 7 8 9

_____

8. $-2.5 + 0.5$

+—+
−9 −8 −7 −6 −5 −4 −3 −2 −1 0 1 2 3 4 5 6 7 8 9

_____

9. $0.5 + 1.5$

+—+
−9 −8 −7 −6 −5 −4 −3 −2 −1 0 1 2 3 4 5 6 7 8 9

_____

10. $-1 + \dfrac{1}{2}$

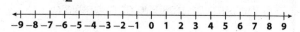

_____

11. $\dfrac{1}{2} + 1\dfrac{1}{2}$

+—+
−9 −8 −7 −6 −5 −4 −3 −2 −1 0 1 2 3 4 5 6 7 8 9

_____

12. $-\dfrac{1}{2} + \dfrac{1}{2}$

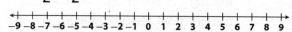

_____

Find each sum without using a number line. The first one is done for you.

13. $5 + (-1)$

_____ **4** _____

14. $\dfrac{2}{3} + \dfrac{5}{3}$

_____

15. $-\dfrac{1}{8} + \dfrac{7}{8}$

_____

16. $-1.5 + (-1.9)$

_____

17. $-2 + (-1.2)$

_____

18. $-4.0 + 3.5$

_____

19. $-1\dfrac{3}{4} + \dfrac{1}{4}$

20. $-7 + 4$

21. $-0.1 + (-0.8)$

Adding Rational Numbers

LESSON 3-2

Reteach

This balance scale "weighs" positive and negative numbers.
Negative numbers go on the left of the balance. Positive numbers go on the right.

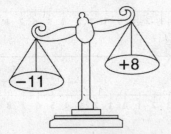  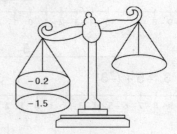

The scale will tip to the left side because the sum of −11 and + 8 is negative.	The scale will tip to the right side because the sum of $-2\frac{1}{2}$ and + 7 is positive.	Both −0.2 and −1.5 go on the left side. The scale will tip to the left side because the sum of −0.2 and −1.5 is negative.
$-11 + 8 = -3$	$-2\frac{1}{2} + 7 = +4\frac{1}{2}$	$-0.2 + (-1.5) = -1.7$

Find 3 + (−9).

Should you add or subtract?

Will the sum be positive or negative?

$$3 + (-9) = -6$$

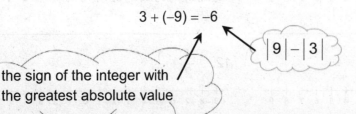

the sign of the integer with the greatest absolute value

$$\left|\,9\,\right| - \left|\,3\,\right|$$

Find each sum.

1. $-2 + 4 =$ _____

2. $3 + (-8) =$ _____

3. $-5 + (-2) =$ _____

4. $2.4 + (-1.8) =$ _____

5. $1.1 + 3.6 =$ _____

6. $-2.1 + (-3.9) =$ _____

7. $\dfrac{4}{5} + \left(-\dfrac{1}{5}\right) =$ _____

8. $-1\dfrac{1}{3} + \left(-\dfrac{1}{3}\right) =$ _____

9. $-\dfrac{7}{8} + \dfrac{3}{8} =$ _____

LESSON 3-2

Adding Rational Numbers

Reading Strategies: Use Graphic Aids

Randy's football team had the ball on the zero yard line. On their first play they gained 6 yards. On the second play they lost 4 yards. On what yard line is the ball now?

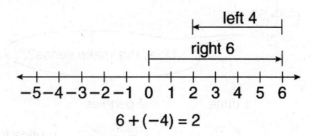

$$6 + (-4) = 2$$

Use the number line to help you answer the questions.

1. On which number do you begin? _____

2. Which direction do you move first? How many places do you move?

_____

3. Which direction do you move next? How many places do you move?

_____

When Angela went to bed, the temperature was zero degrees. Two hours later, the temperature had gone down 5.5 degrees. By the time Angela got up the temperature had gone down another 3 degrees. What was the temperature when she got up?

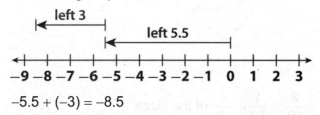

$$-5.5 + (-3) = -8.5$$

Use the number line to help you answer the questions.

4. On which number do you begin? _____

5. In which direction do you move first? How many spaces?

_____

6. In which direction do you move next? How many spaces?

_____

LESSON 3-2
Adding Rational Numbers
Success for English Learners

Problem 1

Add $3.62 and $18.57.

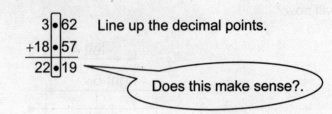

$$\begin{array}{r} 3\bullet62 \\ +18\bullet57 \\ \hline 22\bullet19 \end{array}$$

Line up the decimal points.

Does this make sense?.

Check

3 dollars	2 quarters	1 dime	2 pennies	
				rounds to $4

18 dollars	2 quarters	1 nickel	2 pennies	
				rounds to $19

4 + 19 = 23, so $22.19 is reasonable.

Problem 2

Add $\frac{3}{10} + \frac{1}{10}$.

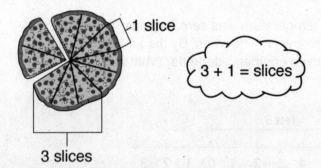

1 slice

3 + 1 = slices

3 slices

$\frac{3}{10}$ of the pizza + $\frac{1}{10}$ of the pizza = $\frac{3}{10} + \frac{1}{10} = \frac{4}{10}$ of the pizza.

1. Why is it important to line up decimals when adding decimal numbers?

_____

_____

2. Explain what the denominator represents in Problem 2.

_____

LESSON 3-3

Subtracting Rational Numbers

Practice and Problem Solving: A/B

Use a number line to find each difference.

1. −5 − 4

−9 −8 −7 −6 −5 −4 −3 −2 1 0 2 3 4 5 6 7 8 9

2. 1 − (−8)

−9 −8 −7 −6 −5 −4 −3 −2 1 0 2 3 4 5 6 7 8 9

Find each difference without using a number line.

3. 4 − (−5)

4. $-5 - \dfrac{1}{2}$

5. $\dfrac{1}{7} - \dfrac{3}{7}$

_____

6. −3.7 − (−4.9)

7. $-2\dfrac{1}{4} - (-3)$

8. −1.6 − 2.1

_____

9. $-4\dfrac{3}{4} - \dfrac{3}{4}$

10. 2 − (−7.5) − 1.2

11. −0.02 − 9.02 − 0.04

_____

12. 4 − (−0.25) − 0.5

13. −5.1 − (−0.1) − 1.2

14. $-\dfrac{3}{5} - \dfrac{7}{5} - \left(-\dfrac{2}{5}\right)$

_____

Solve.

15. The temperature on Monday was −1.5°C. The temperature on Tuesday was 2.6°C less than the temperature on Monday. What was the temperature on Tuesday?

_____

16. A diver dove to a location $6\dfrac{3}{5}$ meters below sea level. He then dove to a second location $8\dfrac{1}{5}$ meters below sea level. How many meters are there between the two locations?

_____

LESSON 3-3

Subtracting Rational Numbers

Practice and Problem Solving: C

Find each difference.

1. $-3\dfrac{1}{3} - 5\dfrac{2}{3} - \left(-2\dfrac{1}{3}\right)$

_____

2. $3\dfrac{3}{7} - 1\dfrac{2}{3} - \dfrac{5}{7}$

_____

3. $-\dfrac{1}{10} - 4\dfrac{3}{5} - 5\dfrac{3}{10}$

_____

4. $-1.5 - 4.9 - 0.8$

_____

5. $-\dfrac{1}{12} - 3\dfrac{3}{8} - \left(-\dfrac{4}{3}\right)$

_____

6. $-9.54 - 1.651 - 0.988$

_____

7. $-\dfrac{5}{6} - \dfrac{17}{18} - \left(-\dfrac{2}{9}\right)$

_____

8. $-0.03 - (-5.51) - 5.12$

_____

9. $-1.099 - 12.001 - 0.09$

_____

10. $-1.02 - 1.99 - 1.34$

_____

11. $-1.65 - (-0.45) - (-0.15)$

_____

12. $-3\dfrac{1}{2} - \left(-5\dfrac{5}{9}\right) - 9\dfrac{1}{18}$

_____

Solve.

13. If x equals $8 - (-2.25)$ and y equals $6 - 4.2 - (-4.9)$, what is the value of $x - y$?

_____

14. Alex's score for a game is given by the expression $9 - 8.2 - (-1.9)$. Beth's score for the same game is $-8 - (-5.4) - 1.8$. Whose score was higher? By how much?

_____

15. The temperature on Monday was 14°C. On Tuesday the temperature decreased by 5°. On Wednesday the temperature decreased another 10°. On Thursday the temperature increased by 8°. What was the temperature at the end of the day on Thursday?

_____

Name _____ Date _____ Class_____

Subtracting Rational Numbers
Practice and Problem Solving: D

Use a number line to find each difference. The first one is done for you.

1. 8 − 6

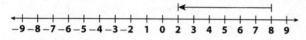

_____2_____

2. 5 − (−1)

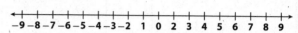

_____

3. −5 − (−2)

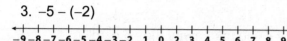

_____−3_____

4. −2 − 5

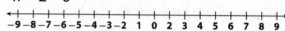

_____

5. 1 − 4

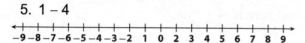

_____

6. 4 − (−4)

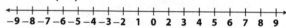

_____

7. 1 − (−0.5)

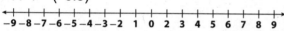

_____

8. −2 − 1

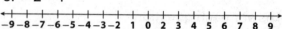

_____

9. 1.5 − 3

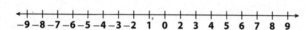

_____

10. $2 - \dfrac{1}{2}$

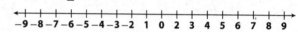

_____

11. $\dfrac{1}{2} - 1\dfrac{1}{2}$

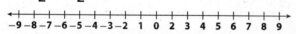

_____

12. $-\dfrac{1}{2} - 1$

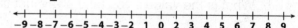

_____

Find each difference without using a number line. The first one is done for you.

13. 6 − (−1)

_____7_____

14. $\dfrac{1}{3} - \dfrac{5}{3}$

_____

15. $-\dfrac{1}{8} - \dfrac{3}{8}$

_____

16. −1.5 − (−2.9)

_____

17. −2 − 0.2

_____

18. −4.0 − 3.8

_____

19. $-1\dfrac{3}{4} - \dfrac{1}{4}$

_____

20. −2 − 4.5

_____

21. −0.2 − 0.8

_____

Subtracting Rational Numbers

Reteach

The total value of the three cards shown is $-4\frac{1}{2}$.

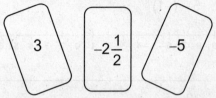

What if you **take away** the $-2\frac{1}{2}$ card?

Cards 3 and −5 are left.
Their sum is −2.

So, $-4\frac{1}{2} - \left(-2\frac{1}{2}\right) = -2$.

What if you **take away** the −5 card?

Cards 3 and $-2\frac{1}{2}$ are left.

Their sum is $\frac{1}{2}$.

So, $-4\frac{1}{2} - (-5) = \frac{1}{2}$

Answer each question.

1. The total value of the three cards shown is 12.

   a. What is the value if you take away just the 7? _____

   b. What is the value if you take away just the 13? _____

   c. What is the value if you take away just the −8? _____

2. Subtract −4 − (−2).

   a. −4 < −2. So the answer will be a _____ number.

   b. |4| − |2| = _____   c. −4 − (−2) = _____

Subtract.

3. 31 − (−9) = _____   4. 15 − 18 = _____   5. −9 − 17 = _____

6. 2.6 − (−1.6) = _____   7. 4.5 − 2.5 = _____   8. −2.0 − 1.25 = _____

9. $\frac{4}{5} - \left(-\frac{1}{5}\right) =$ _____   10. $-2\frac{1}{3} - \left(-\frac{1}{3}\right) =$ _____   11. $-\frac{7}{8} - \frac{3}{8} =$ _____

LESSON 3-3

Subtracting Rational Numbers

Reading Strategies: Use a Graphic Organizer

A graphic organizer is useful for subtracting decimals.

Find 19.2 – 7.54.

Step 1: Draw a table that has three rows. Include enough columns for each place that has a digit in either of the numbers. Include a separate column for the decimal points.

Step 2: Write one digit in each square. Carefully line up the decimals.

1	9	.	2	
–	7	.	5	4

Step 3: If there is a square without a number, insert a zero as a placeholder.

1	9	.	2	0
–	7	.	5	4

Step 4: Subtract each column to find the answer.

1	9	.	2	0
–	7	.	5	4
1	1	.	6	6

1. How do you place the numbers in the table?

_____

2. Why was a zero added to 19.2?

_____

3. Write the problem 40.3 – 6.54 in the grid.

4. Did you need to add a zero as a placeholder? If so, where?

_____

5. Subtract 6.54 from 40.3 using the grid. What is the answer? _____

LESSON 3-3

Subtracting Rational Numbers
Success for English Learners

Problem 1

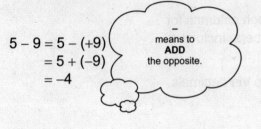

$5 - 9 = 5 - (+9)$
$\qquad = 5 + (-9)$
$\qquad = -4$

means to **ADD** *the opposite.*

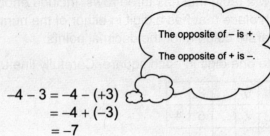

The opposite of − is +.

The opposite of + is −.

$-4 - 3 = -4 - (+3)$
$\qquad = -4 + (-3)$
$\qquad = -7$

Problem 2

From January 1 to March 14

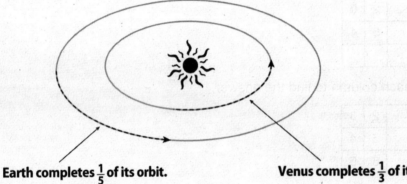

Earth completes $\frac{1}{5}$ of its orbit. Venus completes $\frac{1}{3}$ of its orbit.

$\frac{1}{3} - \frac{1}{5}$ describes how much more of its orbit Venus completes than Earth does.

1. Look at Problem 1. What is the opposite of 9? _____

2. In the second part of Problem 1, why don't you change the −4 to +4?

_____

3. Is 3 − 5 the same as 5 − 3? Explain.

_____

4. In Problem 2, what is the first thing you need to do to find $\frac{1}{3} - \frac{1}{5}$?

_____

5. How much more of its orbit does Venus complete? _____

Name _____ Date _____ Class_____

LESSON 3-4

Multiplying Rational Numbers

Practice and Problem Solving: A/B

Use the number line to find each product.

1. $4\left(-\frac{1}{2}\right)$ _____

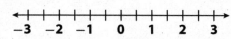

2. $-5\left(-\frac{2}{3}\right)$ _____

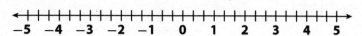

Find the product.

3. $-2\,(3.1)$	4. $4\,(-5.4)$	5. $-3.3\,(6)$	6. $-3\,(-5.6)$
_____	_____	_____	_____

7. $4.5\,(8)$	8. $2\,(-1.05)$	9. $-2.05\,(4)$	10. $-3.5\,(-9)$
_____	_____	_____	_____

Find the product. Show your work.

11. $\left(\frac{2}{3}\right) \times (-6) \times 5 =$ _____

12. $\left(-\frac{3}{5}\right)\left(-\frac{10}{3}\right)\left(-\frac{2}{9}\right) =$ _____

13. $-7 \times \left(-\frac{3}{5}\right) \times \left(\frac{15}{7}\right) =$ _____

14. $2\,(4)\left(\frac{1}{16}\right) =$ _____

Solve. Show your work.

15. A landscaper installs 12 sections of trellis. Each section of trellis is $\frac{3}{4}$ yard long. How many yards of trellis are installed altogether?

_____

16. A biologist uses a box-shaped fish trap that measures $\frac{1}{4}$-meter by $\frac{2}{3}$-meter by $\frac{3}{5}$-meter. What is the volume of the trap in cubic meters?

_____

17. The temperature at noon is 75°F. The temperature drops 3 degrees every half hour. What is the temperature at 4 P.M.?

_____

LESSON 3-4

Multiplying Rational Numbers

Practice and Problem Solving: C

Compare the products by writing < or >. Without doing the calculations, explain how you know your answers are correct.

1. $\frac{1}{2} \times \frac{1}{2} \times \frac{1}{2} = \left(\frac{1}{2}\right)^3$ ◯ 1

   _____

2. $\left(-\frac{1}{2}\right) \times \left(-\frac{1}{2}\right) \times \left(-\frac{1}{2}\right) = \left(-\frac{1}{2}\right)^3$ ◯ 0

   _____

3. $\frac{1}{2} \times \frac{1}{2} \times \frac{1}{2}$ ◯ $\left(-\frac{1}{2}\right) \times \left(-\frac{1}{2}\right) \times \left(-\frac{1}{2}\right)$

   _____

4. $0.5\,(-1.1)$ ◯ 0

   _____

Tell whether each statement is *True* or *False*. Without doing the calculations, explain how you know your answers are correct.

5. $\left(-\frac{1}{2}\right)^6 < 0$ _____

   _____

6. $(1.5)^7 > 1$ _____

   _____

7. $(0.9)^4 > 1$ _____

   _____

Solve. (The formula for the volume of a sphere is $V = \frac{4}{3}\pi r^3$.)

8. The radius of a spherical balloon is $\frac{1}{2}$ foot. The radius of a second one

   is $\frac{3}{4}$ foot. How do the volumes of the balloons compare?

   _____

9. The radius of a sphere is reduced by one third. How does its volume change?

   _____

Name _____ Date _____ Class_____

Multiplying Rational Numbers
Practice and Problem Solving: D

Fill in the blanks to complete the computation. Refer to the number line if you need help. The first one is done for you.

1. $6\left(-\dfrac{1}{2}\right) = \underline{\left(-\dfrac{1}{2}\right)} + \underline{\left(-\dfrac{1}{2}\right)} + \underline{\left(-\dfrac{1}{2}\right)} + \underline{\left(-\dfrac{1}{2}\right)} + \underline{\left(-\dfrac{1}{2}\right)} + \underline{\left(-\dfrac{1}{2}\right)} = \underline{-\dfrac{6}{2}}$ or -3 _____

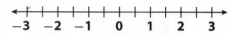

2. $-3\left(-\dfrac{2}{3}\right) = -\underline{\hspace{1cm}} - \underline{\hspace{1cm}} - \underline{\hspace{1cm}} = \underline{\hspace{1cm}}$

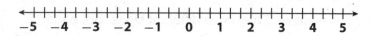

Write each addition expression as a multiplication expression. Then, solve. The first one is done for you.

3. $\dfrac{5}{8} + \dfrac{5}{8} + \dfrac{5}{8} + \dfrac{5}{8} = \underline{\quad 4 \quad} \times \underline{\dfrac{5}{8}} = \underline{\dfrac{20}{8}}$ or $2\dfrac{1}{2}$ _____

4. $(-2.5) + (-2.5) = \underline{\hspace{3cm}} = \underline{\hspace{1.5cm}}$

5. $\left(-\dfrac{2}{9}\right) + \left(-\dfrac{2}{9}\right) + \left(-\dfrac{2}{9}\right) = \underline{\hspace{3cm}} = \underline{\hspace{1.5cm}}$

Fill in the missing steps. Then, find the answer. The first one is started for you.

6. $\left(-\dfrac{1}{4}\right) \times \dfrac{3}{5} \times \left(-\dfrac{2}{5}\right) = \underline{-\dfrac{1}{4}} \times \underline{\left(\dfrac{3 \times (-2)}{5 \times 5}\right)} = \underline{-\dfrac{1}{4}} \times \underline{\hspace{1.5cm}} = \underline{\hspace{1.5cm}}$

7. $4(2.5)0.8 = \underline{\hspace{1.5cm}} \times \underline{\hspace{1.5cm}} \times 0.8 = \underline{\hspace{1.5cm}} \times 0.8 = \underline{\hspace{2.5cm}}$

Solve. The first one is started for you.

8. A seal dives when it see a whale. The seal dives for 5 seconds at an average rate of 3.5 meters per second.

   a. Write an addition expression to represent how far the seal dives in 5 seconds. Find the sum.

   $(-3.5) + (-3.5) + (-3.5) + (-3.5) + (-3.5) =$

   _____

   b. Write a multiplication expression to represent how far the seal dives in 5 seconds. Find the product.

   _____

LESSON 3-4

Multiplying Rational Numbers

Reteach

You can use a number line to multiply rational numbers.

$$5 \times \left(-\frac{1}{2}\right)$$

How many times is the $-\frac{1}{2}$ multiplied?

Five times, so there will be 5 jumps of $\frac{1}{2}$ unit each along the number line.

Your first jump begins at 0. In which direction should you move?

$-\frac{1}{2}$ is negative, and 5 is positive. They have different signs. So, each jump will be to the *left*.

(When both numbers have the same sign, each jump will be to the *right*.)

Name the numbers where each jump ends, from the first to the fifth jump.

$$-\frac{1}{2}, \ -1, \ -1\frac{1}{2}, \ -2, \ -2\frac{1}{2}$$

So, $5 \times \left(-\frac{1}{2}\right) = -2\frac{1}{2}$.

Find each product. Draw a number line for help.

1. $6 \times \frac{1}{4}$

   Multiply $\frac{1}{4}$ how many times? _____

   Which direction on the number line? _____

   Move from 0 to where? _____   Product: _____

2. $-8 \ (-3.3)$

   Multiply (-3.3) how many times? _____

   Move from 0 to where? _____   Product: _____

3. 4.6×5

   Multiply 4.6 how many times? _____

   Move from 0 to where? _____   Product: _____

LESSON 3-4 Multiplying Rational Numbers

Reading Strategies: Understand Symbols

Each number and symbol in a multiplication problem tells you something about how to use a number line to solve it.

$-3\left(-\dfrac{1}{2}\right)$ ⟵ The $\dfrac{1}{2}$ *inside* the parentheses signals that each jump along a number line will be half a unit.

$-3\left(-\dfrac{1}{2}\right)$ ⟵ The 3 *outside* the parentheses signals that there will be a total of 3 jumps.

$-3\left(-\dfrac{1}{2}\right)$ ⟵ Both numbers have the same sign in front of them, a "−" sign. So, in this case, each jump along the number line will be to the *right*, starting from 0.

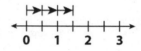

So, $-3\left(-\dfrac{1}{2}\right) = 1\dfrac{1}{2}$.

Put the steps together.

$4\left(-\dfrac{2}{3}\right)$

Step 1: The number inside the parentheses is the length of each jump along the number line. Here, each jump is $\dfrac{2}{3}$.

Step 2: The 4 outside the parentheses signals that a total of 4 jumps must be made.

Step 3: The two numbers have different signs, so each jump along the number line is to the left.

So, $4\left(-\dfrac{2}{3}\right) = -\dfrac{8}{3}$ or $-2\dfrac{2}{3}$.

Use the steps to read the numbers and symbols. Then, multiply.

1. $\left(-\dfrac{2}{3}\right)(-6)$ 2. $-7\,(0.75)$ 3. $4\left(\dfrac{1}{5}\right)(-3)$

_____   _____   _____

Name _____ Date _____ Class_____

LESSON 3-4

Multiplying Rational Numbers

Success for English Learners

Problem 1

Multiply: −3(1.5)

Use a number line.

THINK: 3 jumps   of 1.5 units

Start at 0. Jump which way?

Rule 1: A negative (−) times a positive (+) makes a negative (−).

The product will be negative, so jump *left*.

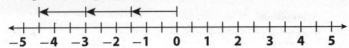

So, −3(1.5) = −4.5

Use Rule 1 to multiply.

1. −2.2(4) _____   2. −6(0.5) _____   3. −1(9.9) _____   4. −3.3(3) _____

Problem 2

Multiply: $-2\left(-\dfrac{3}{4}\right)$

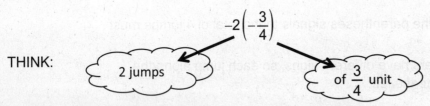

THINK: 2 jumps   of $\dfrac{3}{4}$ unit

Rule 2: A negative (−) times a negative (−) makes a positive (+).

The product will be positive, so jump *right*.

So, $-2\left(-\dfrac{3}{4}\right) = 1\dfrac{2}{4} = 1\dfrac{1}{2}$.

Use Rule 2 to multiply.

5. $-\dfrac{6}{5}(-10) =$ _____   6. $-4\left(-\dfrac{3}{7}\right) =$ _____   7. $\left(-\dfrac{1}{4}\right)(-16) =$ _____

LESSON 3-5

Dividing Rational Numbers

Practice and Problem Solving: A/B

Find each quotient.

1. $\dfrac{1}{2} \div (-3)$

2. $-6 \div \left(-\dfrac{3}{4}\right)$

3. $\dfrac{5}{6} \div 10$

_____

_____

_____

4. $\dfrac{5.25}{15}$

5. $24 \div (-3.2)$

6. $-0.125 \div (-0.5)$

_____

_____

_____

7. $-\dfrac{1}{7} \div -\dfrac{3}{14}$

8. $\dfrac{\left(\dfrac{3}{2}\right)}{\left(-\dfrac{9}{8}\right)} =$

9. $-1\dfrac{1}{2} \div 3\dfrac{1}{3}$

_____

_____

_____

10. $2\dfrac{1}{4} \div \dfrac{3}{8}$

11. $\dfrac{4.2}{-2.4}$

12. $-\dfrac{5}{8} \div \left(-\dfrac{5}{16}\right)$

_____

_____

_____

Fill in the blank with a number to make a true statement.

13. $0.25 \div$ _____ $= -0.25$

14. $-\dfrac{1}{2} \div$ _____ $= -\dfrac{7}{3}$

15. $\dfrac{1}{7} \div$ _____ $= 14$

Write a division problem for each situation. Then, solve it.

16. How many quarter-pound $\left(\dfrac{1}{4}\right)$ packets of plant food can a garden shop make out of 8 pounds of the plant food?

_____

17. The assembly of a machine takes $\dfrac{3}{4}$ hour. There are twelve steps in the assembly process. What is the average time for each step?

_____

18. A 35-meter length of cable is cut into pieces that measure 1.25 meters each. Into how many pieces is the cable cut?

_____

19. $4\dfrac{1}{8}$ tons of gravel is spread evenly across $2\dfrac{1}{6}$ acres. How many tons of gravel are on each acre?

_____

Dividing Rational Numbers
Practice and Problem Solving: C

Write each quotient two other ways by moving the negative sign.

1. $\dfrac{-1}{5}$ = _____

   = _____

2. $-\dfrac{7}{30}$ = _____

   = _____

3. $\dfrac{1}{-2}$ = _____

   = _____

Use >, <, or = to compare the quotients. Show the quotients.

4. $\left(4 \times \dfrac{1}{3}\right) \div \dfrac{2}{5}$ $\bigcirc$ $4 \times \left(\dfrac{1}{3} \div \dfrac{2}{5}\right)$

   _____

5. $(4.5 \div 0.5) \div 3$ $\bigcirc$ $4.5 \div (0.5 \div 3)$

   _____

6. $\left(6 \div -\dfrac{1}{5}\right) \times -\dfrac{4}{3}$ $\bigcirc$ $6 \div \left(-\dfrac{1}{5} \times -\dfrac{4}{3}\right)$

   _____

7. $5.5\,(-3 \times 7.5)$ $\bigcirc$ $7.5\,(-3 \times 5.5)$

   _____

Use decimals to rewrite each quotient. Then, solve.

8. $\dfrac{\left(\dfrac{2}{5}\right)}{\left(-\dfrac{5}{8}\right)}$

   _____

9. $\dfrac{\left(-5\dfrac{2}{5}\right)}{\left(-\dfrac{5}{16}\right)}$

   _____

10. $\dfrac{\left(\dfrac{1}{4}\right)}{\left(\dfrac{3}{5}\right)}$

    _____

Write each quotient as a decimal and as a fraction. Show your work.

11. $\dfrac{\left(1 + \dfrac{1}{2} + \dfrac{1}{4}\right)}{\left(1 - \dfrac{1}{2} - \dfrac{1}{4}\right)}$ _____

12. $\dfrac{\left(1 + \dfrac{1}{3} + \dfrac{1}{6}\right)}{\left(1 - \dfrac{1}{3} - \dfrac{1}{6}\right)}$ _____

13. $\dfrac{\left(1 + \dfrac{1}{4} + \dfrac{1}{8}\right)}{\left(1 - \dfrac{1}{4} - \dfrac{1}{8}\right)}$ _____

14. If the 4s in question 13 are replaced with 5s, and the 8s are replaced with 10s, how will the quotient compare to the other three quotients? Explain.

_____

_____

LESSON 3-5

Dividing Rational Numbers

Practice and Problem Solving: D

Write the missing number. Then, solve. The first one is done for you.

1. $-6 \div \dfrac{3}{4} = -6 \times \dfrac{\underline{4}}{\underline{3}}$

   $\underline{\quad -8 \quad}$

2. $\dfrac{4}{5} \div 8 = \dfrac{4}{5} \times \underline{\quad}$

   _____

3. $\dfrac{-7}{8} \div \dfrac{7}{-4} = \dfrac{-7}{8} \times \underline{\quad}$

   _____

4. $\dfrac{\left(\dfrac{5}{-3}\right)}{\left(\dfrac{7}{8}\right)} = \left(\dfrac{5}{-3}\right) \times \underline{\quad}$

   _____

5. $\dfrac{-2}{\left(\dfrac{4}{9}\right)} = -2 \times \underline{\quad}$

   _____

6. $\dfrac{\left(-4\dfrac{3}{4}\right)}{4} = -\dfrac{19}{4} \times \underline{\quad}$

   _____

Solve. The first one is done for you.

7. $\dfrac{-1}{8} \div -5 = \dfrac{-1}{8} \times -\dfrac{1}{5} = \underline{\quad}$

   $\underline{\quad \dfrac{1}{40} \quad}$

8. $\dfrac{\left(2\dfrac{1}{4}\right)}{\left(-\dfrac{6}{7}\right)} = \dfrac{9}{4} \times -\dfrac{7}{6} = \underline{\quad}$

   _____

9. $3 \div \dfrac{6}{7} = \dfrac{3}{1} \times \dfrac{7}{6} = \underline{\quad}$

   _____

**Find the missing numbers. Add zeros as needed. Then, solve.
The first one is done for you.**

10. $0.4 \div 2.5 \rightarrow 2.5\overline{)?}$

    $\underline{\quad 0.40; \; 0.16 \quad}$

11. $\dfrac{-4.75}{0.3} \rightarrow ?\overline{)-4.75}$

    _____

12. $8 \div 2.5 \rightarrow 2.5\overline{)?}$

    _____

Solve.

13. The town's highway department marks a new road with reflective markers. The road is $6\dfrac{3}{4}$ miles in length. The markers are spaced every eighth $\left(\dfrac{1}{8}\right)$ of a mile.

    a. Write a division problem to find how many markers are installed.

    _____

    b. Solve the problem.

    _____

    c. Explain the answer.

    _____

LESSON 3-5

Dividing Rational Numbers

Reteach

To divide fractions:

- Multiply the first, or "top," number by the reciprocal of the second, or "bottom," number.

- Check the sign.

    Divide: $-\dfrac{3}{5} \div \dfrac{2}{3}$

Step 1: Rewrite the problem to multiply by the reciprocal.

$$-\dfrac{3}{5} \div \dfrac{2}{3} = -\dfrac{3}{5} \times \dfrac{3}{2}$$

Step 2: Multiply.

$$-\dfrac{3}{5} \times \dfrac{3}{2} = \dfrac{-3 \times 3}{5 \times 2} = \dfrac{-9}{10}$$

Step 3: Check the sign.
A negative divided by a positive is a negative.

So, $\dfrac{-9}{10}$ is correct.

$$-\dfrac{3}{5} \div \dfrac{2}{3} = -\dfrac{9}{10}$$

Write the sign of each quotient.

1. $4\dfrac{1}{4} \div 3\dfrac{1}{2}$

2. $-3.5 \div 0.675$

3. $\dfrac{5}{\left(-\dfrac{3}{5}\right)}$

4. $-\dfrac{2}{9} \div \left(-\dfrac{3}{8}\right)$

_____   _____   _____   _____

Complete the steps described above to find each quotient.

5. $-\dfrac{1}{7} \div \left(-\dfrac{5}{9}\right)$

6. $\dfrac{7}{8} \div \dfrac{8}{9}$

Step 1: _____

Step 2: _____

Step 3: _____

Step 1: _____

Step 2: _____

Step 3: _____

LESSON 3-5 Dividing Rational Numbers

Reading Strategies: Read a Table

Writing the signs of the numbers in a table can help you write the correct sign for the answer to division problems.

Look at these rules for signs for two numbers, A and B:

If A is	and B is	then A ÷ B is
+	+	+
+	−	−
−	−	+

Write the correct sign for each quotient: + or −.

	−4	8.25	$-\frac{6}{11}$	$2\frac{1}{12}$
−7.5 ÷	1. ___	2. ___	3. ___	4. ___
$\frac{3}{8}$ ÷	5. ___	6. ___	7. ___	8. ___
$-5\frac{2}{3}$ ÷	9. ___	10. ___	11. ___	12. ___

The rules for signs apply for more than two numbers. Write + or − in the empty cells for the division problem (A ÷ B) ÷ C.

If A	B	and C	then (A ÷ B) ÷ C is
+	−	13. ___ ,	+
+	−	+	14. ___ .
−	−	15. ___ ,	+

LESSON 3-5

Dividing Rational Numbers
Success for English Learners

Problem 1

How to divide mixed numbers . . .

Step 1: Rewrite each mixed number as an improper fraction.

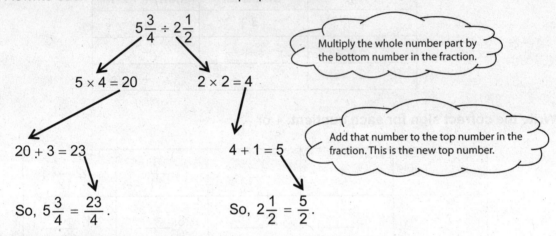

$$5\frac{3}{4} \div 2\frac{1}{2}$$

$$5 \times 4 = 20 \qquad\qquad 2 \times 2 = 4$$

Multiply the whole number part by the bottom number in the fraction.

$$20 + 3 = 23 \qquad\qquad 4 + 1 = 5$$

Add that number to the top number in the fraction. This is the new top number.

So, $5\frac{3}{4} = \frac{23}{4}$. So, $2\frac{1}{2} = \frac{5}{2}$.

Step 2: Which fraction are you dividing by? "Flip" it to get the reciprocal.

"Flip" $\frac{5}{2}$. $\longrightarrow$ $\frac{2}{5}$

Step 3: Multiply the first fraction by this "flipped" fraction:

$$\frac{23}{4} \times \frac{2}{5} = \frac{23 \times 2}{4 \times 5} = \frac{46}{20}$$

Step 4: Simplify the fraction.

$$\frac{46}{20} = \frac{46 \div 2}{20 \div 2} = \frac{23}{10}$$

What number can 46 and 20 both be divided by?

Step 5: Change that improper fraction back to a mixed number.

$$\frac{23}{10} = 2\frac{3}{10}$$

How many 10s in 23? How many left over?

Solve. Use the 5 steps.

1. $7\frac{5}{8} \div 3\frac{2}{3}$ _____

2. $6\frac{1}{5} \div 3\frac{1}{10}$ _____

LESSON 3-6 Applying Rational Number Operations

Practice and Problem Solving: A/B

Estimate each answer. Explain your reasoning.

1. Sections of prefabricated fencing are each $4\frac{1}{3}$ feet long. How long are

   $6\frac{1}{2}$ sections placed end to end?

   _____

2. One half liter of lemonade concentrate is added to 3 liters of water.
   How many $\frac{1}{3}$-liter servings of lemonade are made?

   _____

3. Two $2\frac{1}{2}$-inch plastic strips and two $5\frac{1}{3}$-inch plastic strips are used to

   form a rectangle. What is the perimeter of the rectangle?

   _____

4. The average mass of the eggs laid by chickens on Ms. Watson's farm
   is 3.5 grams. About how many grams does a dozen eggs weigh?

   _____

5. An 8.5-centimeter green bean pod contains peas that average
   0.45- centimeter in diameter. How many peas are in the pod?

   _____

**Solve by converting to the easiest form of the rational numbers to use
in the problem. Show your work**

6. Arwen uses a dropper that produces drops that have a volume of
   $\frac{1}{8}$-milliliter to fill a 30-milliliter test tube. How many drops does it take

   to fill the test tube?

   _____

   _____

7. Three strips of 2-yard-wide outdoor carpet are used to cover a sidewalk. One is
   3.5 yards long, the second is 25 percent longer than the first, and the third is

   $6\frac{1}{4}$ yards long. How long are the three carpets placed end to end?

   _____

   _____

Name _____ Date _____ Class_____

 # Applying Rational Number Operations
Practice and Problem Solving: C

Use the information given in the table below to complete Exercises 1–4.

Planets' Orbital Velocity

Planet	Orbital Velocity (mi/s)
Mercury	29.74
Venus	21.76
Earth	18.5
Mars	14.99
Jupiter	8.12
Saturn	6.02
Uranus	4.23

Solve. Show your work. Express the answer in fraction form.

1. How many miles does Mercury travel in an hour? Simplify the fractions in your answer.

   _____

2. How much greater is the orbital velocity of Mercury than Jupiter? Simplify the fractions in your answer.

   _____

3. During the time it takes Saturn to travel 32,508 miles, how much time in seconds has elapsed on Earth? Simplify the fractions in your answer.

   _____

4. How many miles does Venus travel in a minute? Simplify the fractions in your answer.

   _____

Name _____ Date _____ Class_____

LESSON 3-6

Applying Rational Number Operations

Practice and Problem Solving: D

Solve. Show your work. The first one has been done for you.

1. A middle school conducts a recycling drive, during which $\frac{1}{5}$ of the materials collected were bottles and $\frac{1}{4}$ was paper. Cardboard boxes made up $\frac{1}{10}$ of the material. How much of the total do these three categories of items represent?

   The LCM of the three denominators, 4, 5, and 10, is 20.

   Multiply each fraction to get a common denominator of 20.

   $$\frac{1}{5} \cdot \frac{4}{4} = \frac{4}{20} \qquad \frac{1}{4} \cdot \frac{5}{5} = \frac{5}{20} \qquad \frac{1}{10} \cdot \frac{2}{2} = \frac{2}{20}$$

   Add the fractions: $\frac{4}{20} + \frac{5}{20} + \frac{2}{20} = \frac{11}{20}$

   Bottles, paper, and cardboard boxes were $\frac{11}{20}$ of the total amount of recycled material collected by the middle school.

2. A family budgets $\frac{1}{2}$ of its income for housing and $\frac{1}{3}$ for food. What fraction of their budget do these expenses cover?

   _____

   _____

3. Decorations for the seventh-grade dance take $\frac{1}{6}$ of the student council's budget. Entertainment takes $\frac{3}{8}$ of the budget. What fraction of the budget do these expenses cover? What fraction is left for other activities? (*Hint*: To answer the second question, subtract the answer to the first question from 1, which represents the whole budget.)

   _____

   _____

   _____

LESSON 3-6
Applying Rational Number Operations
Reteach

To multiply fractions and mixed numbers:
Step 1: Write any mixed numbers as improper fractions.
Step 2: Multiply the numerators.
Step 3: Multiply the denominators.
Step 4: Write the answer in simplest form.

> Remember, positive times negative equals negative.

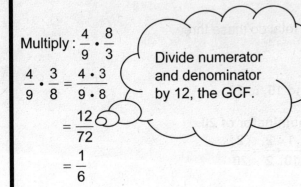

Multiply: $\dfrac{4}{9} \cdot \dfrac{8}{3}$

$\dfrac{4}{9} \cdot \dfrac{3}{8} = \dfrac{4 \cdot 3}{9 \cdot 8}$

> Divide numerator and denominator by 12, the GCF.

$= \dfrac{12}{72}$

$= \dfrac{1}{6}$

Multiply: $6\dfrac{1}{4} \cdot \left(-1\dfrac{4}{5}\right)$

$6\dfrac{1}{4} \cdot \left(-1\dfrac{4}{5}\right) = \dfrac{25}{4} \cdot \left(\dfrac{-9}{5}\right)$

$= \dfrac{25 \cdot (-9)}{4 \cdot 5}$

$= \dfrac{-225}{20}$

$= -11\dfrac{1}{4}$

Use the models to solve the problems.

1. One cup of dog food weighs $1\dfrac{4}{5}$ ounces. A police dog eats $6\dfrac{1}{3}$ cups of food a day. How many ounces of food does the dog eat each day?

   _____

2. A painter spends 3 hours working on a painting. A sculptor spends $2\dfrac{2}{3}$ as long working on a sculpture. How long does the sculptor work?

   _____

3. A meteorite found in the United States weighs $\dfrac{7}{10}$ as much as one found in Mongolia. The meteorite found in Mongolia weighs 22 tons. How much does the one found in the United States weigh?

   _____

4. A chicken salad recipe calls for $\dfrac{1}{8}$ pound of chicken per serving. How many pounds of chicken are needed to make $8\dfrac{1}{2}$ servings?

   _____

LESSON 3-6

Applying Rational Number Operations

Reading Strategies: Use a Visual Model

The Smith family has a two-and-a-half-foot-long sandwich to share. One-half foot of the sandwich will serve one person. How many one-half foot servings are in this sandwich?

$$\longleftarrow 2\frac{1}{2} \text{ feet} \longrightarrow$$

$\frac{1}{2}$	$\frac{1}{2}$	$\frac{1}{2}$	$\frac{1}{2}$	$\frac{1}{2}$

Use the model to answer each question.

1. How long is the sandwich?

   _____

2. How long is each serving?

   _____

3. If you divided the sandwich into $\frac{1}{2}$-foot servings, how many would you have?

   _____

4. What is $2\frac{1}{2} \div \frac{1}{2}$?

   _____

Suppose you have two sandwiches.

$\frac{1}{2}$	$\frac{1}{2}$	$\frac{1}{2}$	$\frac{1}{2}$	$\frac{1}{2}$

$\frac{1}{2}$	$\frac{1}{2}$	$\frac{1}{2}$	$\frac{1}{2}$	$\frac{1}{2}$

5. How many feet are in both sandwiches?

   _____

6. What is $2\frac{1}{2} \times 2$?

   _____

7. Compare the answers to $2\frac{1}{2} \div \frac{1}{2}$ and $2\frac{1}{2} \times 2$. What do you notice?

   _____

   _____

LESSON 3-6

Applying Rational Number Operations

Success for English Learners

Problem 1

Add $\frac{3}{10} + \frac{1}{10}$.

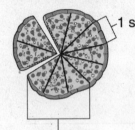

-1 slice

3 slices

$\frac{10}{10} = 1$ whole pizza

$3 + 1 = 4$ slices

$\frac{3}{10}$ of the pizza $+ \frac{1}{10}$ of the pizza

$\frac{3}{10} + \frac{1}{10} = \frac{4}{10}$ of the pizza

Simplify. $\frac{4}{10} = \frac{2}{5}$.

Problem 2

From January 1 to March 14:

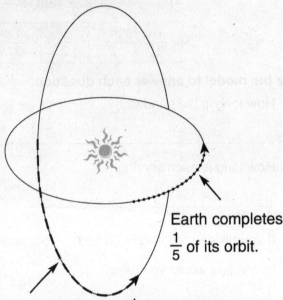

Earth completes $\frac{1}{5}$ of its orbit.

Venus completes $\frac{1}{3}$ of its orbit.

$\frac{1}{3} - \frac{1}{5}$ describes how much more of its orbit Venus completes than Earth.

1. Explain what the denominator represents in Problem 1.

_____

2. In order to find the answer to $\frac{1}{3} - \frac{1}{5}$ in Problem 2, what is the first thing you need to do?

_____

3. If the denominators of two fractions are the same, how do you add the fractions?

_____

MODULE 3 # Rational Numbers
Challenge

1. A meteorologist is measuring the change in temperature in three cities.
   For five days, she recorded the daily temperature in each city.

Temperatures (°C) in Three Cities

City	Monday	Tuesday	Wednesday	Thursday	Friday
City A	$-\dfrac{1}{8}$	$2\dfrac{1}{4}$	$-3\dfrac{1}{2}$	$5\dfrac{4}{5}$	$-12\dfrac{1}{2}$
City B	$4\dfrac{1}{5}$	$-1\dfrac{3}{5}$	$-8\dfrac{1}{10}$	$11\dfrac{1}{5}$	$3\dfrac{3}{10}$
City C	$11\dfrac{1}{3}$	$2\dfrac{5}{6}$	$-3\dfrac{2}{3}$	$-9\dfrac{1}{6}$	$2\dfrac{1}{3}$

The temperature change is the difference between the temperature on
a certain day and the temperature the day before.

For example, in City A the temperature change from Monday to
Tuesday was $2\dfrac{1}{4} - \left(-\dfrac{1}{8}\right) = 2\dfrac{3}{8}$.

The meteorologist defines the "temperature volatility" to be the sum of
the daily temperature changes over a certain period of time.

Which city had the greatest temperature volatility for the five-day
period shown?

_____

2. In the mathematical expression below, the three boxes can be filled
   with any operation symbol (+, −, ×, or ÷).

$$2 \ \square \ -\dfrac{1}{8} \ \square \ -10 \ \square \ 16$$

Each operation symbol can only be used once.

For example, the boxes can be filled as shown below:

$$2 \ \boxed{\div} \ -\dfrac{1}{8} \ \boxed{-} \ -10 \ \boxed{+} \ 16, \text{ which equals 10.}$$

How can the operations be placed in the boxes to yield the greatest
possible value for the expression? (Hint: Remember to multiply and
divide before you add and subtract.)

_____

LESSON
4-1

Unit Rates

Practice and Problem Solving: A/B

Solve.

1. To make 2 batches of nut bars, Jayda needs to use 4 eggs. How many eggs are used in each batch of nut bars?

   _____

2. On her way to visit her parents, Jennifer drives 265 miles in 5 hours. What is her average rate of speed in miles per hour?

   _____

3. Last week Alexander was paid $56 for 7 hours of work. How much money does Alexander's job pay per hour?

   _____

4. Ned has scored 84 points in the first 6 games of the basketball season. How many points per game has Ned scored?

   _____

5. At the local grocery store, a 16-ounce bottle of apple juice costs $3.20. What is the cost of the apple juice per ounce?

   _____

6. An above-ground swimming pool is leaking. After $\frac{1}{2}$ hour the pool has

   leaked $\frac{7}{8}$ of a gallon of water. How many gallons of water per hour is

   the swimming pool leaking?

   _____

7. After $\frac{3}{4}$ of a minute a sloth has moved just $\frac{3}{8}$ of a foot. What is the

   sloth's speed in feet per minute?

   _____

8. Food A contains 150 calories in $\frac{3}{4}$ of a serving. Food B contains

   250 calories in $\frac{2}{3}$ of a serving. Find each unit rate. Which food has

   fewer calories per serving?

   _____

LESSON 4-1

Unit Rates

Practice and Problem Solving: C

Solve.

1. Sasha can mow $\frac{3}{8}$ of an acre of grass in 45 minutes. How many acres of grass does Sasha mow per hour?

   _____

2. Ammar hikes $2\frac{3}{4}$ miles of nature trail in 1 hour and 15 minutes. How many miles of trail does Ammar hike per hour?

   _____

3. Melinda paints $\frac{7}{8}$ of a wall in $1\frac{1}{6}$ hours. What part of a wall does Melinda paint in 1 minute?

   _____

4. There is $\frac{1}{4}$ ounce of yeast in every $2\frac{1}{4}$ teaspoons of yeast. A recipe for bread calls for 2 teaspoons of yeast. How many ounces of yeast are needed for this recipe?

   _____

5. Every $5\frac{1}{2}$ cups of flour weighs $1\frac{9}{16}$ pounds. Use a unit rate to show how you could determine if there are more than or less than 35 cups of flour in a 10-pound bag of flour.

   _____

   _____

6. One tank is filling at a rate of $\frac{5}{8}$ gallon per $\frac{7}{10}$ hour. A second tank is filling at rate of $\frac{5}{9}$ gallon per $\frac{2}{3}$ hour. Which tank is filling faster? Explain how you know.

   _____

   _____

   _____

LESSON 4-1

Unit Rates

Practice and Problem Solving: D

Solve. The first one is done for you.

1. To make 2 loaves of banana bread, Leandra needs 6 eggs.
   How many eggs are needed to make 1 loaf of banana bread?

$$\frac{6 \text{ eggs}}{2 \text{ loaves}} = \frac{\textbf{3} \text{ eggs}}{1 \text{ loaf}}$$

   Leandra needs _____**3**_____ eggs to make 1 loaf of banana bread.

2. On his way to visit his sister at college, Gregg drives 135 miles in
   3 hours. What is his average rate of speed in miles per hour?

$$\frac{135 \text{ miles}}{3 \text{ hours}} = \frac{\text{miles}}{1 \text{ hour}}$$

   Gregg's average rate of speed is _____ miles per hour.

3. Jan designs a new logo for Kim's website. Kim pays Jan $45 for
   5 hours of work. How much money does Kim pay Jan per hour?

   _____

4. At a discount grocery store, Jessica paid $0.72 for an 8-ounce bottle of
   spring water. What is the cost of the spring water per ounce?

   _____

5. A bucket is leaking. After 3 hours the bucket has leaked $\frac{3}{4}$ of an

   ounce. How many ounces per hour is the bucket leaking?

$$\frac{\frac{3}{4} \text{ oz}}{3 \text{ h}} = \frac{3}{4} \div \frac{3}{1} = \underline{\quad} \times \underline{\quad} = \frac{\text{oz}}{1 \text{ h}}$$

6. After 15 minutes a train has moved $\frac{9}{2}$ miles toward its destination.

   How many miles per minute is the train moving?

   _____

7. A snack that Reginald just bought has 150 calories in $\frac{3}{4}$ of a serving.

   How many calories per serving is this?

$$\frac{150 \text{ cal}}{\frac{3}{4} \text{ serving}} = \frac{150}{1} \div \underline{\quad} = \frac{150}{1} \times \underline{\quad} = \frac{\text{cal}}{1 \text{ serving}}$$

   _____

LESSON 4-1

Unit Rates

Reteach

A **rate** is a ratio that compares two *different* kinds of quantities or measurements.

3 aides for 24 students	135 words in 3 minutes	7 ads per 4 pages
$\dfrac{3 \text{ aides}}{24 \text{ students}}$	$\dfrac{135 \text{ words}}{3 \text{ minutes}}$	$\dfrac{7 \text{ ads}}{4 \text{ pages}}$

Express each comparison as a rate in ratio form.

1. 70 students per 2 teachers   2. 3 books in 2 months   3. $52 for 4 hours of work

_____   _____   _____

In a **unit rate**, the quantity in the denominator is 1.

300 miles in 6 hours	275 square feet in 25 minutes
$\dfrac{300 \text{ miles}}{6 \text{ hours}} = \dfrac{300 \div 6}{6 \div 6} = \dfrac{50 \text{ miles}}{1 \text{ hour}}$	$\dfrac{275 \text{ ft}^2}{25 \text{ min}} = \dfrac{275 \div 25}{25 \div 25} = \dfrac{11 \text{ ft}^2}{1 \text{ min}}$

Express each comparison as a unit rate. Show your work.

4. 28 patients for 2 nurses _____

5. 5 quarts for every 2 pounds _____

When one or both of the quantities being compared is a fraction, the rate is expressed as a **complex fraction**. Unit rates can be used to simplify rates containing fractions.

15 miles every $\frac{1}{2}$ hour	$\frac{1}{4}$ cup for every $\frac{2}{3}$ minute
$\dfrac{15 \text{ miles}}{\frac{1}{2} \text{ hour}} = 15 \div \dfrac{1}{2} = \dfrac{15}{1} \times \dfrac{2}{1} = \dfrac{30 \text{ miles}}{1 \text{ hour}}$	$\dfrac{\frac{1}{4} \text{ c}}{\frac{2}{3} \text{ min}} = \dfrac{1}{4} \div \dfrac{2}{3} = \dfrac{1}{4} \times \dfrac{3}{2} = \dfrac{\frac{3}{8} \text{ c}}{1 \text{ min}}$

Complete to find each unit rate. Show your work.

6. 3 ounces for every $\frac{3}{4}$ cup   7. $3\frac{2}{3}$ feet per $\frac{11}{60}$ hour

_____   _____

LESSON
4-1

Unit Rates

Reading Strategies: Build Vocabulary

A **rate** is a special ratio that compares two values that are measured in different units. When one or both quantities being compared are fractions, the rate is expressed as a **complex fraction**.

$8 for 2 pounds of beef

↓

$$\frac{\$8}{2 \text{ lb}}$$

↓

pounds compared to dollars

3 miles in $\frac{1}{4}$ hour

↓

$$\frac{3 \text{ mi}}{\frac{1}{4} \text{ h}}$$

↓

miles compared to hours

Answer each question.

1. Is the ratio $\frac{5 \text{ hours}}{12 \text{ hours}}$ a rate? Explain.

_____

2. Is the ratio $\frac{50 \text{ yards}}{18 \text{ seconds}}$ a rate? Explain.

_____

3. What does the rate $\frac{25 \text{ miles}}{\frac{2}{3} \text{ gallon}}$ compare?

_____

In a **unit rate**, the second quantity in the rate is 1 unit. To rewrite a rate as a unit rate, rewrite the rate as a fraction with a denominator of 1.

Write *yes* or *no* to tell whether each rate is a unit rate. If a rate is not a unit rate, rewrite it as a unit rate.

4. $\frac{\$2.75}{1 \text{ h}}$ _____

5. $\frac{100 \text{ mi}}{4 \text{ gal}}$ _____

6. $\frac{200 \text{ ft}^2}{\frac{1}{4} \text{ h}}$ _____

7. $\frac{\frac{2}{3} \text{ lb}}{15 \text{ min}}$ _____

LESSON 4-1

Unit Rates

Success for English Learners

Problem 1

The Lawsons drive 288 miles in 6 hours. What is their average speed per hour?

Write the rate as a fraction.

$$\frac{\text{number of miles}}{\text{number of hours}} = \frac{288 \text{ miles}}{6 \text{ hours}}$$

Think: What can I do to change the denominator to a 1?

$$\frac{288 \text{ miles}}{6 \text{ hours}} \div \frac{6}{6} = \frac{48}{1}$$

$$288 \div 6 = 48$$

 The unit rate is:

$$48 \text{ miles per hour} = \frac{48 \text{ miles}}{1 \text{ hour}}.$$

So, their average speed is 48 miles per hour.

Problem 2

Bucket A is filling at a rate of $\frac{1}{2}$ cup per $\frac{2}{3}$ minutes. Bucket B is filling at a rate of $\frac{1}{3}$ cup per $\frac{1}{4}$ minutes. Which bucket is filling faster?

Write each rate as a fraction.

Bucket A	Bucket B
$\dfrac{\frac{1}{2} \text{ c}}{\frac{2}{3} \text{ min}}$	$\dfrac{\frac{1}{3} \text{ c}}{\frac{1}{4} \text{ min}}$

Rewrite each fraction as division, then solve.

Bucket A

$$\frac{\frac{1}{2}}{\frac{2}{3}} = \frac{1}{2} \div \frac{2}{3}$$

$$= \frac{1}{2} \times \frac{3}{2}$$

$$= \frac{3}{4} \text{ c per min}$$

Bucket B

$$\frac{\frac{1}{3}}{\frac{1}{4}} = \frac{1}{3} \div \frac{1}{4}$$

$$= \frac{1}{3} \times \frac{4}{1}$$

$$= \frac{4}{3}, \text{ or } 1\frac{1}{3} \text{ c per min}$$

Compare the unit rates.

Bucket A		Bucket B
$\dfrac{3}{4}$	$<$	$1\dfrac{1}{3}$

So, Bucket B is filling faster.

Solve.

1. Seth walks $1\frac{1}{4}$ miles in $\frac{5}{12}$ hour. What is Seth's unit rate? _____

2. Briana walks $\frac{3}{4}$ mile in $\frac{1}{5}$ hour. What is Briana's unit rate? _____

3. Compare the walking speeds of Seth and Briana from questions 1 and 2. Who has the faster speed per hour?

_____

Constant Rates of Change

Practice and Problem Solving: A/B

Use the table to determine whether the relationship is proportional. If so, write an equation for the relationship. Tell what each variable you used represents.

1.

Number of tickets	2	3	4	5
Total Cost ($)	54	81	108	135

a. Proportional? _____

b. Equation: _____

c. Number of tickets: _____

d. Total Cost: _____

2.

Weight (lb)	4	5	46
Total Cost ($)	17.40	21.75	200.10

a. Proportional? _____

b. Equation: _____

c. Weight: _____

d. Total cost: _____

3.

Time (h)	2	3	4	5	6
Pages Read	50	75	90	110	120

_____

_____

4.

Time (h)	2	3	4
Distance (mi)	80	120	160

_____

_____

The tables show proportional relationships. Find the constant of proportionality, _k_. Write an equation to represent the relationship between the two quantities. Tell what each variable represents.

5.

Pens	3	6	9	12
Boxes	1	2	3	4

_____

_____

6.

Pack	1	2	4	5
Muffins	6	12	24	30

_____

_____

7. a. Create a table to show how the number of days is related to the number of hours. Show at least 5 days.

b. Is the relationship proportional? _____

c. Write an equation for the relationship. _____

LESSON 4-2

Constant Rates of Change

Practice and Problem Solving: C

Answer the following questions.

1. Three tickets to attend an Off-Broadway show cost $81, 4 tickets cost $108, and 5 tickets cost $135.

   a. Show that the relationship between number and the cost is a proportional relationship by making a table of tickets for 1 to 5 tickets.

Number of Tickets					
Total Cost ($)					

   b. The constant of proportionality k is _____.

   c. Write an equation for the relationship: _____

2. On the seventh-grade trip to Washington, D.C., for every 8 students, there were 3 chaperones. Twelve chaperones were needed. How many students went on the trip?

   _____

Determine whether the relationship is a proportional relationship. If so, write an equation for the relationship, and tell what each of your variables represents. If the relationship is not proportional, explain.

3. Ty takes 1 hour to read 35 pages, 2 hours to read 70 pages, and 3 hours to read 105 pages.

   _____

4. There are 12 grams of protein in 2 ounces of almonds.

   _____

5.
Weight (lb)	4	5	6	7
Cost ($)	18	22.5	27	31.5

   _____

6.
Time (h)	1	2	3	4
Distance (mi)	35	80	120	145

   _____

Constant Rates of Change

Practice and Problem Solving: D

Use the table to determine whether the relationship is proportional. If so, write an equation to show the relationship between the two quantities. Tell what each of the variables you used represents. The first one has been done for you.

1.

Teams	1	2	3	4
Number of Players	6	12	18	24

a. Proportional? _____**yes**_____

b. Equation: _____$y = 6x$_____

c. Number of teams: _____x_____

d. Number of players: _____y_____

2.

Time (h)	1	2	3	4
Cars Washed	3	6	9	12

a. Proportional? _____

b. Equation: _____

c. Number of hours: _____

d. Cars washed: _____

3.

Weight (lb)	3	4	5
Cost ($)	2.25	3.00	3.75

_____

_____

_____

4.

Time (min)	2	3	4
Songs Played	10	14	20

_____

_____

_____

The following tables show proportional relationships. Find the constant of proportionality, *k*. Then write an equation to show the relationship between the two quantities. Tell what each of the variables you used represents. The first one has been done for you.

5.

Apples	5	10	15	20
Bags	1	2	3	4

$k = \dfrac{1}{5}$

$y = \dfrac{1}{5}x;$

$x = apples; y = bags$

6.

Cartons	1	2	4	5
Eggs	12	24	48	60

$k =$ _____

_____

_____

LESSON 4-2

Constant Rates of Change
Reteach

A **proportion** is an equation or statement that two rates are the same.

> *In 1 hour of babysitting, Rajiv makes $8.*
> *He makes $16 in 2 hours, and $24 in 3 hours.*

The same information is shown in the table below.

Time Worked (h)	1	2	3
Total Wage ($)	8	16	24

To see if this relationship is proportional, find out if the rate of change is constant. Express each rate of change shown in the table as a fraction.

$$\frac{8}{1} = 8 \qquad \frac{16}{2} = 8 \qquad \frac{24}{3} = 8$$

The rate of change for each column is the same. Because the rate of change is constant, the relationship is *proportional*.

You can express a proportional relationship by using the equation $y = kx$, where k represents the constant rate of change between x and y.

In this example: $k = 8$. Write the equation as $y = 8x$.

The table shows the number of texts Terri received in certain periods of time.

Time (min)	1	2	3	4
Number of Texts	3	6	9	12

1. Is the relationship between number of texts and time a proportional

   relationship? _____

2. For each column of the table, write a fraction and find k, the constant of proportionality.

   _____

3. Express this relationship in the form of an equation: _____

4. What is the rate of change? _____

Write the equation for each table. Let x be time or weight.

5.
Time (h)	1	2	3	4
Distance (mi)	35	70	105	140

6.
Weight (lb)	3	4	5	6
Cost ($)	21	28	35	42

_____   _____

Name _____ Date _____ Class_____

Constant Rates of Change
Reading Strategies: Use Graphic Aids

A **proportion** is a statement where two rates of change, or ratios, are **equivalent**. The statement below is one example of a proportional statement.

> *For 1 hour of garden work, Kathy makes $7.*
> *She makes $14 in 2 hours, and $21 in 3 hours.*

You can use a table to help you see whether the relationship between two quantities is proportional. The table below shows the relationship between the number of hours Kathy works and the amount she is paid.

Time Worked (hr)	1	2	3
Total Wages ($)	7	14	21

To tell whether the relationship between Kathy's time worked and her total wages is proportional, take the numbers in each column of the table, and write each pair as a ratio in the form of a fraction. Use time as your denominator and total wages as your numerator.

$$\frac{7}{1} = 7 \qquad\qquad \frac{14}{2} = 7 \qquad\qquad \frac{21}{3} = 7$$

All three fractions are equivalent, so the relationship is proportional.

The table shows the number of lengths of a swimming pool that Mario swam in certain time periods.

Time (min)	1	2	3	4
Distance (lengths)	3	6	9	12

1. Find the rate at which Mario swam for each time period. Write the pair of numbers in each column of the table as a ratio in the form of a fraction. Use distance as the numerators and time as the denominators.

   _____

2. What is the constant rate of change? _____

3. Is the relationship between distance and time a proportional

   relationship? _____

Find the rate of change shown in each table.

4.
Time (h)	1	2	3	4
Distance (mi)	35	70	105	140

5.
Weight (lb)	4	5	6	7
Cost ($)	17.40	21.75	26.10	30.45

_____   _____

LESSON 4-2 Constant Rates of Change
Success for English Learners

Problem 1

Write a proportion.

2 of the 3 objects are squares.

$\dfrac{2}{3}$

If there are 2 sets of objects, 4 will be squares.

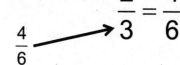

$\dfrac{4}{6}$

$\dfrac{2}{3} = \dfrac{4}{6}$

How many ☐ would you have, if you had **4** △ ?

△	1	2	3	**4**
☐	2	4	6	**8**

For every 2 squares, there is 1 triangle. The relationship is proportional.

Answer the following questions. First, complete the table below. Then, find the proportional relationship.

1. There are 6 ◯ for every 2 ⬭ . Complete the table below to find the proportional relationship.

◯	6			12	15
⬭	2	1	3		

2. For every ⬭ , there are ____ ◯ .

Name _____ Date _____ Class_____

Proportional Relationships and Graphs

Practice and Problem Solving: A/B

Complete each table. Explain why the relationship is a proportional relationship.

1. A cashier earns $8 per hour.

Time (h)	2	4		
Pay ($)	16		40	72

_____

_____

2. Tomatoes cost $0.70 per pound.

Weight (lb)	2		6	8
Price ($)	1.40	2.10		

_____

_____

Tell whether the relationship is a proportional relationship. Explain your answer.

3.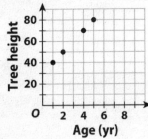

_____

_____

4.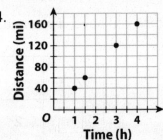

_____

_____

The graph shows the relationship between the distance traveled by a car and the amount of fuel used by the car.

5. Explain the meaning of (2, 40).

_____

6. Write an equation for this relationship.

_____

7. Suppose a compact car uses 1 gallon of fuel for every 27 miles traveled. How would the graph for the compact car compare to the graph for the car shown?

_____

_____

Name _____ Date _____ Class_____

Proportional Relationships and Graphs

Practice and Problem Solving: C

The graph shows the relationship between hours worked and money earned (in dollars) for two employees, A and B.

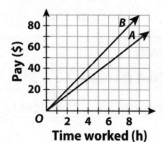

1. Suppose both employees work the same amount of time. Determine which employee earns more money. Explain.

   _____

   _____

2. Using the pay rates shown, determine the amount of money each employee earns for 15 hours of work.

   _____

   _____

3. The pay rate for employee C is less than the pay rate for employee B and greater than the pay rate for employee A. Write an equation for the possible pay *y* in dollars that employee C earns working *x* hours.

   _____

4. Two companies offer digital cable television as described below.

   Company A: $39.99 per month with no installation fee

   Company B: $34.99 per month with a $50 installation fee

   For each company, tell whether the relationship between months of service and total cost is a proportional relationship. Explain why or why not.

   _____

   _____

The table shows the relationship between the length and width of 5 different U.S. flags.

Width (ft), *x*	1.5	4.5	8	10.5	12.5
Length (ft), *y*	3	9	16	21	25

5. Is the relationship is a proportional relationship? If so, write an equation of the form $y = kx$ for the relationship.

   _____

6. Explain how to determine whether a relationship shown in a table is a proportional relationship.

   _____

   _____

Name _____ Date _____ Class _____

Proportional Relationships and Graphs
Practice and Problem Solving: D

Tell whether the relationship is a proportional relationship. Explain your answer. The first one is done for you.

1. Each shirt costs $10.

Shirts	1	2	3	4
Cost ($)	10	20	30	40

__proportional; The cost is always__

__10 times the number of shirts.__

2. There are 50 crayons in each box.

Boxes of crayons	1	2	3
Crayons	50	100	150

_____

_____

3. A person walks 5 feet per second.

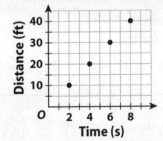

_____

4. A gym costs $20 per month plus a fee.

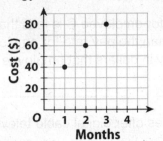

_____

Write an equation for the proportional relationship with the given constant of proportionality *k*. The first one is done for you.

5. $k = 6$

__$y = 6x$__

6. $k = 4$

_____

7. $k = \dfrac{1}{3}$

_____

8. The graph shows the relationship between the money earned and the number of hours worked. Determine the constant of proportionality for this relationship. Show your work.

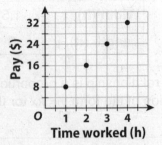

_____

LESSON 4-3 Proportional Relationships and Graphs
Reteach

The graph of a proportional relationship is a line that passes through the origin. An equation of the form $y = kx$ represents a proportional relationship where k is the constant of proportionality.

The graph below shows the relationship between the number of peanut butter sandwiches and the teaspoons of peanut butter used for the sandwiches.

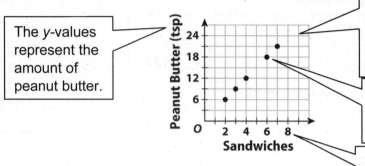

The y-values represent the amount of peanut butter.

A line through the points passes through the origin, which shows a proportional relationship.

Point (6, 18) represents the amount of peanut butter (18 tsp) used for 6 sandwiches.

The x-values represent the number of sandwiches.

The constant of proportionality k is equal to y divided by x. Use the point (6, 18) to find the constant of proportionality for the relationship above.

$$k = \frac{y}{x} = \frac{\text{amount of peanut butter}}{\text{number of sandwiches}} = \frac{18}{6} = 3$$

Using $k = 3$, an equation for the relationship is $y = 3x$.

Fill in the blanks to write an equation for the given proportional relationship.

1.

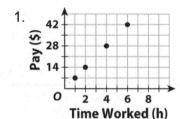

The x-values represent _____.

The y-values represent _____.

Using point _____, $k = \dfrac{y}{x} =$ _____ = _____.

An equation for the graph is _____.

2.

The x-values represent _____.

The y-values represent _____.

Using point _____, $k = \dfrac{y}{x} =$ _____ = _____.

An equation for the graph is _____.

Proportional Relationships and Graphs

LESSON 4-3

Reading Strategies: Reading Tables and Graphs

When two quantities are related by a constant multiplier, the quantities have a **proportional relationship.** The graph of a proportional relationship is a straight line through the origin.

The table below shows the relationship between the number of glasses filled and the amount of juice needed to fill them. The relationship between these two quantities is a proportional relationship.

Glasses	1	2	3	4
Juice Needed (oz)	8	16	24	32

1. What are the quantities used to form this relationship?

    _____

2. How are the two quantities related?

    _____

The data from the table is shown in the graph below. Notice that a line drawn through the points passes through the origin.

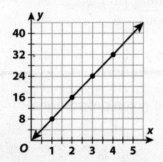

3. What do the *x*-values in the graph represent?

    _____

4. What do the *y*-values in the graph represent?

    _____

5. What does the ordered pair (2, 16) represent?

    _____

6. Write an ordered pair for 3 glasses and the amount of juice needed.

    _____

LESSON 4-3

Proportional Relationships and Graphs

Success for English Learners

Problem 1

Does the graph show a proportional relationship? Use a flowchart to help you.

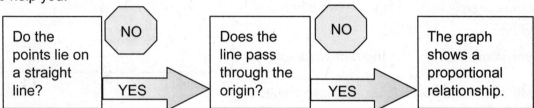

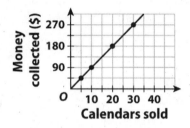

Question	NO	YES
Points on straight line?		✓
Does line go through (0, 0)?		✓
Proportional relationship?		✓

Problem 2

Write an equation for the proportional relationship in the graph above.

1 Pick a point on the graph.

2 Find the constant of proportionality *k*.

3 Write an equation of the form *y* = *kx*.

(10, 90)

$k = \dfrac{y}{x} = \dfrac{\text{money collected}}{\text{calendars sold}} = \dfrac{90}{10} = 9$

$y = 9x$

1. Complete the following statements about the constant of proportionality *k* in a proportional relationship.

   • constant of proportionality = $\dfrac{\text{change in } \boxed{} - \text{values}}{\text{change in } \boxed{} - \text{values}}$

   • The constant of proportionality is the ratio of the

   _____ to the _____.

2. Do all straight lines represent proportional relationships? Explain.

   _____

MODULE 4

Ratios and Proportionality
Challenge

Variations on Variation

An equation with the general form $y = kx$ represents a proportional relationship called **direct variation**. The variable y varies directly with x. Here are two other kinds of variation.

quadratic variation: $y = kx^2$ **indirect variation**: $y = \dfrac{k}{x}$

Examples with real-world contexts usually have values of k greater than 0. The graphs are often shown only in the first quadrant, quadrant I. But k doesn't have to be positive. For values of x less than 0, the graphs will be in more than one quadrant.

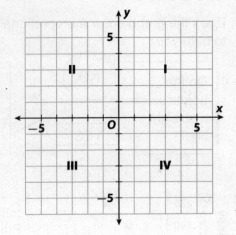

Use a graphing calculator or computer graphing program. For each problem, analyze all three variation equations: direct, quadratic, and indirect.

1. Let $k = 1$. Describe what the three graphs look like in the first quadrant.

   direct: _____

   quadratic: _____

   indirect: _____

2. Let $k = 1$. Tell which quadrants contain the graphs for *all* values of the independent variable x.

   direct: _____   quadratic: _____   indirect: _____

3. For each type of variation, describe what happens in the first quadrant as k gets larger than 1. Try several different values for k.

   direct: _____

   quadratic: _____

   indirect: _____

4. Explore what happens when k is negative. Which quadrants contain the graphs?

   direct: _____   quadratic: _____   indirect: _____

LESSON 5-1

Percent Increase and Decrease

Practice and Problem Solving: A/B

Find each percent increase. Round to the nearest percent.

1. From 24 teachers to 30 teachers _____

2. From $18 to $45 _____

3. From 75 pencils to 225 pencils _____

4. From $65 to $144 _____

5. From 42 acres to 72 acres _____

6. From 95 trees to 145 trees _____

Find each percent decrease. Round to the nearest percent.

7. From 20 miles to 11 miles _____

8. From $16 to $4 _____

9. From 126 ounces to 48 ounces _____

10. From 84 seconds to 8 seconds _____

11. From 90 apples to 75 apples _____

12. From 248 workers to 200 workers _____

Given the original amount and the percent of change, find the new amount.

13. $25; 300% increase _____

14. 160 bananas; 20% decrease _____

15. 56 books; 75% decrease _____

16. 52 companies; 25% increase _____

17. 12,000 miles; 5% increase _____

18. 710 points; 10% decrease _____

Solve.

19. Last year, there were 380 students at Woodland Middle School. This year, the student population will increase by 5%. What will be the school's increased student population?

_____

20. A backpack that normally sells for $39 is on sale for 33% off. Find the amount of the discount and the sale price.

_____

21. In August, the Simons' water bill was $48. In September, it was 15% lower. What was the Simons' water bill in September?

_____

22. A gallery owner purchased a very old painting for $3,000. The painting sells at a 325% increase in price. What is the retail price of the painting?

_____

LESSON 5-1

Percent Increase and Decrease
Practice and Problem Solving: C

Solve.

1. Enrollment in the school orchestra was 340 last year. This year, it dropped 15%.

   a. What is the enrollment this year? _____

   b. If enrollment increases 15% next year, what will the enrollment be?

      Round to the nearest whole number. _____

2. Rodrigo and Samantha work part-time selling magazine subscriptions. Their boss said that he wanted them to increase sales by 15% each week. As an incentive, whoever increases their sales by the higher percentage each week would get a bonus. The table below shows subscription sales for four weeks in a row.

   ### Number of Subscriptions Sold

Worker	Week 1	Week 2	Week 3	Week 4
Rodrigo	17	25	18	27
Samantha	15	18	21	23

   a. Find Rodrigo's percent increase or decrease in sales each week.

      _____

   b. Find Samantha's percent increase or decrease in sales each week.

      _____

   c. Who received a bonus in weeks 2, 3, and 4?

      _____

   d. After four weeks, did Rodrigo or Samantha meet their boss's goal? Explain.

      _____

3. The Kelvin scale is an absolute temperature scale that can be used to calculate percent change in temperatures. The formula to convert Celsius to Kelvin is $K = C + 273.15$. What is the percent change if the temperature rises from 21°C to 29°C? Round to the nearest tenth.

   _____

Percent Increase and Decrease
Practice and Problem Solving: D

Find each percent increase. Round to the nearest percent. The first one is done for you.

1. From $15 to $21 __40%__

2. From 12 teachers to 48 teachers _____

3. From 80 pencils to 152 pencils _____

4. From 40 cans to 70 cans _____

Find each percent decrease. Round to the nearest percent. The first one is done for you.

5. From 80 miles to 15 miles __81%__

6. From 100 ounces to 25 ounces _____

7. From $60 to $40 _____

8. From 39 seconds to 13 seconds _____

Find the new amount given the original amount and the percent of change. The first one is done for you.

9. $25; 10% increase __$27.50__

10. 160 bananas; 20% decrease _____

11. 200 books; 75% decrease _____

12. 52 companies; 25% increase _____

Solve.

13. Last year, there were 400 students at Woodland Middle School. This year, the student population will increase by 5%. What will be the school's student population this year?

_____

14. A backpack that normally sells for $39 is on sale for 30% off. Find the amount of the sale price.

_____

LESSON 5-1

Percent Increase and Decrease
Reteach

A change in a quantity is often described as a percent increase or percent decrease. To calculate a percent increase or decrease, use this equation.

$$\text{percent of change} = \frac{\text{amount of increase or decrease}}{\text{original amount}} \cdot 100$$

Find the percent of change from 28 to 42.

- First, find the amount of the change. $42 - 28 = 14$
- What is the original amount? 28
- Use the equation. $\frac{14}{28} \cdot 100 = 50\%$

An increase from 28 to 42 represents a 50% increase.

Find each percent of change.

1. 8 is increased to 22

   amount of change: 22 – 8 = _____

   original amount: _____

   _____ • 100 = _____%

2. 90 is decreased to 81

   amount of change: 90 – 81 = _____

   original amount: _____

   _____ • 100 = _____%

3. 125 is increased to 200

   amount of change: 200 – 125 = _____

   original amount: _____

   _____ • 100 = _____%

4. 400 is decreased to 60

   amount of change: 400 – 60 = _____

   original amount: _____

   _____ • 100 = _____%

5. 64 is decreased to 48

   _____

6. 140 is increased to 273

   _____

7. 30 is decreased to 6

   _____

8. 15 is increased to 21

   _____

9. 7 is increased to 21

   _____

10. 320 is decreased to 304

    _____

Percent Increase and Decrease
Reading Strategies: Analyze Information

Percent can be used to describe change. It is shown as a ratio.

$$\text{Percent of change} = \frac{\text{amount of change}}{\text{original amount}}$$

The following steps describe how the percent of change is figured on a savings account that starts with $50.

    Original amount in the account: $50
    Current amount in the account: $30
    Amount the account decreased by: $20

$$\text{Percent of change} = \frac{\text{amount of change}}{\text{original amount}} = \frac{\$20}{\$50}$$

Savings went down, so this ratio is a **percent of decrease** in savings.

1. How much money was placed into the savings account when it

    opened? _____

2. Did the number of dollars in the account increase or decrease?

    _____

3. When you are finding the percent of change, where do you place the original number in the fraction?

_____

Use the information below to solve 4–6.

A clothing salesman sold 25 shirts his first day on the job and 45 shirts the second day.

4. What is the original number of shirts he sold?

_____

5. How many more shirts did he sell the second day than the first day?

_____

6. Write the fraction that shows the amount of change over the original amount. What is the percent of change? Is it a percent increase or percent decrease?

_____

LESSON 5-1 Percent Increase and Decrease
Success for English Learners

Problem 1

$$\text{percent of change} = \frac{\text{amount of change}}{\text{original amount}}$$

27 is **DECREASED** to 20

The new amount is less than the original amount, so SUBTRACT to find the amount of change

$$\text{percent decrease} = \frac{\text{original amount} - \text{new amount}}{\text{original amount}}$$

$$= \frac{27 - 20}{27}$$

$$= \frac{7}{27}$$

$$= 27\overline{)7}$$

$$= 27\overline{)7.000} \quad \overset{0.259}{}$$

$$\approx 25.9\%$$

Problem 2

How do you find the retail price?

| Buys snow globes for $9.20. | Sells snow globes at a 95% increase. |

Step 1

Find 95% of $9.20 → $9.20 × 0.95 = $8.74

Step 2

To get the retail price, add the amount from Step 1 to the original price, $9.20.

$$\$9.20 + \$8.74 = \$17.94$$

---

1. Explain the difference between a percent increase and a percent decrease.

   _____

   _____

2. Give a real-life example of a percent increase.

   _____

3. Explain the difference between retail and wholesale.

   _____

   _____

4. Fill in the blank: retail = _____ + amount of increase

5. Write your own problem using percent of change.

   _____

   _____

   _____

LESSON
5-2

Rewriting Percent Expressions

Practice and Problem Solving: A/B

Use the situation below to complete Exercises 1–6 in the table below.

Discounts R Us buys items at wholesale, then marks them up to set a retail sale price. Some of the items the store sells are shown in the table below.

Item	Wholesale Price	% Markup	$ Markup	Retail Sale Price
1. Notebook	$1.50	20%		
2. Scissors	$3.25	40%		
3. Calculator	$9.60	25%		
4. Sunglasses	$12.50	78%		
5. Bicycle	$78.00	55%		
6. Picture frame	$2.99	150%		

Find the retail sale price of each item below. Round to two decimal places when necessary.

7. Original price: $65.00; Markdown: 12%

_____

8. Original price: $29.99; Markdown: $33\frac{1}{3}$%

_____

9. Original price: $119.00; Markdown: 70%

_____

10. Original price: $325.50; Markdown: 15%

_____

Use the information to complete 11–14.

A jewelry supply shop buys silver chains from a manufacturer for *c* dollars each, and then sells the chains at a 57% markup.

11. Write the markup as a decimal. _____

12. Write an expression for the retail price of a silver chain.

_____

13. What is the retail price of a silver chain purchased for $45.00?

_____

14. How much was added to the original price of the chain? _____

LESSON 5-2

Rewriting Percent Expressions

Practice and Problem Solving: C

Answer the questions about each situation.

A clothing store offers various promotions to attract customers but wants to maintain the same amount of profit. To do this, the store marks up prices above retail and then advertises a deal that results in a markdown equivalent to the retail price. The retail price of a necktie is $59.99. The store offers a "buy 2, get one free" deal on neckties.

1. What is the new retail price during this promotion? _____

2. What is the markup? _____

3. What is the markup percent on a tie during the promotion? _____

A sporting goods store sells jerseys with the name of the local football team. The store owner buys 80 jerseys at a wholesale price of $55 each and applies his standard retail markup of 65%. When the local team made it to the playoffs, the store owner marked up the retail price by 25%. After the local team lost the championship, the store owner marked down that price by 33%.

4. What was the standard retail price of each jersey? _____

5. What was the price when the team was in the playoffs? _____

6. What was the price after the team lost the championship? _____

Two jewelry stores buy silver chains from a manufacturer for c dollars each, and then sell the chains at a 57% markup. Store A has a sale and marks down all chains by 20% off retail. In addition, customers can use a coupon worth 15% off the price of any item, including sale items. Store B offers a coupon worth 35% off any one item.

7. At Store A, Aurelie used a 15%-off coupon to buy a chain already marked down by 20%. Write an expression for the price of this chain.

_____

8. At Store B, Tucker used a 35%-off coupon to buy a chain. Write an expression for the price of this chain.

_____

9. Which store offers a better price on chains?

_____

LESSON 5-2

Rewriting Percent Expressions

Practice and Problem Solving: D

Answer each question. The first one is done for you.

1. Abdul buys dress pants from a clothing company for *p* dollars. He then sells each pair of pants in his men's clothing shop at a 40% markup.

   a. Write the markup as a decimal. _____**0.40*p***_____

   b. Write an expression for the retail price of a pair of dress pants.

   _____

   c. What is the retail price of the pants that Abdul purchased for $56.00?

   _____

   d. How much did Abdul add to the original price of the pants?

   _____

Complete the table. The first row is done for you.

Item	Price	% Markup	$ Markup	Retail Price
2. Tie	$30	20%	**$6.00**	**$36.00**
3. Cufflinks	$10	35%		
4. Belt	$40	25%		

Find the sale price of each item. Round to two decimal places when necessary. The first one is done for you.

5. Original price: $65; Markdown: 10%

   _____**58.50**_____

6. Original price: $30.50; Markdown: 30%

   _____

7. Original price: $105; Markdown: 75%

   _____

8. Original price: $325; Markdown: 15%

   _____

9. A jewelry supply shop buys silver chains from a manufacturer for *c* dollars each, and then sells the chains at a 40% markup. Write an expression for the retail price of a silver chain.

   _____

LESSON
5-2
Rewriting Percent Expressions
Reteach

A **markup** is an example of a percent increase.	A **markdown,** or discount, is an example of a percent decrease.
To calculate a markup, write the markup percentage as a decimal and add 1. Multiply by the original cost.	To calculate a markdown, write the markdown percentage as a decimal and subtract from 1. Multiply by the original price.
A store buys soccer balls from a supplier for $5. The store's markup is 45%. Find the retail price.	A store marks down sweaters by 20%. Find the sale price of a sweater originally priced at $60.
Write the markup as a decimal and add 1.	Write the markup as a decimal and subtract it from 1.
$0.45 + 1 = 1.45$	$1 - 0.2 = 0.8$
Multiply by the original cost.	Multiply by the original cost.
Retail price = $5 × 1.45 = $7.25	Sale price = $60 × 0.8 = $48

Apply the markup for each item. Then, find the retail price. Round to two decimal places when necessary.

1. Original cost: $45; Markup %: 20%

   _____

2. Original cost: $7.50; Markup %: 50%

   _____

3. Original cost: $1.25; Markup %: 80%

   _____

4. Original cost: $62; Markup %: 35%

   _____

Apply the markdown for each item. Then, find the sale price. Round to two decimal places when necessary.

5. Original price: $150; Markdown %: 40%

   _____

6. Original price: $18.99; Markdown: 25%

   _____

7. Original price: $95; Markdown: 10%

   _____

8. Original price: $75; Markdown: 15%

   _____

9. A clothing store bought packages of three pairs of socks for $1.75. The store owner marked up the price by 80%.

   a. What is the retail price? _____

   b. After a month, the store owner marks down the retail price by 20%.

      What is the sales price? _____

LESSON 5-2

Rewriting Percent Expressions

Reading Strategies: Use a Model

A toy store buys kites from a supplier for k dollars. The store owner decides to mark up the price of each kite by 30%. What is the retail price of a kite that the supplier sells for $60?

You can use a bar model to help you solve this problem.

Step 1: Draw a bar to show the cost of the kite, k.

Step 2: Draw a bar that shows the markup: 30% of k, or $0.3k$.

Step 3: These bars together represent the original cost plus the markup, $k + 0.3k$.

Step 4: Use the expression to find the retail price of a kite.

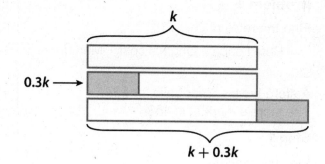

Retail price = Original cost + Markup

$$= k + 0.3k$$

$$= 1.3k = 1.3(\$60) = \$78$$

The retail price of each kite is $78.

Answer each question. As you do, draw each step of the bar model in the space at the right.

A store buys cameras from a supplier for c dollars. The store owner decides on a markup of 70%. What is the retail price of a camera that the supplier sells for $80?

1. When you use a bar model to solve the problem, which bar should you draw first?

   _____

2. Which bar should you draw next?

   _____

3. What do these bars together represent?

   _____

4. What is the retail price of the camera?

   _____

LESSON 5-2

Rewriting Percent Expressions

Success for English Learners

A **markup** is a percent *increase*. With a markup, the price goes **UP.** ↑

A **markdown** is a percent *decrease*. With a markdown, the price goes **DOWN.** ↓

Problem 1

Find the retail price.

    Retail price = Original cost + Markup

A store buys soccer balls for $5.
The store's markup is 45%.

Step 1

Find the markup.

    $5 × 0.45 = $2.25

Step 2

ADD the markup to the original cost.

    $5 + $2.25 = $7.25

The retail price of a soccer ball is $7.25.

Problem 2

Find the sale price.

    Sale price = Original price − Markdown

The original price of a sweater is $60.
On sale, the markdown is 20%.
Find the sale price.

Step 1

Find the markdown.

    $60 × 0.20 = $12

Step 2

SUBTRACT the markdown from the original price.

    $60 − $12 = $48

The sale price of the sweater is $48.

1. Explain the difference between a markup and a markdown.

   _____

   _____

2. Explain the difference between a retail price and a sale price.

   _____

   _____

3. Write your own word problem using a markup or a markdown.

   _____

   _____

   _____

LESSON 5-3 Applications of Percent
Practice and Problem Solving: A/B

1. Complete the table.

Sale Amount	5% Sales Tax	Total Amount Paid
$67.50		
$98.75		
$399.79		
$1250.00		
$12,500.00		

2. Complete the table.

Principal	Rate	Time	Interest Earned	New Balance
$300	3%	4 years		
$450		3 years	$67.50	
$500	4.5%		$112.50	
	8%	2 years	$108.00	

Solve.

3. Joanna wants to buy a car. Her parents loan her $5,000 for 5 years at 5% simple interest. How much will Joanna pay in interest?

_____

4. This month Salesperson A made 11% of $67,530. Salesperson B made 8% of $85,740. Who made more commission this month? How much did that salesperson make?

_____

5. Jon earned $38,000 last year. He paid $6,840 for entertainment. What percent of his earnings did Jon pay in entertainment expenses?

_____

6. Nora makes $3,000 a month. The circle graph shows how she spends her money. How much money does Nora spend on each category?

   a. rent _____

   b. food _____

   c. medical _____

   d. clothes _____

   e. miscellaneous _____

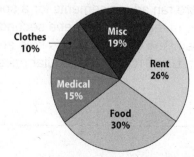

Name _____ Date _____ Class_____

LESSON
5-3

Applications of Percent
Practice and Problem Solving: C

1. Complete the table.

Sale Amount	Tax	Amount of Tax	Total Cost
$49.95		$4.00	$53.95
	5%	$6.43	
$499.99	7.5%		
		$103.96	$2,702.96
$12,499.00	7%		

2. Complete the table.

Principal	Annual Rate	Time	Interest Earned	New Balance
$2,400		6 months		$2,442.00
	4.9%	2 years	$4.41	
$9,460.12		5 years		$12,061.65
$3,923.87	2.2%		$64.74	

Solve.

3. Jorge earns a 9% commission on all of his sales. He had sales of $89,400 for the month. Harris works for a different company, and also sold $89,400 for the month but made $447 more than Jorge. What is Harris' commission rate?

_____

4. Danielle wants to buy a video game. At the local Big Box store, it costs $49.95. Danielle has a coupon for 10% off at the store, and she will pay a 6.5% sales tax. At an online store, the game is $44.95, with $4.00 shipping charge and no sales tax. Which purchase would be cheaper?

_____

5. A clothing store ran advertisements for a special sale. The store's ads read "Buy one at regular price, get a second one for half price." Explain how the terms of the clothing store's sale are different from offering a 50% discount. Use $100 as the regular price for the item to write your explanation.

_____

**LESSON
5-3**

Applications of Percent

Practice and Problem Solving: D

Complete the table to find the amount of sales tax to the nearest whole cent. The first one has been done for you.

1.

Sale Amount	5% Sales Tax
$50	$0.05 \times \$50 = 2.5 = \$2.50$
$120	
$480	
$2,240	
$12,500	

Complete the table. The first one has been done for you.

2.

Principal	Rate	Time	Interest Earned
$400	5%	2 years	$40
$950	10%	5 years	
$50	4%	1 year	
$1,000	8%	2 years	

Write the correct answer. The first one has been done for you.

3. Karl just had a birthday. Karl's age is now 50% of his uncle's age. Karl's uncle is 32 years old. How old is Karl?

   $0.5 \times 32 = 16$, **Karl is 16 years old.**

4. The cost of Jacquie's gym membership is $20 per month. Jacquie gets a 10% discount of the monthly cost in any month in which she refers a friend who also becomes a member. How much does Jacquie save in a month when one of her friends joins the gym?

   _____

5. Yesterday Tyler ate lunch at his local diner. The bill for his meal came to $8.40, not including sales tax. Tyler wants to leave a 15% tip for his waiter. How much should his tip be?

   _____

LESSON 5-3

Applications of Percent

Reteach

For any problem involving percent, you can use a simple formula to calculate the percent.

$$amount = \text{percent} \times \text{total}$$

The amount will be the amount of tax, tip, discount, or whatever you are calculating. Use the formula that has your unknown information before the equal sign.

For simple-interest problems, time is one factor.
So, you must also include time in your formula.

$$amount\ (interest) = \text{total (principal)} \times \text{percent (rate)} \times \text{time}$$

A. Find the sale price after the discount.

Regular price = $899

Discount rate = 20%

You know the total and the percentage.
You don't know the discount amount.
Your formula is:

amount = % × total

= 0.20 × $899

= $179.80

The amount of discount is $179.80.
The sale price is the original price minus the discount.
$899 − $179.80 = $719.20

The sale price is $719.20

B. A bank offers simple interest on a certificate of deposit. Jamie invests $500 and after one year earns $40 in interest. What was the interest rate on his deposit?

You know the total deposited—the principal. You know the amount earned in interest. You don't know the percentage rate of interest. Since the time is 1 year, your formula is:

% = amount ÷ total

= $40 ÷ $500

= 0.08

= 8%

The interest rate is 8%.

Johanna purchases a book for $14.95. There is a sales tax of 6.5%. How much is the final price with tax?

1. What is the total in this problem? _____

2. What is the percent? _____

3. Use the formula *amount* = total × percent to find the amount of the sales tax.

   _____

4. To find the final price, add the cost of the book to the amount of tax.

   _____

LESSON 5-3

Applications of Percent

Reading Strategies: Build Vocabulary

Sales tax is added to the price of an item or service. Sales tax is a percent of the purchase price. A sales tax of 6.5% means that all taxable items will have an additional 6.5% added to the total cost.

sales tax rate × sale price = sales tax

The **total sale price** is computed by adding the sales tax to the cost of all the items purchased.

sale price + sales tax = total sale price

Find the amount of sales tax for each purchase to the nearest whole cent.

1. sale price: $9,450

   sales tax rate: 8%

   _____

2. sale price: $1,089

   sales tax rate: 6.25%

   _____

3. sale price: $21,097

   sales tax rate: 5.5%

   _____

Interest is the amount of money the bank pays to use your money, or the amount of money you pay the bank to borrow its money.

Principal is the amount of money you save or borrow from the bank.

Rate of interest is the percent rate on money you save or borrow.

Time is the number of years the money is saved or borrowed.

Answer each question.

4. You put $800 in a savings account at 4% annual interest and leave it there for five years.

   a. What is the principal? _____

   b. What is the interest rate? _____

   c. What is the amount of time the money will stay in the account?

   _____

Find out how much interest you would earn by using this formula:

Interest	=	Principal	×	Rate	×	Time	⟵	words
i	=	p	×	r	×	t	⟵	symbols
		$800	×	4%	×	5		
		$800	×	0.04	×	5	⟵	Change % to decimal.
		$160					⟵	Multiply to solve.

5. To find out how much interest you will earn by keeping your money in a bank, what three things do you need to know?

   _____

Applications of Percent

LESSON 5-3

Success for English Learners

Problem 1

Find the tax on the sale.

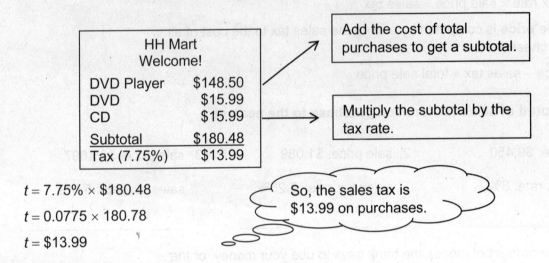

```
            HH Mart
            Welcome!

DVD Player      $148.50
DVD             $15.99
CD              $15.99
Subtotal        $180.48
Tax (7.75%)     $13.99
```

Add the cost of total purchases to get a subtotal.

Multiply the subtotal by the tax rate.

$t = 7.75\% \times \$180.48$

$t = 0.0775 \times 180.78$

$t = \$13.99$

So, the sales tax is $13.99 on purchases.

Problem 2

Use this diagram to help you set up an equation for simple interest.

Simple interest $= P \times r \times t$

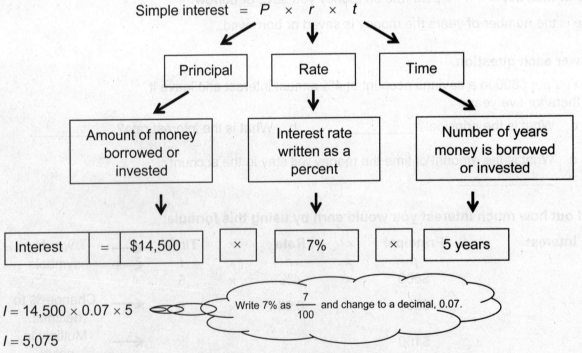

Principal → Amount of money borrowed or invested

Rate → Interest rate written as a percent

Time → Number of years money is borrowed or invested

| Interest | = | $14,500 | × | 7% | × | 5 years |

$I = 14,500 \times 0.07 \times 5$

Write 7% as $\frac{7}{100}$ and change to a decimal, 0.07.

$I = 5,075$

The simple interest on $14,500 invested or loaned for 5 years at 7% is $5,075.

1. Jon invested $6,200 for 6 years at 3%. Calculate the simple interest.

_____

Proportions and Percent
Challenge

Multi-Step Unit Conversion

Length (customary)	Length (metric)	Time	Metric-Customary
1 ft = 12 in.	1 cm = 10 mm	1 h = 60 m	1 in. = 2.54 cm
1 yd = 3 ft	1 m = 100 cm	1 m = 60 s	1 m = 39.37 in.
1 mi = 5,280 ft	1 km = 1,000 m	1 y = 365 d	

Using a method called "dimensional analysis," you can convert any units for length, time, or speed using just the information in the chart.

This example shows converting 30 miles per hour (mi/h) to meters per second (m/s). Notice how the units cancel out.

$$\overset{\text{length}}{\frac{30\ \text{mi}}{1\ \text{h}} \times \frac{5{,}280\ \text{ft}}{1\ \text{mi}} \times \frac{12\ \text{in.}}{1\ \text{ft}} \times \frac{1\ \text{m}}{39.37\ \text{in.}}} \times \overset{\text{time}}{\frac{1\ \text{h}}{60\ \text{min}} \times \frac{1\ \text{min}}{60\ \text{sec}}}$$

Convert these units. Show your steps.

1. Complete the calculation above to change 30 mi/h to meters per second.

_____

2. Change 2.3 km to inches.

_____

3. Change 67.3 ft/s to kilometers per hour.

_____

Try these area and volume conversions. (Hint: Square factors for area; cube factors for volume.)

4. A water tower is filled at 750 cubic feet per minute. Find the rate in gallons per hour. (1 gallon is about 0.134 cubic feet)

_____

5. A field is 130 ft by 274 ft. Find the area in square meters.

_____

6. A basement measures 9.6 m wide, 4.2 m tall, and 15.6 m long. Find the volume of space in the basement in cubic yards.

_____

Name _____ Date _____ Class _____

Algebraic Expressions

Practice and Problem Solving: A/B

Write an algebraic expression for each phrase.

1. Four more than the price, *p*

2. Five less than three times the length, *L*

_____   _____

Write a word phrase for each algebraic expression.

3. $25 - 0.6x$

_____

4. $\frac{2}{3}y + 4$

_____

Use the Distributive Property to simplify each expression.

5. $(100 + 4z)20$

6. $0.75(3.5a - 6b)$

_____   _____

Factor each expression.

7. $45c + 10d$

8. $27 - 9x + 15y$

_____   _____

Solve. Show each step.

9. A construction worker bought several bottles of juice for $3 at the convenience store. She paid for them with a $20 bill. If *j* represents the number of bottles of juice, write an expression for the change she should receive.

_____

10. A giant bamboo plant grew an average of 18 centimeters per year. The botanist started measuring the plant when it was 5 centimeters tall. If *y* represents the number of years the botanist has measured the plant, what expression represents its height?

_____

LESSON 6-1

Algebraic Expressions

Practice and Problem Solving: C

An electrician has $120 to spend on interior light fixtures. The wholesale price for a 13-watt low-energy lamp is $4. The price for a high-energy lamp is $5.

1. Write the algebraic expression for how much the electrician spends for *a* units of the low-energy lamp and *b* units of the high-energy lamp.

   _____

2. Write an *equation* that relates your answer to Exercise 1 to the amount of money the electrician has to spend.

   _____

3. Complete the table for the electrician's purchase. Assume that all of the $120 is spent.

Number of low-energy lamps	Total Cost of low-energy lamps	Number of high-energy lamps	Total Cost of high-energy lamps	Total
5	a. $_____	b. _____	c. $ _____	$120
d. _____	e. $_____	16	f. $_____	$120
15	g. $_____	h. _____	i. $_____	$120
j. _____	k. $_____	l. _____	m. $_____	$120

4. How does the *total* price for the high-energy lamps relate to the total price of the low-energy lamps? How does the *total* price for the low-energy lamps relate to the total price of the high-energy lamps?

   _____

5. The electrician wants to spend all of the $120 and buy some of both types of lamps. If he wants to buy as many high-energy lamps as possible, how many of each type of lamp should he buy?

   _____

LESSON
6-1

Algebraic Expressions
Practice and Problem Solving: D

Write an algebraic expression for each phrase by filling in the blanks.
The first is done for you.

1. Fifty decreased by two tenths of *m*.

   Write the expression for "Fifty decreased by"

   <u>50 –</u>

   Two tenths = 0.<u>2</u>

   0.<u>2</u> "of *m*" is written as

   0.<u>2</u> × *m*, or

   0.<u>2</u>*m*
   Put the steps together.

   "Fifty decreased by" <u>50 –</u>

   "two tenths of *m*" <u>0.2*m*</u> or

   <u>50 – 0.2*m*</u>

2. Ten minus three tenths of *n*.

   Write the expression for "Ten minus"

   _____

   Three tenths = 0._____

   Three tenths of *n* is written as

   0._____ _____ *m*, or

   0._____*n*.
   Put the steps together:

   "Ten minus than three tenths of *n*"

   _____

Use the Distributive Property. Simplify the answer. The first one is
done for you.

3. $\frac{1}{4}(6x + 14y) =$

   $\frac{1}{4} \bullet \underline{6x} + \frac{1}{4} \bullet \underline{14y} =$

   $\frac{6}{4}\underline{x} + \frac{14}{4}\underline{y} = \frac{3}{2}x + \frac{7}{2}y$

4. $\frac{1}{6}(15a + 20b) =$

   _____ • _____ + _____ • _____ =

   _____ + _____ = _____ + _____

Factor. The first one is done for you.

5. $5x + 10y + 30z =$

   $\underline{5} \bullet x + \underline{5} \bullet 2y + \underline{2} \bullet \underline{3} \bullet \underline{5}z =$

   $\underline{5} \bullet (x + 2y + \underline{6}z)$

6. $7a + 21b + 42c =$

   ___ • *a* + ___ • 3*b* + ___ • ___ • ___*c* =

   _____ • (*a* + 3*b* + _____*c*)

7. $4x + 12$

   _____

8. $6s + 18t + 3w$

   _____

LESSON 6-1
Algebraic Expressions
Reteach

Algebraic expressions can be written from verbal descriptions. Likewise, verbal descriptions can be written from algebraic expressions. In both cases, it is important to look for word and number clues.

Algebra from words
"One third of the participants increased by 25."

Clues
Look for "number words," like
• "One third."
• "Of" means multiplied by.
• "Increased by" means add to.

Combine the clues to produce the expression.

• "One third of the participants." $\frac{1}{3}p$ or $\frac{p}{3}$.

• "Increased by 25." $+25$

"One third of the participants increased by 25."
$\frac{1}{3}p + 25$ or $\frac{p}{3} + 25$

Words from algebra
"Write $0.75n - \frac{1}{2}m$ with words."

Clues
Identify the number of parts of the problem.
• "$0.75n$" means "three fourths of n" or 75 hundredths of n. The exact meaning will depend on the problem.
• "$-$" means "minus," "decreased by," "less than," etc., depending on the context.

• "$\frac{1}{2}m$" is "one half of m" or "m over 2."

Combine the clues to produce a description. "75 hundredths of the population minus half the men."

Write a verbal description for each algebraic expression.

1. $100 - 5n$

2. $0.25r + 0.6s$

3. $\dfrac{3m - 8n}{13}$

_____   _____   _____

_____   _____   _____

Write an algebraic expression for each verbal description.

4. Half of the seventh graders and one third of the eighth graders were divided into ten teams.

_____

5. Thirty percent of the green house flowers are added to 25 ferns for the school garden.

_____

6. Four less than three times the number of egg orders and six more than two times the number of waffle orders.

_____

LESSON 6-1 Algebraic Expressions

Reading Strategies: Compare and Contrast

This lesson shows how the **Distributive Property** is used with
expressions. It also presents the idea of **factoring**, which is related to the
Distributive Property in some types of problems. Knowing how the two
concepts are alike and how they are different can help you solve problems.
The problems illustrate the two concepts.

Problem 1

Thirty-five percent of the revenue produced at the auction will go to the
charity. The morning participants spent an average of $50 each. The
afternoon attendees spent an average of $75 each.

a. Write an algebraic expression for the amount contributed to the charity
   by all participants. Use *m* for morning participants and *a* for afternoon
   participants.

   _____

b. Use the Distributive Property to simplify the expression in part **a**.

   _____

c. How do these expressions differ in the information they convey?

   _____
   _____

Problem 2

Twenty customers bought the portable drill when it was on sale. Twelve of
the customers also bought the charger that goes with it.

a. Write an algebraic expression for how much money was spent on the
   drills and chargers.

   _____

b. Factor the expression in part **a**. What does the factored expression
   represent?

   _____

c. How do these expressions differ in the information they convey?

   _____
   _____

LESSON 6-1

Algebraic Expressions
Success for English Learners

Problem 1a

Write the expression:

"Three times the number of chairs increased by 10."

"Three times the number..." = **3n**

"...increased by 10" = + **10**.
So, **3n** and + **10** give
3n + **10**

Problem 1b

Write the words: "$\frac{2}{3}x - 12$"

"$\frac{2}{3}$" ⟶ "Two thirds"

"$\frac{2}{3}x$" ⟶ "Two thirds **of x**."

"– 12" ⟶ "less 12," "reduced by 12," "minus 12," etc.

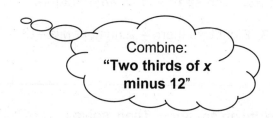

Combine:
"Two thirds of x minus 12"

Problem 2

Distributive Property or Factoring?

⟶ $5(2a + 3b) = 5(2a) + 5(3b) = 10a + 15b$

⟶ $100x - 300y = 100(x - 3y)$

⟶ "Three times the price of a pizza and six times the price of a drink."

⟶ "Three times the price of a pizza and two drinks."

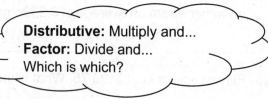

Distributive: Multiply and...
Factor: Divide and...
Which is which?

1. In Problem 1a, what is another way to write the expression?

_____

2. In Problem 2, write expressions for the two word problems.

_____

3. Write the expressions from Exercise 2 in an equation to show the Distributive Property.

_____

LESSON 6-2 One-Step Equations with Rational Coefficients

Practice and Problem Solving: A/B

Solve.

1. $\frac{1}{3}n = 4$

2. $y + 0.4 = 2$

3. $12 = 0.5a$

4. $-1 = \frac{1}{3}v$

_____ _____ _____ _____

$n = $ _____ $y = $ _____ $a = $ _____ $v = $ _____

5. $15.5z = -77.5$

6. $\frac{t}{-11} = 11$

7. $0.5m = 0.75$

8. $\frac{r}{4} = 250$

_____ _____ _____ _____

$z = $ _____ $t = $ _____ $m = $ _____ $r = $ _____

Write each sentence as an equation.

9. Eight less than $\frac{1}{3}$ a number n is -13.

10. A number f multiplied by -12.3 is -73.8.

_____ _____

Write an equation. Then, solve.

11. During unusually cold weather, the temperature in Miami Beach was 10°C. This was 12 degrees more than in Tallahassee. What is the temperature in Tallahassee?

_____

12. A swimmer swam 48 kilometers in d days. What is the value of d if the swimmer swam an average of 3.2 kilometers daily?

_____

13. Fifteen tickets cost $193.75. What is the average cost of each ticket?

_____

14. A student walks $\frac{1}{4}$ mile from her home to the store on her way to a friend's house. If the store is $\frac{1}{3}$ of the way to her friend's house, how far is her friend's house from her home?

_____

LESSON 6-2 **One-Step Equations with Rational Coefficients**

Practice and Problem Solving: C

Solve using addition, subtraction, multiplication, or division.

1. $0.6x = 3.2$

2. $m + 2.3 = 9.4$

3. $\dfrac{y}{0.23} = 12$

4. $z - 2.3 = 0.46$

_____ _____ _____ _____

5. $s + \dfrac{3}{7} = 6$

6. $\dfrac{5}{6}r = 4\dfrac{3}{5}$

7. $f - \dfrac{3}{4} = 1\dfrac{1}{2}$

8. $\dfrac{3m}{\frac{2}{3}} = 7$

_____ _____ _____ _____

Answer the questions.

9. a. A painter works 37.5 hours one week. If she worked 5 days, how many hours did she work on average per day?

_____

b. At $15.75 per hour, how much did she make per day?

_____

10. A recipe calls for $3\dfrac{2}{3}$ cups of flour. Earl used $7\dfrac{1}{3}$ cups. By how much did he increase the recipe?

_____

11. Explain how you could use either of two operations to solve Exercise 10.

_____

_____

12. A bottle of fruit juice holds 1.89L. If Shakira bought almost 6L of fruit juice, how many bottles did she buy?

_____

13. Eric had 15.3 feet of fishing line. He cut off a piece and had 38.4 inches left. How long was the piece he cut?

_____

One-Step Equations with Rational Coefficients
Practice and Problem Solving: D

Solve by adding or subtracting. The first one is done for you.

1. $x - 8 = 11$

    $x - 8 + \underline{\textbf{8}} = 11 + \underline{\textbf{8}}$

    $x \qquad = \underline{\textbf{19}}$

2. $y - 3 = -2$

    $y - 3 + \underline{\hspace{1.5cm}} = -2 + \underline{\hspace{1.5cm}}$

    $y \qquad = \underline{\hspace{1.5cm}}$

3. $w + 5 = 8$

    $w + 5 - \underline{\hspace{1.5cm}} = 8 - \underline{\hspace{1.5cm}}$

    $w \qquad = \underline{\hspace{1.5cm}}$

4. $z + 7 = -14$

    $z + 7 - \underline{\hspace{1.5cm}} = -14 - \underline{\hspace{1.5cm}}$

    $z \qquad = \underline{\hspace{1.5cm}}$

Solve by multiplying or dividing. The first one is done for you.

5. $\dfrac{a}{3} = 5$

    $\underline{\textbf{3}} \times \dfrac{a}{3} = \underline{\textbf{3}} \times 5$

    $a = \underline{\textbf{15}}$

6. $4.5b = 27$

    $\dfrac{4.5b}{\underline{\hspace{1.2cm}}} = \dfrac{27}{\underline{\hspace{1.2cm}}}$

    $\underline{\hspace{1.5cm}} \quad \underline{\hspace{1.5cm}}$

    $b = \underline{\hspace{2cm}}$

7. $\dfrac{c}{5} = 6$

    $\underline{\hspace{1.5cm}} \times \dfrac{c}{5} = \underline{\hspace{1.5cm}} \times 6$

    $c = \underline{\hspace{2cm}}$

8. $7.35d = 29.4$

    $\dfrac{7.35d}{\underline{\hspace{1.2cm}}} = \dfrac{29.4}{\underline{\hspace{1.2cm}}}$

    $\underline{\hspace{1.5cm}} \quad \underline{\hspace{1.5cm}}$

    $d = \underline{\hspace{2cm}}$

Solve by completing the steps. The first is done for you.

9. Two angles of a triangle have a sum of 110°. The sum of all three angles in the triangle is 180°. What is the measure of the third angle?

    Add the angle measures: $\underline{\textbf{110°}} + \underline{\textbf{x}}$

    What is the sum? $\underline{\textbf{180°}}$

    Write the equation: $\underline{\textbf{110} + \textbf{x} = \textbf{180}}$

    Solve the equation: $\underline{\textbf{x} = \textbf{70°}}$

10. A driver uses 2.7 gallons of gasoline to drive her car 72.9 miles. What was her car's mileage?

    Define mileage: _____ per _____

    Substitute and solve: _____ ÷ _____

    _____ = _____

    The mileage is _____ miles per gallon.

One-Step Equations with Rational Coefficients

LESSON 6-2

Reteach

Using Addition to Undo Subtraction

Addition "undoes" subtraction. Adding the same number to both sides of an equation keeps the equation balanced.

$$x - 5 = -6.3$$
$$x - 5 + \mathbf{5} = -6.3 + \mathbf{5}$$
$$x = -1.3$$

Using Subtraction to Undo Addition

Subtraction "undoes" addition. Subtracting a number from both sides of an equation keeps the equation balanced.

$$n + \frac{3}{4} = -15$$
$$n + \frac{3}{4} - \frac{3}{4} = -15 - \frac{3}{4}$$
$$n = -15\frac{3}{4}$$

Be careful to identify the correct number that is to be added or subtracted from both sides of an equation. The numbers and variables can move around, as the problems show.

Solve using addition or subtraction.

1. $6 = m - \dfrac{7}{8}$

2. $3.9 + t = 4.5$

3. $10 = -3.1 + j$

Multiplication Undoes Division

To "undo" division, multiply both sides of an equation by the number in the denominator of a problem like this one.

$$\frac{m}{3} = 6$$
$$3 \times \frac{m}{3} = 3 \times 6$$
$$m = 18$$

Division Undoes Multiplication

To "undo" multiplication, divide both sides of an equation by the number that is multiplied by the variable as shown in this problem.

$$4.5p = 18$$
$$\frac{4.5p}{4.5} = \frac{18}{4.5} = 4$$

Notice that decimals and fractions can be handled this way, too.

Solve using division or multiplication.

4. $\dfrac{y}{2.4} = 5$

5. $0.35w = -7$

6. $-\dfrac{a}{6} = 1$

LESSON 6-2 One-Step Equations with Rational Coefficients

Reading Strategies: Use a Table

The procedure for solving a one-step equation can be shown in a table.
As the lesson title suggests, there is **one step** to do before you write the
answer. That step is the middle row below.

Problem	Problem	Problem	Problem
$a - 8 = -5.3$	$6 = b + 11.2$	$0.4c = 220$	$10.4 = \dfrac{d}{2}$
One Step Add 8: $a - 8 + 8 = -5.3 + 8$	**One Step** Subtract 11.2: $6 - 11.2 =$ $b + 11.2 - 11.2$	**One Step** Divide by 0.4: $\dfrac{0.4c}{0.4} = \dfrac{220}{0.4}$	**One Step** Multiply by 2: $2 \times 10.4 = 2 \times \dfrac{d}{2}$
Answer $a = 2.7$	**Answer** $-5.2 = b$ or $b = -5.2$	**Answer** $c = 550$	**Answer** $20.4 = d$ or $d = 20.4$

Use the table to solve each equation.

1. **Problem:** $\dfrac{p}{8} = -2$ 2. **Problem:** $1.5 + q = -0.6$ 3. **Problem:** $-9.5a = -38$

    One Step: **One Step:**   **One Step:**

    _____   _____   _____

    Answer: $p = $ _____   **Answer:** $q = $ _____   **Answer:** $a = $ _____

Write the equation for "Problem." Then, fill in the blanks.

4. A cat owner paid the vet a fee of $269.50 for a year's worth of visits.
   He made 14 visits that year. What was the average cost per visit?

   Problem: _____

   One Step: _____

   Answer: _____

5. A soccer team won three fourths of its games. The team won
   18 games. How many games did the team play?

   Problem: _____

   One Step: _____

   Answer: _____

LESSON 6-2

One-Step Equations with Rational Coefficients
Success for English Learners

Problem 1

What is the slowest time s?

Slowest time s Fastest time 7.2 seconds

3.84 seconds

The difference between the fastest and slowest time is 3.84 seconds.

The slowest time is s.

The fastest time is 7.2 seconds.

$$s - 3.84 = 7.2$$
$$\underline{+3.84} \quad \underline{+3.84}$$
$$s \qquad = 11.04$$

Problem 2

Sometimes you need to multiply both sides by a number in order to isolate the variable.

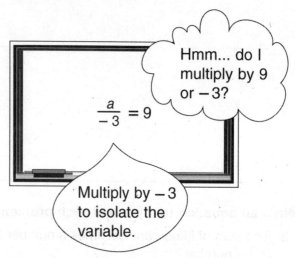

Hmm... do I multiply by 9 or -3?

$$\frac{a}{-3} = 9$$

Multiply by -3 to isolate the variable.

The solution to the equation is $a = -27$.

Problem 3

A fraction-and-a-whole-number problem: $\dfrac{1}{4}x = 9 \longrightarrow 4\left(\dfrac{1}{4}\right)x = 4(9) = 36$

How is this problem like Problem 2? How is it different from Problem 2? Both deal with rational numbers. One is written with the variable divided by a number, and the other shows the variable multiplied by a fraction.

1. In Problem 1, how do you get the result "11.04" by adding "7.2" and "3.84" since they have different numbers of decimal places?

   _____

2. In Problem 2, what rational number is a coefficient of a?

   _____

3. What is another way to write $\dfrac{1}{4}x$ in Problem 3? _____

LESSON 6-3 Writing Two-Step Equations
Practice and Problem Solving: A/B

Model each two-step operation by drawing algebra tiles.

1. $3m + 5 = 8$

_____

2. $-2x - 3 = 5.$

_____

Write an equation to represent each problem.

3. The sum of fifteen and six times a number t is eighty-one. What
   is the number?

   _____

4. An electrician charges $40 to come to your house. She also charges
   $55 for each hour that she works. The electrician charges you a total
   of $190. How many hours does the electrician work at your house?
   Use h for the number of hours.

   _____

5. A taxi charges $1.75 plus a fee of $0.75 for each mile traveled. The
   total cost of a ride, without a tip, is $4.75. How many miles is the trip?
   Use m for the number of miles traveled.

   _____

LESSON 6-3

Writing Two-Step Equations
Practice and Problem Solving: C

Write a two-step equation for each word problem.

1. The sum of a number p and seven is divided by twelve. The result is three. What is the number?

   _____

2. Sixteen is divided by the sum of a number q and 1. The result is four. What is the number?

   _____

3. A number s is subtracted from seven. When the result is divided by three, the quotient is two. What is the number?

   _____

Write a two-step equation to represent each problem.

4. Twelve and three tenths more than five and thirteen thousandths of a number d is equal to fifteen and three hundred two thousandths. What is the value of d?

   _____

5. When the sum of an unknown number z and twenty-two is divided by the same unknown number, the quotient is twelve. What is the unknown number?

   _____

6. A home repair crew charges seventy-five dollars per day plus two hundred fifty-five dollars for each hour the crew works. One day the crew works c hours and charges a total amount of one thousand, six hundred five dollars. How many hours does the crew work?

   _____

Writing Two-Step Equations
LESSON 6-3
Practice and Problem Solving: D

**Model each two-step equation by drawing algebra tiles.
The first one is done for you.**

1. $2p + 3 = 7$

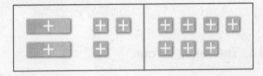

_____

2. $3t + 10 = 16$

_____

3. $-q - 3 = 7$

_____

**Write an equation for each word problem. The first one is
done for you.**

4. The sum of three times a number d and 5 is 17. What is the number?

   $3d + 5 = 17$

   _____

5. As a membership fee, a health club charges a one-time amount of $40
   and charges $25 for each month. The total fee after m months is $240.
   What is the value of m?

   _____

6. A runner warms up for ten minutes and then takes seven minutes to
   run each mile. The total time after r miles is 45 minutes. How many
   miles are run?

   _____

LESSON 6-3 Writing Two-Step Equations
Reteach

Many real-world problems look like this:

   one-time amount + number × variable = total amount

You can use this pattern to write an equation.

Example:

At the start of a month a customer spends $3 for a reusable coffee cup. She pays $2 each time she has the cup filled with coffee. At the end of the month she has paid $53. How many cups of coffee did she get?

one-time amount:	$3
number × variable:	$2 \times c$ or $2c$, where c is the number of cups of coffee
total amount:	$53

The equation is: $3 + 2c = 53$.

Write an equation to represent each situation.
Each problem can be represented using the form:
   one-time amount + number × variable = total amount

1. The sum of twenty-one and five times a number f is 61.

   _____   _____   _____
      one-time amount   +   number × variable   =   total amount

2. Seventeen more than seven times a number j is 87.

   _____

3. A customer's total cell phone bill this month is $50.50. The company charges a monthly fee of $18 plus five cents for each call. Use n to represent the number of calls.

   _____

4. A tutor works with a group of students. The tutor charges $40 plus $30 for each student in the group. Today the tutor has s students and charges a total of $220.

   _____

Writing Two-Step Equations
LESSON 6-3

Reading Strategies: Analyze Information

It is important to know whether an equation is a one-step equation or a two-step equation. It is also important to know whether each step is addition, subtraction, multiplication, or division.

Equation	Number of Steps and Description
$2x = 7$	One step: Multiply x by 2.
$y + 5 = 11$	One step: Add 5 to y.
$3z - 1 = 11$	Two steps: Multiply z by 3, then subtract 1.
$\dfrac{w+3}{2} = 4$	Two steps: Add 3 to w, then divide the result by 2.

Knowing the steps helps you write a two-step equation. Knowing the steps is even more important in the next lesson on *solving* two-step equations.

Write an equation for each problem. State whether the problem should be written as a one-step equation or a two-step equation. Then describe the step or steps.

1. Five times a number subtracted from 50 is 15. What is the number?

   Equation: _____

   Number of steps and description:

   _____

2. Eight more than a number is twenty-seven. What is the number?

   Equation: _____

   Number of steps and description:

   _____

3. At a bookstore, you buy a calendar for $3 and some books for $4 each. You spend a total of $23. How many books do you buy?

   Equation: _____

   Number of steps and description:

   _____

4. You are giving away equal groups of paper clips to some number of friends. Each friend receives 15 paper clips and you started with 90 paper clips. How many friends receive paper clips?

   Equation: _____

   Number of steps and description:

   _____

LESSON 6-3

Writing Two-Step Equations
Success for English Learners

Problem 1

To write an equation from the words, remember clues:

"Six times a number" ⟶ $6n$

"Two less than a number" ⟶ $n - 2$

"Eight more than a number" ⟶ $n + 8$

"The opposite of 7" ⟶ -7

Combine the clues to write an equation with numbers:

"Four less than two times a number is equal to the opposite of nine."

$$2x - 4 = -9$$

Problem 2

Look at the boldfaced numbers and words in the problem.

A group of students want to raise **$3,000** for hurricane victims. They were **given $750** by local businesses, but they have to raise the rest. If there are **50 students**, how much does each student need to raise?

Put the information in a chart like this:

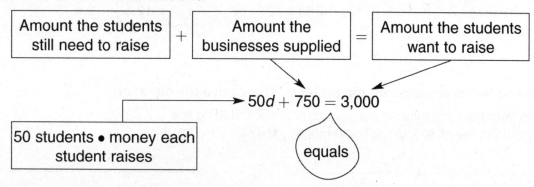

1. Write the words for the numbers and symbols: $18 - 3x = 3$

_____

_____

2. Write the numbers and symbols for this problem: "Five times a number minus seven is equal to the opposite of eleven."

_____

_____

LESSON 6-4

Solving Two-Step Equations
Practice and Problem Solving: A/B

Solve each equation. Cross out each number in the box that matches a solution.

| -18 | -8 | -6 | -4 | -3 | -2 | 2 | 3 | 4 | 6 | 8 | 18 |

1. $5x + 8 = 23$

2. $-2p - 4 = 2$

3. $6a - 11 = 13$

4. $4n + 12 = 4$

5. $9g + 2 = 20$

6. $\dfrac{k}{6} + 8 = 5$

7. $\dfrac{s}{3} - 4 = 2$

8. $\dfrac{c}{2} + 5 = 1$

9. $9 + \dfrac{a}{6} = 8$

Solve. Check each answer.

10. $3v - 12 = 15$

11. $8 + 5x = -2$

12. $\dfrac{d}{4} - 9 = -3$

Write an equation to represent the problem. Then solve the equation.

13. Two years of local Internet service costs $685, including the installation fee of $85. What is the monthly fee?

14. The sum of two consecutive numbers is 73. What are the numbers?

LESSON 6-4 Solving Two-Step Equations

Practice and Problem Solving: C

Rewrite each equation so it is in the form $ax + b = c$ or $\dfrac{x + d}{e} = f$, where x is a variable. Then solve the equation.

1. $3x - 17 = x + 3$

_____

_____

2. $6 + \dfrac{5x - 1}{3} = 10$

_____

_____

3. $7 + \dfrac{3 - 4x}{5} = 0$

_____

_____

4. $8 + 5x - 2 = -14$

_____

_____

5. $x + 7 = 5x - 9$

_____

_____

6. $\dfrac{x + 11}{3} - 5 = 1$

_____

_____

In each equation, one of the letters represents a variable and the other letters represent constants. Solve for the indicated variable and describe what operations you performed to solve for the variable.

7. Solve $rs + t = u$ for the variable s.

_____

_____

8. Solve $r(s + t) = u$ for the variable t.

_____

_____

9. Solve $\dfrac{n + m}{p} = q$ for the variable n.

_____

_____

10. Solve $\dfrac{m + n}{p} = q$ for the variable p.

_____

_____

<table>
<tr><td>LESSON
6-4</td><td></td></tr>
</table>

Solving Two-Step Equations
Practice and Problem Solving: D

Tell how to solve each two-step equation. Then solve it. The first one is done for you.

1. $5x + 3 = 33$

   Subtract 3 from both sides; $5x = 30$. Then divide both sides by 5; $x = 6$.

2. $8y - 1 = 31$

   _____

3. $\frac{1}{2}z + 5 = 11$

   _____

4. $15 - 4t = 3$

   _____

5. $\frac{1}{3}(q + 3) = 5$

   _____

Solve. Check each answer.

6. $2m + 7 = 9$

7. $3p - 5 = 19$

Write an equation to represent the problem. Then solve the problem. The first one is done for you.

8. When 3 is subtracted from two times a number, the result is 17. What is the number?

   $2n - 3 = 17; n = 10$

9. The sum of half a number and 5 is 9. What is the number?

   _____

10. The sum of 15 and two times a number is 29. What is the number?

   _____

LESSON 6-4   Solving Two-Step Equations
Reteach

Here is a key to solving an equation.

Example: Solve $3x - 7 = 8$.

Step 1: • Describe how to form the expression $3x - 7$ from the variable x:
  • Multiply by 3. Then subtract 7.

Step 2: • Write the parts of Step 1 in the reverse order and use inverse operations:
  • Add 7. Then divide by 3.

Step 3: • Apply Step 2 to *both sides* of the original equation.
  • Start with the original equation. $3x - 7 = 8$
  • Add 7 to both sides. $3x = 15$
  • Divide both sides by 3. $x = 5$

Describe the steps to solve each equation. Then solve the equation.

1. $4x + 11 = 19$

_____

2. $-3y + 10 = -14$

_____

3. $\dfrac{r - 11}{3} = -7$

_____

4. $5 - 2p = 11$

_____

5. $\dfrac{2}{3}z + 1 = 13$

_____

6. $\dfrac{w - 17}{9} = 2$

_____

LESSON 6-4

Solving Two-Step Equations

Reading Strategies: Analyze Information

An equation such as $-3x + 7 = -5$ is called a *two-step equation* because:

It takes two steps to form *the expression* $-3x + 7$.

It also takes two steps to solve *the equation* $-3x + 7 = -5$.

To form the expression $-3x + 7$ from x: Step 1. Multiply x by -3.
Step 2. Add 7.

To solve the equation $-3x + 7 = -5$: Step A. Subtract 7 from both sides.
Step B. Divide both sides by -3.

Look at the two pairs of steps. To find Step A and Step B, reverse the order of Step 1 and Step 2 and use inverse operations.

Before you solve each equation, list each pair of steps.

1. to form $-2x - 3$ from x: _____

   to solve $-2x - 3 = -25$: _____

   The solution to the equation $-2x - 3 = -25$ is: _____

2. to form $\dfrac{x + 1}{3}$ from x: _____

   to solve $\dfrac{x + 1}{3} = -5$: _____

   The solution to the equation $\dfrac{x + 1}{3} = -5$ is: _____

3. to form $5 - 4x$ from x: _____

   to solve $5 - 4x = 17$: _____

   The solution to the equation $5 - 4x = 17$ is: _____

4. to form $\dfrac{1}{3}(x - 7)$ from x: _____

   to solve $\dfrac{1}{3}(x - 7) = 1$: _____

   The solution to the equation $\dfrac{1}{3}(x - 7) = 1$ is: _____

LESSON 6-4 Solving Two-Step Equations

Success for English Learners

Expression

$$5x - 3 = 32$$

Equation

Expression

$$\frac{x + 12}{4} = -3$$

Equation

Problem 1

Steps to form the expression $5x - 3$:

1. Multiply a variable by 5.
2. Subtract 3.

Steps to solve the equation $5x - 3 = 32$:

A. Add 3 to both sides: $5x = 35$

B. Divide both sides by 5. $x = 7$

Problem 2

Steps to form the expression $\frac{x + 12}{4}$:

1. Add 12 to a variable.
2. Divide by 4.

Steps to solve the equation $\frac{x + 12}{4} = -3$:

A. Multiply both sides by 4: $x + 12 = -12$

B. Subtract 12 from both sides: $x = -24$

Here is the pattern:

Steps to form an expression	Reverse the steps and use inverse operations. →	Steps to solve the equation

Answer part a and part b for each equation.

1. $13x + 2 = 41$

   a. List the steps to form $13x + 2$.

   b. List the steps to solve $13x + 2 = 41$. Solve.

   _____   _____

   _____   _____

2. $\frac{x - 3}{5} = -1$

   a. List the steps to form $\frac{x - 3}{5}$.

   b. List the steps to solve $\frac{x - 3}{5} = -1$. Solve.

   _____   _____

   _____   _____

MODULE 6

Expressions and Equations
Challenge

Five brothers hired a builder to build fence around their house. Each brother has a different requirement for the length of the fence. The requirements are shown in the table below.

Name	Requirement
Adam	"The sum of twice the length of the fence and 250 feet must be less than 2,000 feet"
Benny	"100 feet more than three times the length of the fence must be greater than 2,200 feet."
Christopher	"500 feet more than one-fourth the length of the fence must be between 700 and 725 feet."
Desmond	"35% of the length of the fence plus 1,000 feet is greater than 1,275 feet."
Eddie	"1,000 feet less than 3 times the length of the fence is greater than 1,550 feet"

1. Write a single inequality that represents the possible values for the length of the fence that meet the requirements of all five brothers.

_____

_____

_____

_____

_____

2. The builder looked at the requirements and laughed. She said, "You didn't need to give me all of these requirements. I only needed requirements from two of you!" Which brother's requirements does the builder need and which ones are unnecessary? Why are some of the requirements unnecessary?

_____

_____

_____

_____

LESSON 7-1 Writing and Solving One-Step Inequalities

Practice and Problem Solving: A/B

Solve each inequality. Graph and check the solution.

1. $\dfrac{e}{2} < 3$ _____

2. $n - 1 > 3$ _____

3. $5 < 3 + w$ _____

4. $8 \le 2m$ _____

5. $r - 4 < 1$ _____

6. $2 \le -1t$ _____

7. $2 \ge s - 2$ _____

8. $2 \ge 5 + p$ _____

Solve each inequality.

9. $\dfrac{1}{5} \le \dfrac{x}{15}$ _____

10. $9 > -r$ _____

11. $-2 + b < 3$ _____

12. $70 - a \ge 25$ _____

Write an inequality for each problem. Then solve.

13. Arthur earned $136 in three weeks. He goes back to school in one more week. He needs at least $189 to buy the new coat that he wants for school. How much must Arthur earn in the next week?

_____

14. Marna is playing a game where you score –5 points each time you guess the correct answer. The goal is to get the lowest score. To win the game, Marna must have a score less than –80 points. How many correct answers does Marna need to win the game?

_____

LESSON 7-1

Writing and Solving One-Step Inequalities

Practice and Problem Solving: C

Solve each inequality. Graph and check the solution.

1. $-3.2a \le 8$ _____

2. $2 > n + 0.8$ _____

3. $b - 4.2 \ge -5$ _____

4. $\dfrac{e}{2} < -0.5$ _____

5. $5.1 - r \ge 5$ _____

6. $-1.44 \le -1.8y$ _____

Write an inequality for each problem. Solve the inequality. Then solve the problem.

7. Ashley took $20 out of her savings account each week on Friday. How many weeks ago did she have at least $250 in her account?

   _____

8. A cube has a volume of greater than 125 cm^3. What are the possible lengths of the side of that cube?

   _____

9. A treasure chest sinks at a rate no less than 20 feet per second. The floor of the ocean is at most at $-4,200$ feet. Will the treasure chest reach the ocean floor in less than 3 minutes? Explain.

   _____

LESSON 7-1

Writing and Solving One-Step Inequalities

Practice and Problem Solving: D

Solve each inequality. Graph and check the solution. The first one is done for you.

1. $-2a \geq 6$ $\underline{\qquad a \leq -3 \qquad}$

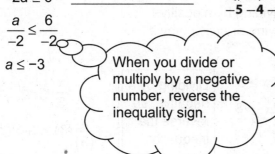

$$\frac{a}{-2} \leq \frac{6}{-2}$$

$$a \leq -3$$

When you divide or multiply by a negative number, reverse the inequality sign.

Check: Think:
−5 is one
solution
because
$-5 \leq -3$.
Substitute −5
for *a*.
$(-2)(-5) ? 6$
$10 \geq 6$ ✓

2. $1 > n + 4$ _____

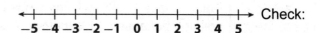

Check:

3. $b - 2 \geq -2$ _____

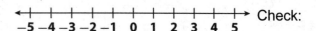

Check:

4. $\dfrac{e}{2} < -1$ _____

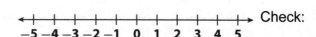

Check:

5. $t + 2 \geq 3$ _____

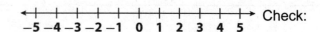

Check:

6. $\dfrac{c}{-2} < -2$ _____

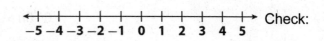

Check:

LESSON 7-1

Writing and Solving One-Step Inequalities
Reteach

When solving an inequality, solve it as if it is an equation. Then decide on the correct inequality sign to put in the answer.

When adding or subtracting a number from each side of an inequality, the sign stays the same. When multiplying or dividing by a positive number, the sign stays the same. When multiplying or dividing by a negative number, the sign changes.

$x + 5 > -5$	$x - 3 \le 8$	$-2x \ge 8$	$\dfrac{x}{3} < -6$
$x + 5 - 5 > -5 - 5$	$x - 3 + 3 \le 8 + 3$	$\dfrac{-2x}{-2} \le \dfrac{8}{-2}$	$\dfrac{x}{(3)}(3) < (-6)(3)$
$x > -10$	$x \le 11$	$x \le -4$	$x < -18$

Dividing by a negative, so reverse the inequality sign.

Check:
Think: 0 is a solution because $0 > -10$. Substitute 0 for x to see if your answer checks.

$x + 5 > -5$

$0 + 5 \ ? -5$

$5 > -5 \ \checkmark$

Check:
Think: 0 is a solution because $0 \le 11$. Substitute 0 for x to see if your answer checks.

$x - 3 \le 8$

$0 - 5 \ ? \ 8$

$-5 \le 8 \ \checkmark$

Check:
Think: -6 is a solution because $-6 \le -4$. Substitute -6 for x to see if your answer checks.

$-2x \ge 8$

$-2 \bullet -6 \ ? \ 8$

$12 \ge 8 \ \checkmark$

Check: Think: -21 is a solution because $-21 < -18$. Substitute -21 for x to see if your answer checks.

$\dfrac{x}{3} < -6$

$\dfrac{-21}{3} \ ? \ -6$

$-7 < -6 \ \checkmark$

Solve each inequality. Check your work.

1. $n + 6 \ge -3$

2. $-2n < -12$

3. $\dfrac{n}{3} \le -21$

4. $n - (-3) \ge 7$

5. $-15 + n < -8$

6. $6n > -12$

7. $-6 + n < -9$

8. $\dfrac{n}{-6} > -2$

LESSON 7-1

Writing and Solving One-Step Inequalities
Reading Strategies: Use a Graphic Organizer

When solving an inequality, solve it as if it is an equation. Then decide on the correct inequality sign to put in the answer.

Solving an inequality when you add or subtract	Solving an inequality when you divide by a negative number
$x + 3 > -4$	$-2x \geq -6$
Think: To solve $x + 3 = -4$, subtract 3. The inequality sign does not change.	Think: To solve $-2x = -6$, divide by -2. The inequality sign reverses.
$x + 3 - 3 > -4 - 3$	$\dfrac{-2x}{-2} \leq \dfrac{-6}{-2}$
$x > -7$	$x \leq 3$
$\updownarrow$ **The inequality signs stay the same.**	$\updownarrow$ **The inequality signs are reversed.**
Solving an inequality when you multiply or divide by a positive number	Solving an inequality when you multiply by a negative number
$2x \leq -4$	$\dfrac{x}{-3} < 3$
Think: To solve $2x = -4$, divide by positive 2. The inequality sign does not change.	Think: To solve $\dfrac{x}{-3} = 3$, multiply by -3. The inequality sign reverses.
$\dfrac{2x}{2} \leq \dfrac{-4}{2}$	$\left(\dfrac{x}{-3}\right)(-3) > (3)(-3)$
$x \leq -2$	$x > -9$

Tell what operation and number you use to solve each inequality. Tell whether the inequality sign reverses. Do not solve the inequalities.

1. To solve $n - 5 > 0$, you _____

   Does the sign of the inequality reverse? _____

2. To solve $\dfrac{n}{-6} \leq -2$, you _____

   Does the sign of the inequality reverse? _____

3. To solve $3n > -9$, you _____

   Does the sign of the inequality reverse? _____

Name _____ Date _____ Class _____

Writing and Solving One-Step Inequalities

Success for English Learners

When adding or subtracting a number from each side of an inequality, the sign stays the same. When multiplying or dividing, sometimes you need to reverse the inequality.

Problem 1

Multiply or divide by a positive number.

The sign stays the same.

$6x > -54$

$\dfrac{6x}{6} > \dfrac{-54}{6}$

$x > -9$

The sign does not change.

$\dfrac{x}{4} \leq 8$

$\left(\dfrac{x}{4}\right)4 \leq (8)(4)$

$x \leq 32$

Check:

$0 > -9;\ 6 \cdot 0\ ?\ -54$

$\qquad\qquad 0 > -54\ \checkmark$

Check:

$28 \leq 32;\ \dfrac{28}{4}\ ?\ 8$

$\qquad\qquad 7 \leq 8\ \checkmark$

Problem 2

Multiply or divide by a negative number.

The sign is reversed.

$-2x \geq 6$

$\dfrac{-2x}{-2} \leq \dfrac{6}{-2}$

$x \leq -3$

The sign changes.

$\dfrac{x}{-3} \leq 9$

$\left(\dfrac{x}{-3}\right)(-3) \geq (9)(-3)$

$x \geq -27$

Check:

$-5 \leq -3;\ -2 \cdot -5\ ?\ 6$

$\qquad\qquad 10 \geq 6\ \checkmark$

Check:

$0 \geq -27;\ \dfrac{0}{-3}\ ?\ 9$

$\qquad\qquad 0 \leq 9\ \checkmark$

Circle the symbol that will be in the answer to each inequality. Do not solve.

1. $n + -6 \geq 3$ <   ≤   >   ≥

2. $-6n < -12$ <   ≤   >   ≥

3. $6n \leq 12$ <   ≤   >   ≥

4. $n - (-6) \geq 3$ <   ≤   >   ≥

5. $-6 + n < -3$ <   ≤   >   ≥

6. $6n > -12$ <   ≤   >   ≥

Complete.

7. Explain how you know when to reverse the inequality sign when solving inequalities.

_____

_____

LESSON 7-2

Writing Two-Step Inequalities

Practice and Problem Solving: A/B

Write an inequality for each description.

1. Ten times a number increased by four is no more than twenty-five.

   _____

2. Thirty subtracted from four times a number is greater than the opposite of ten.

   _____

3. One fourth of the opposite of the difference of five and a number is less than twenty.

   _____

Write a description of each inequality.

4. $-5a + 3 > 1$

   _____

5. $27 - 2b \leq -6$

   _____

6. $\frac{1}{2}(c + 1) \geq 5$

   _____

Use the following situation to complete Exercise 7.

7. The school photography club charges $10 for each photo in its annual pet photo contest. The club wants to save $75 of its earnings for a pizza party. The club members also want to have at least $50 left over after the pizza party to pay for other club expenses. Write an expression for:

   a. how much money the club earns by taking p pet photos

      _____

   b. the difference between the amount the club earns and the amount for the pizza party

      _____

   c. Now write a two-step inequality for finding the smallest number of photographs that need to be made to pay for the club's pizza party and have at least $50 left over to pay club expenses.

      _____

Name _____ Date _____ Class_____

Writing Two-Step Inequalities

Practice and Problem Solving: C

Write an inequality for each situation. Then, combine the inequalities into a *compound inequality*.

1. A barge can safely haul no more than 400 tons across the river. The barge has an empty weight of 24 tons. The average weight of the railroad cars is 4 tons each. How many railroad cars can the barge haul?

   _____

2. In order for the barge operator to meet his expenses, he has to haul at least 120 tons of freight. How many railroad cars must the barge operator haul on each trip to at least break even?

   _____

3. Write a compound inequality that gives the range of the number of railroad cars that the barge can haul which will allow the barge operator to at least break even.

   _____

Write a two-step inequality for the graph on each number line. Include addition, subtraction, multiplication or division.

4.

   _____

5.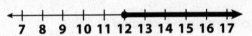

   _____

6.

   _____

7. Explain why the compound inequality, $-5 < 3x < 10$, is not considered a two-step inequality in the sense in which it used in this lesson.

   _____

LESSON 7-2

Writing Two-Step Inequalities

Practice and Problem Solving: D

Write an inequality for each phrase. The first one is done for you.

1. Four times a number is at least 2.

   $4x \geq 2$

2. One third of the opposite of a number is less than 12.

   _____

3. A number increased by 5 is less than 7.

   _____

4. Ten less than a number is more than 30.

   _____

5. Two more than 5 times a number is greater than or equal to 3.

   _____

6. Six less than two times a number is no more than 17.

   _____

Write an inequality for each situation. Show your work. The first one is done for you.

7. An employee of a car wash earns $12 for each car she washes. She always saves $50 of her weekly earnings. This week, she wants to have at least $100 in spending money. What is the fewest number of cars she must wash?

   Twelve times the number of cars she washes minus $50 for her savings must be

   greater than or equal to $100. Twelve times the number of cars, *n*, is 12*n*. Subtract

   $50 for her savings: 12*n* – 50. This has to be at least $100, so 12*n* – 50 ≥ 100.

8. A video-game enthusiast saved $750 to spend on a video game player and games. The player costs $400. The games cost $49 each. At most, how many games can the enthusiast buy along with the player?

   _____

   _____

9. A health-food producer has 250 samples of a new snack to distribute in the mall. The producer has to keep at least 50 samples for display in the health-food store for the product launch. How long will the samples last if consumers are taking the samples at a rate of 25 every hour?

   _____

   _____

LESSON 7-2

Writing Two-Step Inequalities
Reteach

Two-step inequalities involve
- a division or multiplication
- an addition or subtraction.

Step 1
The description indicates whether division or multiplication is involved:

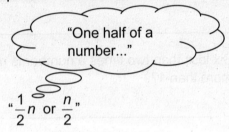

Step 2
The description indicates whether addition or subtraction is involved:

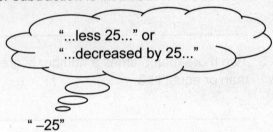

Step 3
Combine the two to give two steps:

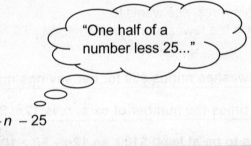

Step 4
Use an inequality symbol:

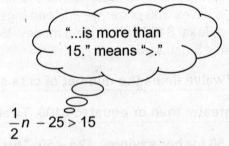

Fill in the steps as shown above.

1. Five less than 3 times a number is greater than the opposite of 8.

   Step 1: _____

   Step 2: _____

   Step 3: _____

   Step 4: _____

2. Thirteen plus 5 times a number is no more than 30.

   Step 1: _____

   Step 2: _____

   Step 3: _____

   Step 4: _____

LESSON 7-2
Writing Two-Step Inequalities
Reading Strategies: Recognize Words and Phrases

Words and phrases in two-step inequality problems can be replaced with numbers, symbols, and the operations of addition, subtraction, multiplication, and division.

As you read inequality problems, watch for these "special" words.

"one half of", "one third of" $\longrightarrow$ $\frac{1}{2}a$, $\frac{1}{3}b$, $\frac{c}{2}$, $\frac{d}{3}$

"four times", "double", "triple" $\longrightarrow$ $4x$, $2y$, $3z$

"five more than", "less 11" $\longrightarrow$ $a + 5$, $b - 11$

"the opposite of" $\longrightarrow$ -6, $-\frac{1}{4}$, -2.5

Inequalities are also described by specific words and phrases.

"no more than 23": ≤ 23 "no less than the opposite of 4": ≥ -4

Two-step inequality problems may combine all of these word clues.

Example Five less than 7 times a number is greater than the opposite of 3.

"...7 times a number..." $\longrightarrow$ $7n$

"Five less than..." $\longrightarrow$ -5

"...greater than the opposite of three." $\longrightarrow$ > -3

"Five less than 7 times a number..." $\longrightarrow$ $7n - 5$

"Five less than 7 times a number is greater than the opposite of 3."

$7n - 5 > -3$

Write an inequality for each description.

1. Half of the sum of a number and 6 is no less than 20.

   _____

2. Twelve more than 3 times a number is no more than the opposite of 11.

   _____

3. Two times a number minus 8 is less than 5.

   _____

Writing Two-Step Inequalities

LESSON 7-2

Success for English Learners

Problem 1

To write an inequality from the words, remember clues:

"Four <u>times</u> a number" ⟶ $4n$

"Five <u>less than</u> a number" ⟶ $n - 5$

"Six <u>more than</u> a number" ⟶ $n + 6$

"The <u>opposite</u> of 3" ⟶ -3

"<u>No more than</u> a number" *or*

"<u>Less than or equal to</u> a number" ⟶ $\leq n$

"<u>No less than</u> a number" *or*

"<u>Greater than or equal to</u> a number" ⟶ $\geq n$

Combine the clues to write an inequality with numbers:

"Five more than three times a number is no greater than the opposite of 6."

$$5 + 3n \leq -6$$

Problem 2

Look at the highlighted parts of the problem.

The seventh-grade students need to raise **at least $5,000** for their class trip. They were **given $850** by local businesses for the trip, but they have to raise the rest. If there are **83 students**, how much does each student need to raise?

Put the information in a chart like this:

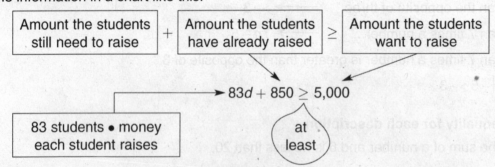

Write the words or the numbers and symbols.

1. Write the words for the numbers and symbols: $5 - 2x > -4$

   _____

2. Write the numbers and symbols for this problem: "Three times a number minus 7 is less than or equal to the opposite of 10."

   _____

LESSON 7-3

Solving Two-Step Inequalities

Practice and Problem Solving: A/B

Fill in the blanks to show the steps in solving the inequality.

1. $3x - 5 < 19$

   $3x - 5 + $ _____ $ < 19 + $ _____

   $3x < $ _____

   $3x \div $ _____ $ < $ _____ $ \div $ _____

   $x < $ _____

2. $-2x + 12 < -4$

   $-2x + 12 - $ _____ $ < -4 - $ _____

   $-2x < $ _____

   $-2x \div $ _____ $ > $ _____ $ \div $ _____

   $x > $ _____

3. Why do the inequality signs stay the same in the last two steps of Exercise 1?

   _____

4. Why is the inequality sign reversed in the last two steps of Exercise 2?

   _____

Solve the inequalities. Show your work.

5. $-7d + 8 > 29$

6. $12 - 3b < 9$

7. $\dfrac{z}{7} - 6 \geq -5$

   _____   _____   _____

   _____   _____   _____

   _____   _____   _____

8. Fifty students are trying to raise at least $12,500 for a class trip. They have already raised $1,250. How much should each student raise, on average, in order to meet the goal? Write and solve the two-step inequality for this problem.

   _____

   _____

9. At the end of the day, vegetables at Farm Market sell for $2.00 a pound, and a basket costs $3.50. If Charlene wants to buy a basket and spend no more than $10.00 total, how many pounds of vegetables can she buy? Write and solve the inequality.

   _____

   _____

LESSON 7-3 Solving Two-Step Inequalities

Practice and Problem Solving: C

Provide the missing steps needed to arrive at the two-step inequality. Work backwards.

1. $a < -3$

_____

_____

$-5a + 2 > 17$

2. $b \geq 1$

_____

_____

$3b + 4 \geq 7$

Use the description below for Exercises 3–5.

In Euclidean geometry, the sum of the lengths of 2 sides of a triangle is greater than the length of the third side. The lengths of 3 sides of a triangle are $3x$, 7, and 12.

3. Write three inequalities that apply for this triangle.

_____

_____

_____

4. Find the value of x for each of the three inequalities.

_____

_____

_____

5. What range of values of x satisfies all three inequalities? Explain your answer.

_____

_____

Write a description of each inequality listed below. Then, solve it.

6. $-3 \geq \frac{1}{3}(6 - x)$

_____

_____

7. $4(2x + 1) < -\frac{1}{2}$

_____

_____

LESSON 7-3 Solving Two-Step Inequalities
Practice and Problem Solving: D

Solve. Then, graph each solution set. The first one is done for you.

1. $7y - 8 > 6$ ___$y > 2$___

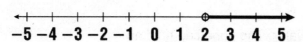

2. $4d + 15 \leq -1$ _____

  +—+—+—+—+—+—+—+—+—+—+—+→

3. $\dfrac{r}{-6} + 5 < 7$ _____

  +—+—+—+—+—+—+—+—+—+—+—+→

Give three solutions for each inequality. The first one is done for you.

4. $5 + 2x > 9$ 5. $\dfrac{1}{5}(y + 10) \leq -25$ 6. $-3(1 - z) < 9$

  ___3, 4, 5___   _____   _____

Solve the inequality for each problem. The first one is done for you.

7. The chess club plans to sell water bottles to raise $425. They have
   $175 already. If they sell water bottles for $8 each, at least how many
   bottles do they need to sell in order to raise enough money?

   $8n + 175 \geq \$425$

   ___Subtract 175 from both sides: $8n + 175 - 175 \geq 425 - 175$; $8n \geq 250$; divide both sides___

   ___by 8: $n \geq 31.25$. The club members need to sell at least 32 bottles.___

8. A gymnasium can hold no more than 650 people. A permanent
   bleacher in the gymnasium holds 136 people. The event organizers
   are setting up 25 rows with an equal number of chairs. At most, how
   many chairs can be in each row?

   _____

   _____

Solving Two-Step Inequalities

Reteach

When you solve a real-world two-step inequality, you have to
- be sure to solve the inequality correctly, and
- interpret the answer correctly in the context of the problem.

Example

The catfish pond contains 2,500 gallons of water. The pond can hold no more than 3,000 gallons. It is being filled at a rate of 110 gallons per hour. How many whole hours will it take to fill but not overfill the pond?

Step 1: Solve the inequality.

- The pond already contains 2,500 gallons.
- The pond can be filled at a rate of 110 gallons per hour, or 110h for the number of gallons added in h hours.
- The pond can hold no more than 3,000 gallons, so $2,500 + 110h \leq 3,000$.
- Solve the inequality:
  $2,500 - 2,500 + 110h \leq 3,000 - 2,500$
  $110h \leq 500$, or $h \leq 4.5$ hours.

Step 2: Interpret the results.

The problem asks for how many *whole* hours would be needed to fill the pond with not more than 3,000 gallons. Since $h \leq 4.5$ hours, 5 hours would fill the pool to overflowing. So, the nearest number of *whole* hours to fill it but not to overfill it would be 4 hours.

---

1. A cross-country racer travels 20 kilometers before she realizes that she has to cover at least 75 kilometers in order to qualify for the next race. If the racer travels at a rate of 10 kilometers per hour, how many whole hours will it take her to reach the 75-kilometer mark?

_____

With inequality problems, many solutions are possible. In real-world problems these solutions need to be examined for sense.

Example

An animal shelter has $2,500 in its reserve fund. The shelter charges $40 per animal placement and would like to have at least $4,000 in its reserve fund. If the shelter places 30 cats and 10 dogs, will that be enough to meet its goal?

Step 1

Write and solve the inequality:
$2,500 + 40a \geq 4,000$, or $40a \geq 1,500$
$a \geq 37.5$

Step 2

If the shelter places 30 cats and 10 dogs, or 40 animals, that will be enough to meet its goal, because $a = 40$ is a solution to the inequality $a \geq 37.5$.

---

2. Alissa has $75 worth of bird seed, which she will put into small bags. She will sell each bag for $7. What is the greatest number of bags she must sell in order to have no less than $10 worth of bird seed left over?

LESSON 7-3

Solving Two-Step Inequalities
Reading Strategies: Analyzing and Interpreting Information

Real-world, two-step inequalities involve data that has to be analyzed and interpreted.

Example

An orchard has 300 fruit trees, but only 250 bore fruit this year. How many days will it take to pick the fruit if pickers pick at most 30 trees per day?

Solution

Step 1 List and analyze the information that is given.

• 250 trees in all to pick

• The pickers pick at most 30 trees per day.

Step 2 Write and solve the inequality.

$30d \le 250$

$d \le 8\dfrac{1}{3}$ days

Step 3 Interpret the answer.

The answer will be either 8 or 9 days. However, notice that the inequality is "less than or equal to."

The pickers will pick at most 240 trees in 8 days. They will not be able to pick all 250 trees in 8 days, and will need to work for 9 days.

List and analyze the information in each problem. Then, write an inequality, and solve and interpret the answer.

1. The community food bank has 750 meals to distribute over a 12-hour period. They need to save at least 50 of the meals for the volunteers. How many people can be served by the food bank in 10 hours, not including the volunteers?

   _____

   _____

2. A vegetable-oil recovery plant has already recycled 1,400 liters out of 2,500 liters of used oil. If the plant can recycle 24 liters of used oil per hour, about how many hours will it take to recycle what is left?

   _____

   _____

Name _____ Date _____ Class_____

LESSON 7-3

Solving Two-Step Inequalities
Success for English Learners

Problem 1

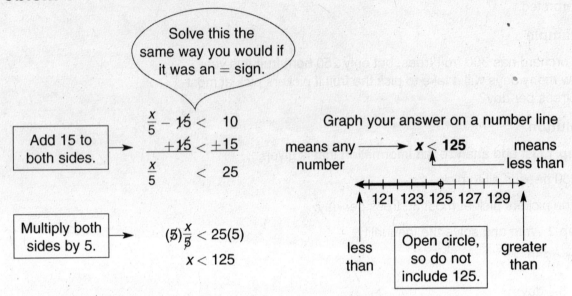

1. In Problem 1, is 125 a solution to the inequality? Explain.

_____

2. In Problem 1, why do you *not* reverse the inequality symbol?

_____

Problem 2

Think of Problem 1 as a real-world problem.

"One fifth of the students less 15 is less than 10. Could there be 120 students or 50 students or 25 students? Why?"

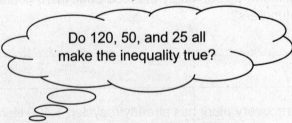

Yes, all make true statements: 120 < 125, 50 < 125, and 25 < 125.

Give three solutions to the inequalities.

3. $100 - 2x > 20$

4. $4y + 3 \leq -13$

_____   _____

_____   _____

Inequalities

Challenge

The Schultz family is planning a garden for part of their back yard. The width of the garden will be 20 feet. Each family member has different requirements. The requirements are shown in the table below.

Name	Requirement
Mr. Schultz	The maximum length of fencing around the garden is 100 feet.
Mrs. Schultz	The area of the garden must be greater than 400 square feet.
Angelica	One-half of the garden will be flowers. At most there will be 350 square feet for flowers.
Robert	At least 15% percent of the garden will be used to grow carrots and lettuce. At least there will be 45 square feet for carrots and lettuce.

Write and solve an inequality that represents the possible values for the lengths of the garden for each family member.

1. Mr. Schultz: _____ _____

2. Mrs. Schultz: _____ _____

3. Angelica: _____ _____

4. Robert: _____ _____

Use the information to decide on the length for the garden. Then make and label a scale drawing of the garden, being sure each family member's requirements are met.

5.

Scale: 1 square: 4 square feet

LESSON 8-1

Similar Shapes and Scale Drawings
Practice and Problem Solving: A/B

1. The plan of a terrace is shown at right. The scale is 2 inches : 6 feet. What are the length and width of the terrace? Find the terrace's area.

   Length: _____

   Width: _____

   Area: _____

   5 in.

   2 in.

2. The floor plan of a ballroom is shown at right. The scale is 3 centimeters : 4 meters. What are the length and width of the ballroom? Find the ballroom's area.

   Length: _____

   Width: _____

   Area: _____

   12 cm

   9 cm

3. A garage floor measures 150 feet by 120 feet. A scale drawing of the floor on grid paper uses a scale of 1 unit : 15 feet. What are the dimensions of the drawing?

   _____

4. The scale model of a skyscraper being built is 4.2 feet tall.

   a. When it is finished, the skyscraper will be 525 meters tall. What scale was used to make the model?

   _____

   b. The model is made out of a stack of plywood sheets. Each sheet is 0.6 inch thick. How many sheets of plywood tall is the model?

   _____

5. You have been asked to build a scale model of a restaurant out of bottle caps. The restaurant is 20 feet tall. Your scale is 2.4 cm : 1 foot.

   a. A bottle cap is 1.2 cm tall. About how many bottle caps tall will your model be?

   _____

   b. You are out of bottle caps, and decide to use popsicle sticks instead. You measure them, and they are 15.2 cm tall. How many popsicle sticks tall will your model be?

   _____

**LESSON
8-1**

Similar Shapes and Scale Drawings

Practice and Problem Solving: C

1. A scale drawing of a patio is shown at right. The scale is 4 inches : 6.8 feet. What are the length and width of the patio? Find the patio's area.

   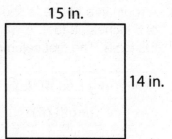
   15 in.

   14 in.

   Length: _____

   Width: _____

   Area: _____

2. The scale for a scale drawing is 8 millimeters : 1 centimeter. Which is larger, the actual object or the scale drawing? Explain.

   _____

   _____

3. Carol has a small copy of a painting. The dimensions of her copy are shown at right. The scale of the copy is 0.5 inches : 12 centimeter.

   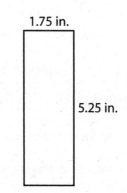
   1.75 in.

   5.25 in.

   a. Find the dimensions of the original painting.

      _____

   b. Find the area of the original painting.

      _____

   c. One centimeter is equal to approximately 0.033 foot. Find the dimensions of the original painting in feet. Round to the nearest thousandth.

      _____

   d. Find the area of the original painting in square feet. Round to the nearest thousandth.

      _____

4. On a scale drawing, a bookshelf is 8 inches tall. The scale factor is $\frac{1}{8}$.

   What is the height of the bookshelf?

   _____

5. On a scale drawing, a school is 1.6 feet tall. The scale factor is $\frac{1}{22}$.

   Find the height of the school.

   _____

Name _____ Date _____ Class_____

Similar Shapes and Scale Drawings

Practice and Problem Solving: D

1. A room in a house is shown on a blueprint. The blueprint has a scale of 5 inches : 8 feet. A wall in the same blueprint is 30 inches. Complete the table. The first column is done for you.

Blueprint Length (in.)	5	10		20		
Actual Length (ft)	8	16	24		40	48

   a. How long is the actual wall? _____

   b. A door in the room has a width of 4 feet. What is the width of the door in the blueprint?

   _____

2. The scale of a room in a blueprint is 2 inches : 1 foot. A window in the same blueprint is 12 inches. Complete the table.

Blueprint Length (in.)	2	4		8		12
Actual Length (ft)	1		3		5	

   a. How long is the actual window? _____

   b. A mantel in the room has an actual width of 8 feet. What is the width of the mantel in the blueprint?

   _____

3. The scale in the drawing is 2 inches : 4 feet. What are the length and width of the actual room? Find the area of the actual room.

   Length: _____

   Width: _____

   Area: _____

12 in.

6 in.

4. A studio apartment has a floor that measures 80 feet by 64 feet. A scale drawing of the floor on grid paper uses a scale of 1 unit : 8 feet. What are the dimensions of the scale drawing?

   _____

   _____

LESSON 8-1

Similar Shapes and Scale Drawings
Reteach

The dimensions of a scale model or scale drawing are related to the actual dimensions by a *scale factor*. The **scale factor** is a ratio.

The length of a model car is 9 in. ⟶

The length of the actual car is 162 in. ⟶

$$\frac{9 \text{ in.}}{162 \text{ in.}} = \frac{9 \div 9}{162 \div 9} = \frac{1}{18}$$

$\frac{9}{162}$ can be simplified to $\frac{1}{18}$. ⟵ The scale factor is $\frac{1}{18}$.

If you know the scale factor, you can use a proportion to find the dimensions of an actual object or of a scale model or drawing.

- The scale factor of a model train set is $\frac{1}{87}$. A piece of track in the model train set is 8 in. long. What is the actual length of the track?

$$\frac{\text{model length}}{\text{actual length}} = \frac{8}{x} \qquad \frac{8}{x} = \frac{1}{87} \qquad x = 696$$

The actual length of track is 696 inches.

- The distance between 2 cities on a map is 4.5 centimeters. The map scale is 1 cm : 40 mi.

$$\frac{\text{distance on map}}{\text{actual distance}} = \frac{4.5 \text{ cm}}{x \text{ mi}} = \frac{1 \text{ cm}}{40 \text{ mi}}$$

$$x = 180$$

The actual distance is 180 miles.

Identify the scale factor.

1. Photograph: height 3 in.
   Painting: height 24 in.

   $$\frac{\text{photo height}}{\text{painting height}} = \frac{\quad \text{in.}}{\quad \text{in.}} = \underline{\quad}$$

2. Butterfly: wingspan 20 cm
   Silk butterfly: wingspan 4 cm

   $$\frac{\text{silk butterfly}}{\text{butterfly}} = \frac{\quad \text{cm}}{\quad \text{cm}} = \underline{\quad}$$

Solve.

3. On a scale drawing, the scale factor is $\frac{1}{12}$. A plum tree is 7 inches tall on the scale drawing. What is the actual height of the tree?

4. On a road map, the distance between 2 cities is 2.5 inches. The map scale is 1 inch:30 miles. What is the actual distance between the cities?

_____ _____

Name _____ Date _____ Class_____

 LESSON 8-1

Similar Shapes and Scale Drawings

Reading Strategies: Read a Map

A **scale drawing** has the same shape, but is not the same size, as the object it represents. A map is an example of a scale drawing.

This is a map of a campground. The scale is 1 cm:10 ft.

To find how far the campground entrance is from the canoe rental office, follow the steps. Use a centimeter ruler to measure.

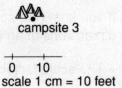

campsite 1

canoe rental office

water

campsite 2

ENTRANCE

campsite 3

```
0    10
scale 1 cm = 10 feet
```

Step 1: Measure the distance in centimeters.

⟶ The distance is 3 centimeters.

Step 2: Set up a proportion using the map scale as one ratio.

⟶ $\dfrac{1\ cm}{10\ ft} = \dfrac{3\ cm}{x\ ft}$

Step 3: Use the proportion. ⟶ $x = 3 \cdot 10$

Step 4: Solve to find the value of x. ⟶ $x = 30$

The campground entrance is 30 feet from the canoe rental office.

Use the map to answer each question.

1. How many centimeters is Campsite 3 from the water?

_____

2. Write a proportion to find the distance from Campsite 3 to the water.

_____

3. How many centimeters is Campsite 3 from the canoe rental office?

_____

4. Write a proportion to find the distance from Campsite 3 to the canoe rental office.

_____

Similar Shapes and Scale Drawings

LESSON 8-1

Success for English Learners

Problem 1

Actual

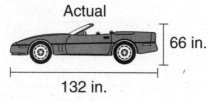

66 in.

132 in.

Model

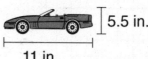

5.5 in.

11 in.

What is the scale factor?

$$\frac{\text{Model length}}{\text{Actual length}} = \frac{11}{132} = \frac{1}{12}; \frac{\text{Model height}}{\text{Actual height}} = \frac{5.5}{66} = \frac{1}{12}$$

Scale factor $= \frac{1}{12}$.

Problem 2

This is a photo of a painting. If you measure the photo, you could find the measurements of the actual painting.

©HMH

Scale factor is $\frac{1}{15}$.

$\frac{1}{15} \rightarrow \frac{\text{photo}}{\text{painting}}$

Write 2 proportions, one for the length and one for the width.

$$\frac{\text{photo length}}{\text{painting length}} = \frac{1}{15} \qquad \frac{\text{photo width}}{\text{painting width}} = \frac{1}{15}$$

1. In Problem 1, what would happen if you used a different scale factor for the length than you did for the width?

   _____

   _____

2. Explain why it is important for the photo and the painting to be in proportion in Problem 2.

   _____

   _____

   _____

LESSON
8-2

Geometric Drawings

Practice and Problem Solving: A/B

Use each set of line segments to sketch a triangle. If a triangle cannot be drawn, explain why.

1.

2.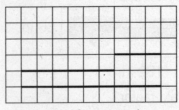

Sketch: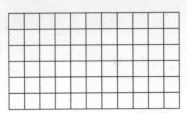

Sketch: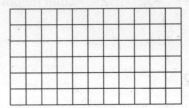

_____

_____

_____

_____

Can each set of line segments form a triangle? Why or why not?

3. $\overline{AB} = \frac{1}{2}$ mile

   $\overline{BC} = \frac{1}{3}$ mile

   $\overline{AC} = \frac{1}{4}$ mile

4. $\overline{DE} = 0.205$ kilometer

   $\overline{EF} = 0.01$ kilometer

   $\overline{DF} = 0.02$ kilometer

_____

_____

_____

_____

How many triangles are formed by the angles and sides—unique triangle, no triangle, or many triangles?

5.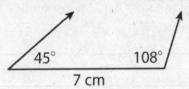

6.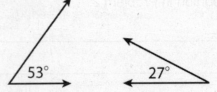

_____

_____

LESSON 8-2

Geometric Drawings

Practice and Problem Solving: C

Astronomers often use triangles to compute the distance between Earth and other planets in the solar system. The diagram below shows how triangles are used in this process.

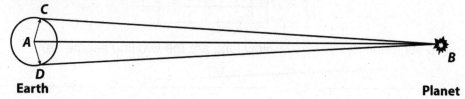

1. Triangles *ABC* and *ABD* are right triangles. Where are the right angles?

   _____

   _____

2. What is the distance *AC* in this diagram called? (*Hint*: What part of the circle is it?) How does it compare to *AD*?

   _____

3. Without using exact numbers, compare the distance *AC* with the distance *BC*?

   _____

4. Without using exact numbers, compare the distances *AB* and *BC*.

   _____

5. Since *ABC* is a right triangle, how does the distance *AB* compare to *BC*? Is it equal, greater than, or less than? Why?

   _____

6. If you did **not** know that *ABC* is a right triangle, what kind of triangle would Exercise 4 suggest that *ABC* is? Why?

   _____

7. The astronomer would like to know the distance *AB* from Earth's center to the planet. The astronomer knows the distance *AC* and that *ABC* is a right triangle. What other angles or sides could the astronomer measure to help find the distance *AB*?

   _____

   _____

Name _____ Date _____ Class_____

Geometric Drawings

Practice and Problem Solving: D

Answer the questions. The first one is started for you.

1.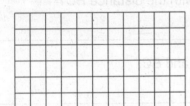

How long are the two line segments?

3 units and 4 units

To form a triangle, how long must
a third line segment be?

less than 7 units but greater

than 1 unit

Choose a third side length, and then
draw the triangle on the grid.

Third side length: _____

2.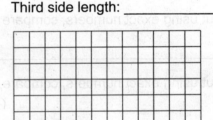

How long are the two line segments?

_____

To form a triangle, how long must
a third line segment be?

_____

_____

Choose a third side length, and then
draw the triangle on the grid.

Third side length: _____

Answer the questions. The first one is started for you.

3.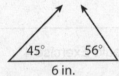

6 in.

What is the sum of the two angle
measures?

101°

If these angles formed a triangle, what
would be the measure of the third angle?

_____

4.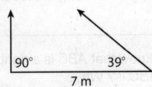

7 m

What is the sum of the two angle
measures?

_____

If these angles formed a triangle, what
would be the measure of the third angle?

_____

LESSON 8-2

Geometric Drawings

Reteach

In this lesson, you learned two different sets of conditions for drawing a triangle.

Three Sides	Two Angles and a Side

Three Sides

Can these three sides form a triangle?

The condition that a triangle can be formed is based on this fact:

The sum of the lengths of two shorter sides is greater than the length of the longest side.

What are the lengths of the shorter sides?

4 and **5** units

What is the length of the longest side?

8 units

Is **4 + 5 > 8**? Yes.

Two Angles and a Side

Why is a common, or included, side needed? Do these angles and side form a triangle?

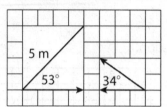

The condition that a triangle can be formed is based on this fact:

The sum of the measures of the angles in a plane triangle is 180 degrees.

What would be the measure of the third angle in a triangle formed from these parts?

180° = 53° + 34° + *x*°

$$x° = 180° − 87°$$

$$x = 93°$$

A triangle can be formed, with the angles 53° and 93° having the 5-meter side in common.

Answer the questions about triangle drawings.

1. Can a triangle be formed with three sides of equal length? Explain using the model above.

   _____

   _____

2. Can a triangle be formed with angles having measures of 30°, 70°, and 110°? Explain using the model above.

   _____

   _____

LESSON 8-2

Geometric Drawings

Reading Strategies: Using Graphic Aids

Real-world problems can be solved more easily in some cases when you draw a diagram to represent the situation.

Example

Two roads meet at a right angle. One road is 5 kilometers in length, and the other is 8 kilometers in length. A third road is constructed connecting the ends of the other two roads. What is its minimum length?

Solution

First sketch the situation.

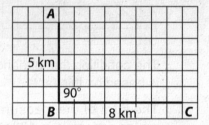

The two sides, *AB*, and *BC*, are the legs of a right triangle. A straight line connecting points *A* and *C* would form the hypotenuse. It would also be the shortest distance between points *A* and *B*.

"Minimum length" and "shortest distance" mean the same thing here.

Since points *A*, *B*, and *C* form a right triangle, the Pythagorean Theorem can be used to find the length of line segment *AC*.

$AC^2 = AB^2 + BC^2$, so $AC^2 = 5^2 + 8^2 = 25 + 64 = 89; \sqrt{AC^2} = AC = \sqrt{89}$.

So, the length of the road represented by *AC* is $\sqrt{89}$ kilometers.

Check

Use this result to check that three sides form a triangle. The long side, $\sqrt{89}$, is between $\sqrt{81}$, or 9, and $\sqrt{100}$, or 10. Add 5 and 8 to get 13. Since 13 > 9 and 13 > 10, the sides form a triangle.

Use another sheet of paper to answer the questions.

1. A carpenter has a 10-foot board and two 4-foot boards. Can these form a triangular wooden brace? Explain.

2. A father is giving his child a 30-inch long softball bat for her birthday. He has a rectangular box that has the dimensions of 5 inches by 6 inches by 25 inches. Will the bat fit in the box? Explain.

LESSON 8-2

Geometric Drawings

Success for English Learners

Problem 1

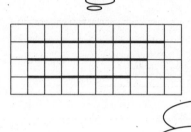

Can these three sides form a triangle?

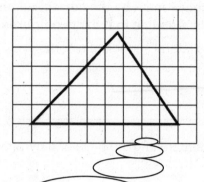

Yes, they can.
If you place the two shorter sides end to end, they are longer than the third side.
So, the three sides can form a triangle.

Problem 2

Describe the triangle formed by these parts and any others you can compute or measure.

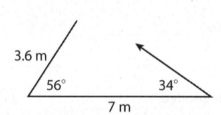

3.6 m
56°
34°
7 m

$180° = 56° + 34° + \mathbf{90°}$

How long are the sides?

3.6 m, 6 m, and 7 m.

Answer the questions.

1. In Problem 1, how would using a compass and a ruler make drawing the triangle easier?

_____

_____

2. Is the triangle in Problem 2 a right triangle? How do you know?

_____

_____

LESSON 8-3

Cross Sections

Practice and Problem Solving: A/B

What is the common set of points for these figures called—an *intersection* or a *cross section*? Place a check mark by the correct name. Describe the geometric figure formed by the common points. Assume that the two figures have more than one point in common.

1. A circle and the lateral surface of a cone.

   Cross section _____   Intersection _____

   Figure formed: _____

2. The edge of a square and the base of a pyramid.

   Cross section _____   Intersection _____

   Figure formed: _____

3. A plane that is perpendicular to the base of a cube and slices through the cube.

   Cross section _____   Intersection _____

   Figure formed: _____

4. A circle with an area bigger than the base of a pyramid and slicing parallel to the base through the pyramid between its apex and its base.

   Cross section _____   Intersection _____

   Figure formed: _____

Name or describe the geometric figure that is shaded. Each shaded region results from a plane passing through the solid.

5.

_____

6.

_____

7.

_____

8.

_____

Name _____ Date _____ Class_____

LESSON
8-3

Cross Sections

Practice and Problem Solving: C

Two identical cubes are intersected by a plane, resulting in two different cross sections as shown. Answer the questions about the two cross sections.

Cross section *X*

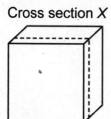

Cross section *Y*

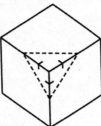

1. The plane that created cross section *X* sliced through the cube parallel to one of its sides. What type of figure is this? Explain.

   _____

   _____

2. The plane that created cross section *Y* sliced through the corner of the cube in such a way that it intersected the midpoints of the sides of the cube. What type of triangle is formed by this cross section? Explain.

   _____

   _____

A plane intersects a cylinder. In Diagram A, the plane is perpendicular to the long axis of the cylinder. In Diagram B, the plane is tilted relative to the cylinder axis. In Diagram C, the plane is tilted even more. In Diagram D, the plane passes through the cylinder along its axis. Answer the questions.

Diagram A   **Diagram B**   **Diagram C**   **Diagram D**

3. What shape are the cross sections in Diagrams A, B, C and D?

   _____

   _____

4. Compare the areas of the four cross sections.

   _____

LESSON
8-3

Cross Sections

Practice and Problem Solving: D

Describe the shape that is formed by the cross section. The first one is done for you.

1.

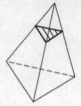

a triangle that is similar to the base

2.

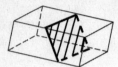

_____

3.

_____

4.

_____

Draw cross sections for these figures that are parallel to their bases.

5.

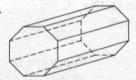

6.

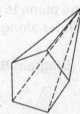

LESSON
8-3

Cross Sections
Reteach

Cross sections can take a variety of shapes, but they are generally related to the parts of the figures from which they are formed. The angle at which the intersecting plane "cuts" the figure is also a factor in determining the shape of the cross section. However, the cross section is always defined as a plane figure in the situations presented here.

Example 1

When the intersecting plane is *parallel* to the base(s) of the figure, the cross section is often related to the shape of the base. In this cylinder, the cross section is congruent to the bases.

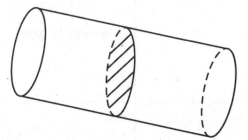

What is the shape of the cross section?
The cross section is a circle that is congruent to each of the bases of the cylinder.

Example 2

When the intersecting plane is *perpendicular* to the base(s) of the figure, the cross section is not always the same shape as the base. In this cylinder, the cross section is a rectangle, not a circle.

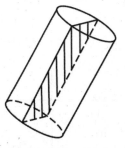

What is the cross section?
A rectangle having a length equal to the height of the cylinder and a width equal to the diameter of the cylinder.

For each solid, draw at least two cross sections with two different shapes. Describe the cross sections.

1.

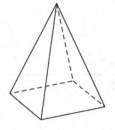

_____

_____

_____

_____

2.

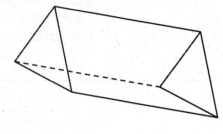

_____

_____

_____

_____

Cross Sections

Reading Strategies: Use a Table

Cross sections are often related to parts of the solids from which they are formed. This makes it possible to organize into a table, information about each solid, its cross section, and the plane that "cut" the figures to form the cross section.

Draw each cross section as described. Complete the table. Be as specific in your descriptions as possible.

Solid	Intersection Direction	Cross Section Shape	How Cross Section Shape Relates to the Solid
1.	parallel to the rectangular base	2.	similar to base
3.	4.	a regular pentagon	5.
6.	passing through the sphere but not through its center	7.	8.
9.	passing through the cone's vertex and bisecting its base	10.	11.

LESSON 8-3

Cross Sections
Success for English Learners

Problem 1

How can you pass a plane through the pyramid so that the cross section is a rectangle?

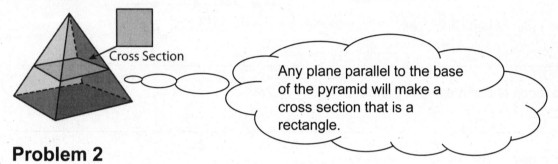

Cross Section

Any plane parallel to the base of the pyramid will make a cross section that is a rectangle.

Problem 2

Cross sections of a cone and a pyramid are shown below.

How are the two cross sections different?

Cone   **Pyramid**

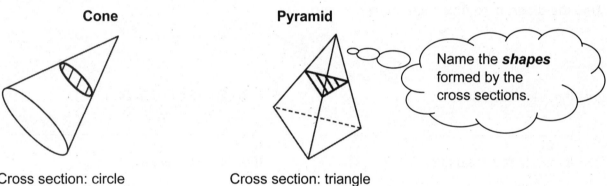

Name the **shapes** formed by the cross sections.

Cross section: circle   Cross section: triangle

Answer the questions.

1. In Problem 1, if the cross section has 4 sides, and one side lies in the base of the pyramid, what shape is the cross section? Explain.

_____

_____

_____

2. In Problem 2, how are the cross sections of the cone and pyramid alike?

_____

_____

**LESSON
8-4**

Angle Relationships
Practice and Problem Solving: A/B

For Exercises 1–3, use the figure.

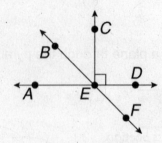

1. Name a pair of vertical angles.

_____

2. Name a pair of complementary angles.

_____

3. Name a pair of supplementary angles.

_____

Use the diagram to find each angle measure.

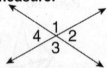

4. If m∠1 = 120°, find m∠3.

_____

5. If m∠2 = 13°, find m∠4.

_____

6. If m∠3 = 110°, find m∠2.

_____

7. If m∠4 = 65°, find m∠1.

_____

Find the value of x in each figure.

8.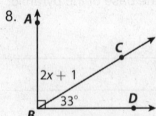

_____

9.

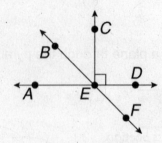

_____

10.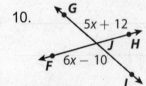

_____

11.

_____

LESSON
8-4

Angle Relationships

Practice and Problem Solving: C

For Exercises 1–4, use the figure.

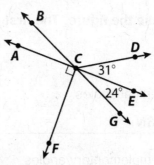

1. Find m∠FCG.

_____

2. Find m∠BCD.

_____

3. Find m∠FCB.

_____

4. Find m∠ACG.

_____

Find the value of *x* in each figure.

5.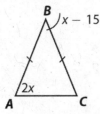

_____

6.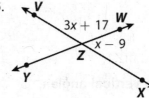

_____

7.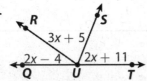

_____

8.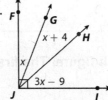

_____

9. The walking paths at a park meet each other as shown. What is the measure of the angle between the Second Path and Third Path?

_____

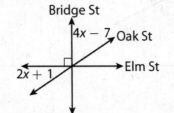

10. Three streets meet each other as shown. What is the measure of the angle between Oak Street and Elm Street?

_____

LESSON 8-4

Angle Relationships
Practice and Problem Solving: D

For Exercises 1–3, use the figure. The first one is done for you.

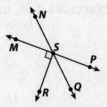

1. Name a pair of vertical angles.

   ∠PSQ and ∠MSN
   _____

2. Name a pair of complementary angles.

   _____

3. Name a pair of supplementary angles.

   _____

**Use the diagram to find each angle measure.
The first one is done for you.**

4. If m∠3 = 60°, find m∠1.

   **∠1 and ∠3 are vertical angles,
   so m∠1 = 60°**
   _____

5. If m∠4 = 100°, find m∠2.

   _____

6. If m∠1 = 50°, find m∠2.

   _____

7. If m∠2 = 125°, find m∠3.

   _____

Find the value of x in each figure. The first one is done for you.

8.

   m∠ABC + m∠CBD = 90, so x = 30
   _____

9.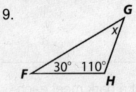

   _____

10.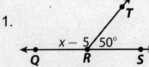

    _____

11.
    _____

LESSON 8-4

Angle Relationships
Reteach

Complementary Angles	Supplementary Angles	Vertical Angles
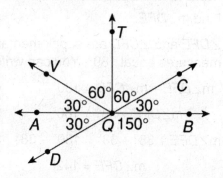 50° 40° A B	155° 25° C D	a c d b
Two angles whose measures have a sum of 90°.	Two angles whose measures have a sum of 180°.	Intersecting lines form two pairs of vertical angles.

Use the diagram to complete the following.

1. Since ∠AQC and ∠DQB are formed by intersecting lines, $\overleftrightarrow{AQB}$ and $\overleftrightarrow{CQD}$, they are:

   _____

2. The sum of the measures of ∠AQV and ∠VQT is: _____
   So, these angles are:

   _____

3. The sum of the measures of ∠AQC and ∠CQB is: _____

   So, these angles are: _____

Find the value of x in each figure.

4.
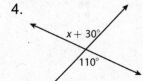
x + 30°
110°

_____

5.
2x + 7
43°

_____

6.
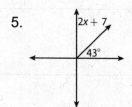
150° 5x

_____

7.
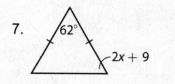
62°
2x + 9

_____

Angle Relationships

LESSON 8-4

Reading Strategies: Understanding Vocabulary

You can use definitions of angles to determine the measures of missing angles.

Pairs of angles can be classified into different types.

Complementary angles	Supplementary angles	Adjacent angles	Vertical angles	Congruent angles
The angle measures equal 90°.	The angle measures equal 180°.	The angles share a common vertex and side.	The angles are nonadjacent angles formed by two intersecting lines.	The angles have the same measure.

Find m∠DFE.

∠DFE and ∠CFD are supplementary angles. So the angle measures equal 180°. You can write an equation to find m∠DFE.

m∠DFE + m∠CFD = 180°	Original equation
m∠DFE + 38° = 180°	Substitute 38° for m∠CFD.
m∠DFE + 38° − 38° = 180° − 38°	Subtract 38° from both sides.
m∠DFE = 142°	Simplify.

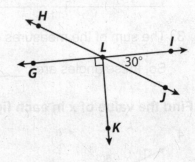

Use the diagram to find each angle measure. Show your work.

1. Find m∠GLH.

   _____

2. Find m∠KLJ.

   _____

3. Find m∠HLI.

   _____

4. Find m∠ILK.

   _____

LESSON 8-4

Angle Relationships
Success for English Learners

Problem 1

Vertical angles

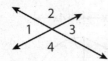

∠1 and ∠3 are vertical angles.
∠2 and ∠4 are vertical angles.
Vertical angles have the same measure.

Complementary angles.

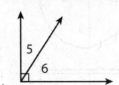

∠5 and ∠6 are complementary angles.
Complementary angles have a sum of 90°.

Supplementary angles.

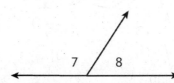

∠7 and ∠8 are supplementary angles.
Supplementary angles have a sum of 180°.

Problem 2

What is m∠x?

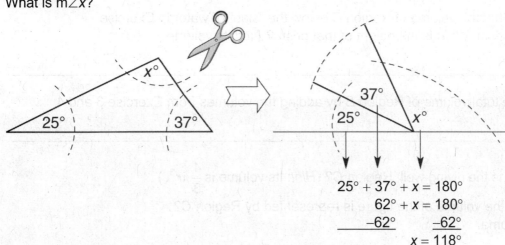

$$25° + 37° + x = 180°$$
$$62° + x = 180°$$
$$\underline{-62° \qquad -62°}$$
$$x = 118°$$

1. What is the sum of complementary angles? Supplementary angles?

_____

2. What is the sum of the measures of the angles in any triangle?

_____

MODULE 8

Modeling Geometric Figures
Challenge

A city has built a combination diving and swimming pool for an international swimming competition. The diagram shows the top and side views of the pool. The dimensions are in feet.

1. What shape is the solid represented by Region *A*? Find its volume in cubic feet.

   _____

   _____

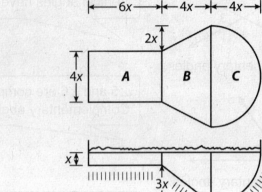

2. What shape is the Region *B* water *surface*? Find its area. (*Hint*: Its area is

   $\frac{1}{2}h(b_1 + b_2)$.)

   _____

   _____

3. To find the volume of Region *B*, start by finding the volume of the "slab" of water that is "*x*" feet deep and in the shape found in Exercise 2.

   _____

4. Next, notice that the volume of Region *B* below the "slab" of water in Exercise 3 is a "half" prism. What is the height of that prism? Find its volume.

   _____

5. Now, find the total volume of Region *B* by adding the volumes from Exercise 3 and 4.

   _____

6. What shape is the diving well, Region *C*? (*Hint*: Its volume is $\frac{4}{3}\pi r^3$.)

   What part of the volume of the figure is represented by Region *C*?
   Find that volume.

   _____

7. Find the *total* volume of the swimming pool, Regions *A*, *B*, and *C*.

   _____

8. What value of *x* would make the total volume of the pool 33,000 cubic feet?

   _____

LESSON 9-1

Circumference

Practice and Problem Solving: A/B

Find the circumference of each circle. Use 3.14 or $\frac{22}{7}$ for π. Round to the nearest hundredth, if necessary.

1.

   _____

2.

   _____

3.

   _____

4.

   _____

5.

   _____

6.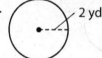

   _____

7.

   _____

8.

   _____

9. 2.5 m

   _____

Solve.

10. A circular swimming pool is 21 feet in diameter. What is the circumference of the swimming pool? Use $\frac{22}{7}$ for π.

    _____

11. A jar lid has a diameter of 42 millimeters. What is the circumference of the lid? Use $\frac{22}{7}$ for π.

    _____

12. A frying pan has a radius of 14 centimeters. What is the circumference of the frying pan? Use $\frac{22}{7}$ for π.

    _____

LESSON
9-1

Circumference

Practice and Problem Solving: C

Find the circumference of each circle. Use 3.14 or $\frac{22}{7}$ for π. Round to the nearest hundredth, if necessary.

1.
   1.25 in.

2.
   3.6 yd

3.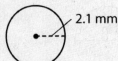
   2.1 mm

_____

_____

_____

4.
   0.75 cm

5.
   $\frac{2}{3}$ ft

6.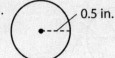
   0.5 in.

_____

_____

_____

Solve each problem.

7. The circumference of a clock is 22 inches. What is the radius of the clock?

_____

8. The circumference of a circular hot tub at a hotel is 56.5 yards. What is the diameter of the hot tub?

_____

9. In NCAA basketball rules, the basketball can have a maximum circumference of 30 inches. What is the maximum diameter of an NCAA basketball to the nearest hundredth?

_____

10. Melanie wants to put ribbon around the circumference of a circular section of the city park. Ribbon comes in rolls of 40 feet. The radius of the section of the park is 100 feet. How many rolls of ribbon should Melanie buy?

_____

Name _____ Date _____ Class _____

Circumference

Practice and Problem Solving: D

Find the circumference of each circle. Use 3.14 or $\frac{22}{7}$ for π. Round to the nearest tenth, if necessary. The first one is done for you.

1.
8 m

$C = 2\pi r \approx 2(3.14)(8) \approx 50.24; 50.2$ m

2.
10 in.

_____

3.
3 ft

_____

4.
7 mm

_____

5.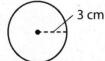
3 cm

_____

6.
4 yd

_____

Solve each problem.

7. A circular patio has a diameter of 35 yards. What is the circumference of the patio? Use $\frac{22}{7}$ for π.

_____

8. A paper plate has a diameter of 9 inches. What is the circumference of the plate? Use $\frac{22}{7}$ for π.

_____

9. A circular light fixture has a radius of 20 centimeters. What is the circumference of the light fixture? Use $\frac{22}{7}$ for π.

_____

LESSON
9-1

Circumference
Reteach

The distance around a circle is called the **circumference.** To find
the circumference of a circle, you need to know the diameter or the
radius of the circle.

The ratio of the circumference of any circle to its diameter $\left(\dfrac{C}{d}\right)$

is always the same. This ratio is known as π (pi) and has a value
of approximately 3.14.

To find the circumference C of a circle if you know the diameter
d, multiply π times the diameter. $C = \pi \bullet d$, or $C \approx 3.14 \bullet d$.

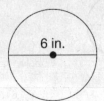

6 in.

$C = \pi \bullet d$
$C \approx 3.14 \bullet d$
$C \approx 3.14 \bullet 6$
$C \approx 18.84$
The circumference is about 18.8 in.
to the nearest tenth.

The diameter of a circle is twice as long as the radius r, or $d = 2r$.
To find the circumference if you know the radius, replace d with $2r$ in
the formula. $C = \pi \bullet d = \pi \bullet 2r$

Find the circumference given the diameter.

1. $d = 9$ cm
   $C = \pi \bullet d$
   $C \approx 3.14 \bullet$ _____

   $C \approx$ _____
   The circumference is _____ cm to
   the nearest tenth of a centimeter.

Find the circumference given the radius.

2. $r = 13$ in.
   $C = \pi \bullet 2r$
   $C \approx 3.14 \bullet (2 \bullet$ _____)

   $C \approx 3.14 \bullet$ _____

   $C \approx$ _____
   The circumference is _____ in. to
   the nearest tenth of an inch.

Find the circumference of each circle to the nearest tenth.
Use 3.14 for π.

3.

   13 cm

   _____

4.

   5 ft

   _____

5.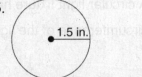

   1.5 in.

   _____

LESSON 9-1

Circumference

Reading Strategies: Using a Graphic Organizer

Perimeter is the distance around a polygon.

The chart below shows formulas for finding the circumference of circles.

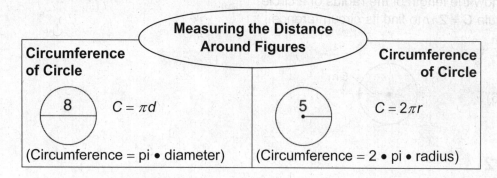

Use the information in the chart above to complete each exercise.

1. If you knew the radius of a circle, what formula would you use to find its circumference?

   _____

2. If you knew the diameter of a circle, what formula would you use to find its circumference?

   _____

3. How does the length of the diameter of a circle relate to the length of the radius of that same circle?

   _____

4. What values of π can you use to approximate the circumference of a circle?

   _____

5. How does the circumference of a circle relate to the perimeter of a polygon?

   _____

   _____

Circumference

Success for English Learners

Problem 1

When you know the length of the radius of a circle, use the formula $C = 2\pi r$ to find its circumference.

$C = 2\pi r$

$C = 2\pi(6)$

$C \approx 2(3.14)(6)$

$C \approx 37.68$ m

6 m

Problem 2

When you know the length of the diameter of a circle, use the formula $C = \pi d$ to find its circumference.

$C = \pi d$

$C = \pi(11)$

$C \approx 3.14(11)$

$C \approx 34.54$ in.

11 in.

1. What information do you need to know to use the formula $C = \pi d$?

   _____

2. A circle has a radius of 9 centimeters. What is the length of its diameter?

   _____

3. Suppose you know a circle has a diameter of 34 feet. How could you use the formula $C = 2\pi r$ to find its circumference?

   _____

   _____

4. Find the circumference of a circle with a diameter of 10 meters using both formulas. Show your work.

   _____

   _____

LESSON 9-2
Area of Circles
Practice and Problem Solving: A/B

Find the area of each circle to the nearest tenth. Use 3.14 for π.

1.

6 m

A   113 m²   C   354.9 m²
B   37.7 m²   D   452.16 m²

2.

8 ft

A   201 ft²   C   25.1 ft²
B   50.2 ft²   D   157.8 ft²

3.
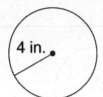
4 in.

4.
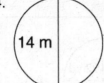
14 m

5.
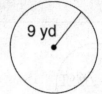
9 yd

_____   _____   _____

Find the area of each circle in terms of π.

6.
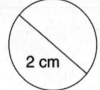
2 cm

7.
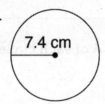
7.4 cm

8.

10 in.

_____   _____   _____

9.

22 mm

10.
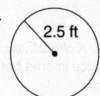
2.5 ft

11.

6 m

_____   _____   _____

Name _____ Date _____ Class_____

LESSON 9-2

Area of Circles
Practice and Problem Solving: C

Find the area of each circle in terms of π. Then find the area to the nearest tenth using 3.14 for π.

1.
2.24 cm

_____
_____

2.
$\frac{1}{2}$ in.

_____
_____

3.
0.4 in.

_____
_____

4.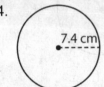
7.4 cm

_____
_____

5.
192 yd

_____
_____

6.
1.4 m

_____
_____

Use the formula $C^2 = 4\pi A$ to find the area A of each circle in terms of π.

7. $C = 2\pi$

_____

8. $C = 5\pi$

_____

9. $C = 8\pi$

_____

Solve.

10. A vanilla cake has a diameter of 8 inches. A chocolate cake has a diameter of 10 inches. What is the difference in area between the top surfaces of the two cakes? Use 3.14 for π.

_____

11. What is the difference in area between a circle with a diameter of 3 meters and a square with a side length of 3 meters? Use 3.14 for π.

_____

Area of Circles
Practice and Problem Solving: D

Find the area of each circle to the nearest tenth. Use 3.14 for π. The first problem is done for you.

1.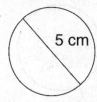
5 cm

19.6 cm²

2.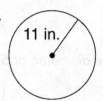
11 in.

_____

3.
3 mm

_____

4.
10 in.

_____

5.
13 cm

_____

6.
7.2 yd

_____

Find the area of each circle in terms of π. The first problem is done for you.

7.
12 cm

36π cm²

8.
9.5 in.

_____

9.
7 yd

_____

10.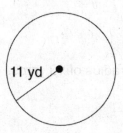
11 yd

_____

11.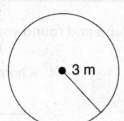
3 m

_____

12.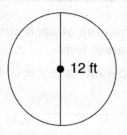
12 ft

_____

Name _____ Date _____ Class_____

LESSON 9-2

Area of Circles

Reteach

The area of a circle is found by using the formula $A = \pi r^2$. To find the area, first determine the radius. Square the radius and multiply the result by π. This gives you the exact area of the circle.

Example:

Find the area of the circle in terms of π.

The diameter is 10 cm. The radius is half the diameter, or 5 cm.
Area is always given in square units.

$$5^2 = 25$$
$$A = 25\pi \text{ cm}^2$$

10 cm

Find the area of each circle in terms of π.

1. A vinyl album with a diameter of 16 inches.

_____

2. A compact disc with a diameter of 120 mm.

_____

Sometimes it is more useful to use an estimate of π to find your answer. Use 3.14 as an estimate for π.

Example:

Find the area of the circle. Use 3.14 for π and round your answer to the nearest tenth.

The radius is 2.8 cm.
Area is always given in square units.

$$2.8^2 = 7.84$$
$$A = 7.84\pi \text{ cm}^2$$
$$A = 7.84 \times 3.14 \text{ cm}^2$$
$$A = 24.6176 \text{ cm}^2$$

Rounded to the nearest tenth, the area is 24.6 cm².

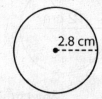

2.8 cm

Find the area of each circle. Use 3.14 for π and round your answer to the nearest tenth.

3. A pie with a radius of 4.25 inches.

_____

4. A horse ring with a radius of 10 yards.

_____

5. A round pond with a diameter of 24 m.

_____

6. A biscuit with a diameter of 9.2 cm.

_____

Name _____ Date _____ Class _____

LESSON 9-2

Area of Circles

Reading Strategies: Make Connections

Radius

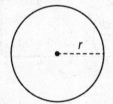

$A = \pi r^2$

$\pi \approx 3.14$ or $\dfrac{22}{7}$

Diameter

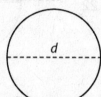

$A = \pi r^2$

$r = \dfrac{d}{2}$

$A = \pi \left(\dfrac{d}{2}\right)^2$

Find the area of each circle in terms of π. Then find the estimated area using 3.14 for π.

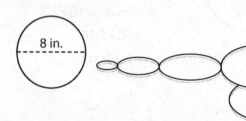

Think: Do I know the diameter or the radius?
The radius goes across half the circle. The diameter goes across the whole circle.

The diameter. I can find the radius by dividing the diameter by 2.

$A = \pi r^2$

$r = \dfrac{d}{2}$

$A = \pi \left(\dfrac{8}{2}\right)^2 = \pi \cdot 4^2 = 16\pi$

In terms of π, the area is 16π in.^{2}
To find the estimated area, use 3.14 for π.

$A = 16\pi$

$= 16 \cdot 3.14$

$= 50.24$ in^2

Find the area of each circle in terms of π. Then find the estimated area using 3.14 for π.

1. _____

_____

7 cm

2. _____

_____

5 yd

LESSON 9-2 — Area of Circles
Success for English Learners

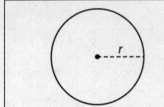   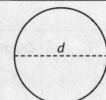

$A = \pi r^2$

$\pi \approx 3.14$ or $\dfrac{22}{7}$

$A = \pi r^2$

$r = \dfrac{d}{2}$

$A = \pi \left(\dfrac{d}{2}\right)^2$

Problem 1

A. The radius is given.

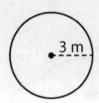

3 m

$A = \pi r^2 \quad r = 3$

$A = \pi \cdot 3^2 = 9\pi$

$\approx 9 \cdot 3.14$

$\approx 28.3 \text{ m}^2$

B. The diameter is given.

8 in.

$A = \pi r^2$

$r = \dfrac{d}{2} = \dfrac{8}{2} = 4$

$A = \pi \cdot 4^2 = 16\pi$

$\approx 16 \cdot 3.14$

$\approx 50.2 \text{ in.}^2$

Problem 2

Find the area in terms of π.

A. The radius is given.

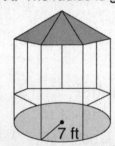

7 ft

$A = \pi r^2 \quad r = 7$

$A = \pi \cdot 7^2 = 49\pi$

$A = 49\pi \text{ ft}^2$

B. The diameter is given.

$d = 9$ in.

$A = \pi r^2$

$r = \dfrac{d}{2} = \dfrac{9}{2} = 4.5$

$A = \pi \cdot 4.5^2 = 20.25\pi$

$A = 20.25\pi \text{ in.}^2$

Find the area in terms of π. Then use 3.14 for π and find the area to the nearest tenth.

1. _____

_____

3.2 mm

2. _____

_____

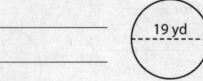

19 yd

Name _____ Date _____ Class_____

Area of Composite Figures

Practice and Problem Solving: A/B

**Estimate the area of each figure. Each square represents
1 square foot.**

1.
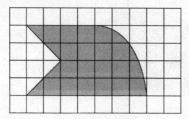

_____

2.
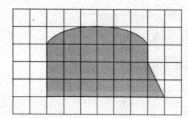

_____

Find the area of each figure. Use 3.14 for π.

3.
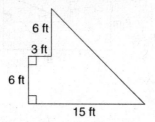

6 ft
3 ft
6 ft
15 ft

_____

4.
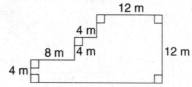

12 m
4 m
8 m 4 m
12 m
4 m

_____

5.
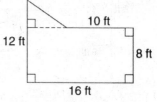

10 ft
12 ft
8 ft
16 ft

_____

6.
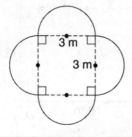

3 m
3 m

_____

7.
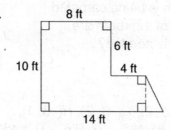

8 ft
6 ft
10 ft
4 ft
14 ft

_____

8.
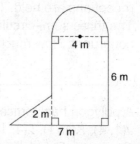

4 m
6 m
2 m
7 m

_____

9. Marci is going to use tile to cover her terrace. How much tile does
she need?

_____

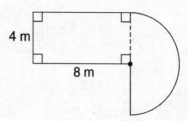

4 m
8 m

**LESSON
9-3**

Area of Composite Figures

Practice and Problem Solving: C

Estimate the area of each figure. Each square represents 1 square foot.

1.
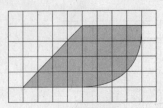

_____

2.
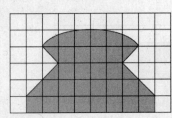

_____

Find the area of each figure. Use 3.14 for π.

3.
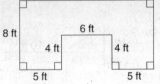

4.
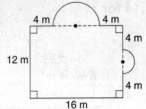

5.
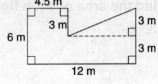

_____   _____   _____

6. The figure shows the dimensions of a room in which
receptions are held. The room is being carpeted.
The three semi-circular parts of the room are
congruent. How much carpet is needed?

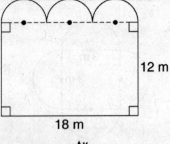

_____

7. A polygon has vertices at *F*(–5, 2), *G*(–3, 2), *H*(–3, 4),
J(1, 4), *K*(1, 1), *L*(4, 1), *M*(4, –2), *N*(6, –2), *P*(6, –3), and
Q(–5, –3). Graph the figure on the coordinate plane.
Then find the area and perimeter of the figure.

_____

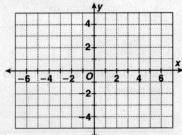

LESSON 9-3 Area of Composite Figures
Practice and Problem Solving: D

Estimate the area of each figure. Each square represents 1 square foot. Choose the letter for the best answer. The first one is done for you.

1.
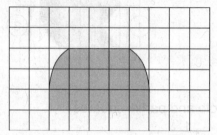

A 10 ft²

Ⓒ 14 ft²

B 11 ft²

D 15 ft²

2.
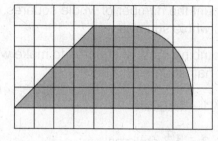

A 24 ft²

C 32 ft²

B 26 ft²

D 36 ft²

Find the area of each figure. Use 3.14 for π. The first one is done for you.

3.
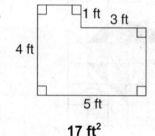

17 ft²

4.
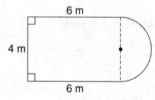

_____

5.
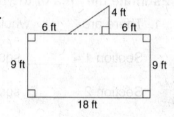

_____

6.
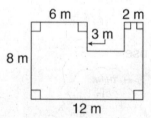

_____

7.
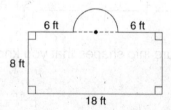

_____

8.
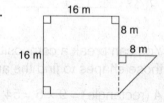

_____

9. The figure shows the dimensions of a room. How much carpet is needed to cover its floor?

_____

LESSON 9-3

Area of Composite Figures

Reteach

When an irregular figure is on graph paper, you can estimate its area by counting whole squares and parts of squares. Follow these steps.

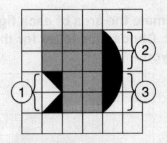

- Count the number of whole squares. There are 10 whole squares.

- Combine parts of squares to make whole squares or half-squares.

Section 1 = 1 square

Section 2 $\approx 1\frac{1}{2}$ squares

Section 3 $\approx 1\frac{1}{2}$ squares

- Add the whole and partial squares

$$10 + 1 + 1\frac{1}{2} + 1\frac{1}{2} = 14$$

The area is about 14 square units.

Estimate the area of the figure.

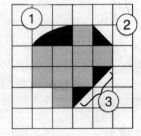

1. There are _____ whole squares in the figure.

   Section 1 $\approx$ _____ square(s)

   Section 2 = _____ square(s)

   Section 3 = _____ square(s)

   $A =$ _____ + _____ + _____ + _____ = _____ square units

You can break a composite figure into shapes that you know. Then use those shapes to find the area.

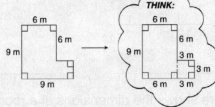

A (rectangle) $= 9 \times 6 = 54$ m^2

A (square) $= 3 \cdot 3 = 9$ m^2

A (composite figure) $= 54 + 9 = 63$ m^2

Find the area of the figure.

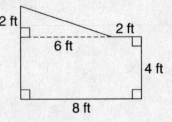

2. A (rectangle) = _____ ft^2

   A (triangle) = _____ ft^2

   A (composite figure) = _____ + _____ = _____ ft^2

**LESSON
9-3**

Area of Composite Figures
Reading Strategies: Make Connections

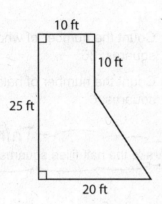

Shape	Area Formula
Triangle	$A = \frac{1}{2}bh$
Square	$A = s^2$
Rectangle	$A = lw$
Parallelogram	$A = bh$
Trapezoid	$A = \frac{1}{2}h(b_1 + b_2)$
Circle	$A = \pi r^2$

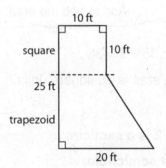

square $= s^2 = 10^2 = 100$ ft^2

trapezoid $= \frac{1}{2} \cdot 15(10 + 20) = 7.5(30) = 225$ ft^2

square + trapezoid $= 100 + 225 = 325$ ft^2

Find the area of each figure. Use 3.14 for π.

1.

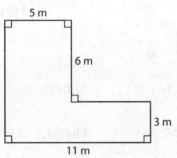

2.

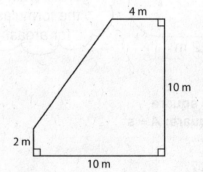

_____

_____

3. The figure shows the
dimensions of a room. How
much carpet is needed to cover
the floor of the room?

_____

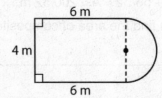

LESSON 9-3

Area of Composite Figures

Success for English Learners

Problem 1

Find the area.

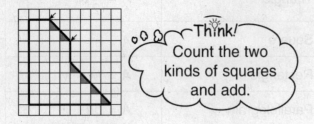

Step 1: Count the number of whole squares: 35

Step 2: Count the number of half squares: 6

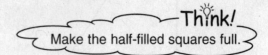
Make the half-filled squares full.

Step 3: $6 \div 2 = 3$

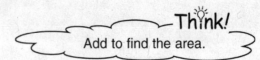
Add to find the area.

Step 4: $35 + 3 = 38$

So, the area is 38 square units.

Problem 2

Find the area.

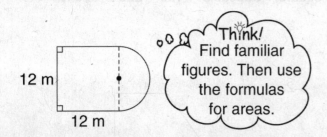

Figure 1 = square
Area of square: $A = s^2$

$s = 12$

$s^2 = 12^2 = 144$

$A = 144 \text{ m}^2$

Total area $\approx 144 + 56.52 \approx A \approx 200.52 \text{ m}^2$

Figure 2 is a semicircle

Area of semicircle:
$$A = \frac{1}{2}\left(\pi r^2\right)$$

Use 3.14 for π.

$r = 6$ so $r^2 = 36$

The radius is $\frac{1}{2}(12)$.

$A \approx \frac{1}{2}(3.14 \cdot 36)$ Substitute.

$A \approx \frac{1}{2}(113.04)$ Multiply.

$A \approx 56.52 \text{ m}^2$ Multiply by $\frac{1}{2}$.

1. How can you find the area of composite figures?

_____

LESSON 9-4

Solving Surface Area Problems
Practice and Problem Solving: A/B

Find the surface area of each solid figure.

1. _____

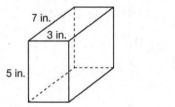

2. _____

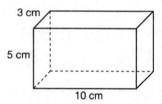

3. _____

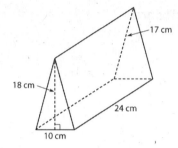

4. _____

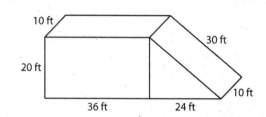

Use the situation below to complete Exercises 5–6.

Cydney built a display stand out of two cubes. The larger cube is 8 inches on each side. The smaller cube is 4 inches on each side. She painted the display stand <u>after</u> she put the two cubes together. She did NOT paint the bottom of the display stand. What was the total area she painted?

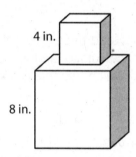

5. Explain your plan for solving the problem.

_____

_____

6. Solve the problem.

_____

Solving Surface Area Problems

LESSON 9-4

Practice and Problem Solving: C

Find the surface area of each solid figure. Round each answer to the nearest tenth.

1. _____

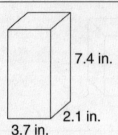

7.4 in.

2.1 in.

3.7 in.

2. _____

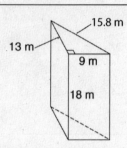

15.8 m

13 m

9 m

18 m

Three students constructed three-dimensional figures of cardboard.

A.

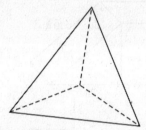

B.

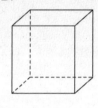

C.

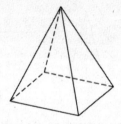

3. Read each description in Exercises 4–6. Before doing any calculations, guess which figure has the greatest surface area and which has the least surface area.

_____

4. Josh made his figure from 6 congruent squares. The edge of each square was 8 inches. Which figure did Josh construct? What is the surface area of his figure?

_____

5. Kayla used 4 isosceles and one square for her figure. Each edge of the square was 10 inches. The two congruent sides of the triangles are 13 inches long. The height of the triangles is 12 inches. Which figure did Kayla construct? What is the surface area of her figure?

_____

6. Angelica used four congruent equilateral triangles. Each side of the triangles was 14 inches. The height of each triangle was 12.1 inches. Which figure did she construct? What is the surface area of her figure?

_____

7. Check your guesses from Exercise 3. Were you correct? _____

Name _____ Date _____ Class_____

LESSON 9-4

Solving Surface Area Problems

Practice and Problem Solving: D

Find the surface area of each solid figure. The first one is done for you.

1. _____**286 ft²**_____

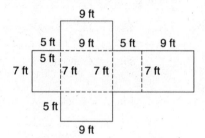

2. _____

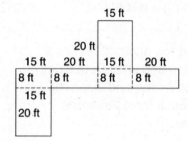

3. _____

4. _____

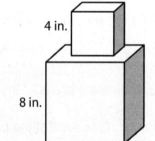

Use the situation below to answer 5–7.

Cydney built a display stand out of two cubes. The larger cube is 8 inches on each side. The smaller cube is 4 inches on each side. She painted the entire outside of each cube before she put the cubes together.

5. What was the surface area she painted for the smaller cube? _____

6. What was the surface area she painted for the larger cube? _____

7. What was the total area that she painted on both cubes? _____

LESSON 9-4

Solving Surface Area Problems

Reteach

The surface area of a three-dimensional figure is the combined areas of the faces.

You can find the surface area of a prism by drawing a **net** of the flattened figure.

Notice that the top and bottom have the same shape and size. Both sides have the same shape and size. The front and the back have the same shape and size.

Remember: $A = lw$

Since you are finding area, the answer will be in square units.

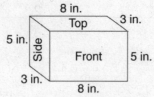
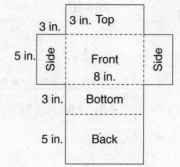

Find the surface area of the prism formed by the net above.

1. Find the area of the front face: A = ____ • ____ = _____ in².

   The area of the front and back faces is 2 • ____ = _____ in².

2. Find the area of the side face: A = ____ • ____ = _____ in².

   The area of the 2 side faces is 2 • ____ = _____ in².

3. Find the area of the top face: A = ____ • ____ = _____ in².

   The area of the top and bottom faces is 2 • ____ = _____ in².

4. Combine the areas of the faces: ____ + ____ + ____ = _____ in².

5. The surface area of the prism is _____ in².

Find the surface area of the prism formed by each net.

6.

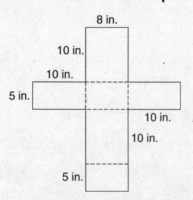

7.

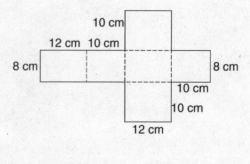

LESSON 9-4 Solving Surface Area Problems

Reading Strategies: Analyze Information

The **surface area** of a three-dimensional figure is the total area of all its surfaces.

If you analyze the net of a rectangular prism, you notice there are six faces. Each face pairs up with another, congruent face:

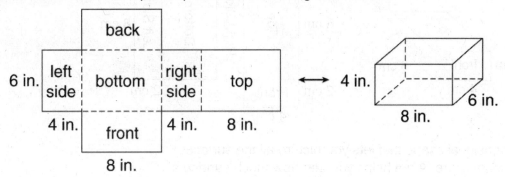

To find the surface area of a rectangular prism, find the sum of the areas of the six faces. Since you are finding area, the answer will be in square units.

Remember: $A = lw$.

Use the congruent pairs of faces to simplify the computation.

Left side and right side:	$2 \times (6 \times 4) = 48$
Back and front:	$2 \times (8 \times 4) = 64$
Top and bottom:	$2 \times (6 \times 8) = 96$
Sum of areas:	$48 + 64 + 96 = 208$
Total surface area:	208 square inches

Find the surface area of each rectangular prism.

1.

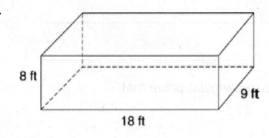

2.

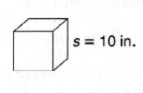

$s = 10$ in.

_____   _____

Solving Surface Area Problems

LESSON 9-4

Success for English Learners

If you unfold a three-dimensional figure and lay it flat, you have made a net.

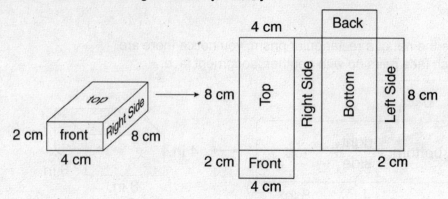

A **net** is a two-dimensional shape that lets you picture all the surfaces of a three-dimensional figure. A net helps you see how much surface a three-dimensional figure covers.

The **surface area** of a three-dimensional figure is the total area of all its surfaces. Surface area is measured in square units. Remember: $A = lw$

Complete.

1. What is the area of the top? _____

2. What is the area of the bottom? _____

3. What is the area of the front? _____

4. What is the area of the back? _____

5. What is the area of the left side? _____

6. What is the area of the right side? _____

7. What is the total surface area of the figure? _____

8. What do you notice about pairs of surfaces of a rectangular prism that have the same areas?

_____

_____

_____

Name _____ Date _____ Class _____

LESSON 9-5

Solving Volume Problems

Practice and Problem Solving: A/B

Find the volume of each figure.

1.

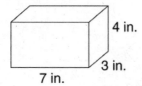

4 in.

3 in.

7 in.

2.

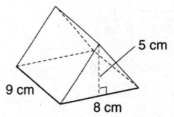

5 cm

9 cm

8 cm

_____

3.

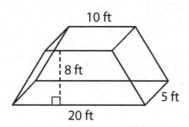

10 ft

8 ft

20 ft

5 ft

4.

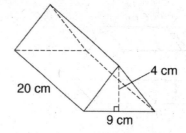

4 cm

20 cm

9 cm

_____

Using cheese, Theo made the display shown at right. Use the figure to complete Exercises 5–7.

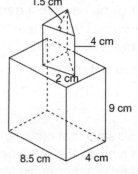

1.5 cm

4 cm

2 cm

9 cm

8.5 cm

4 cm

5. How many cubic centimeters of cheese are in the completed display?

_____

6. Each kilogram of the cheese Theo used takes up a volume of about 20 cubic centimeters. What is the approximate mass of Theo's display?

_____

7. Theo's friend made a display with dimensions that were each half as long as those Theo used. What is the approximate mass of Theo's friends display?

_____

LESSON
9-5

Solving Volume Problems

Practice and Problem Solving: C

Find the volume of each figure.

1.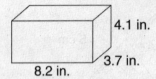
   4.1 in.
   3.7 in.
   8.2 in.

   _____

2.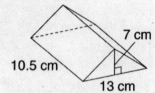
   7 cm
   10.5 cm
   13 cm

   _____

3.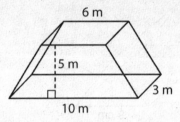
   6 m
   5 m
   3 m
   10 m

   _____

4.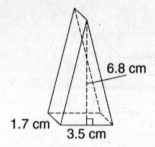
   6.8 cm
   1.7 cm
   3.5 cm

   _____

For the school carnival, Pietro built a clear plastic container to be used in a game called Guess How Many Marbles. The container is to be filled with marbles that are 12 millimeters in diameter.

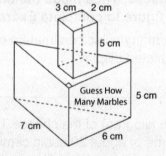
3 cm   2 cm
5 cm
Guess How
Many Marbles   5 cm
7 cm   6 cm

5. Find the volume of the entire container.

   _____

6. Marsha says that one marble has a volume of 904.3 cm^2, so the container can't hold any marbles. What error did Marsha make?

   _____

   _____

7. Can you find how many marbles fit in the container by dividing the volume of the container by the volume of 1 marble? Explain your reasoning.

   _____

   _____

LESSON
9-5

Solving Volume Problems

Practice and Problem Solving: D

Tell how many cubes are in each figure. The first one is done for you.

1.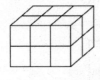

Think: There are 3 × 2 cubes in each layer. There are 2 layers. So, there are 3 × 2 × 2 cubes.

_____ **12 cubes** _____

2.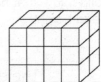

_____

Find the volume of each figure. The first one is done for you.

3.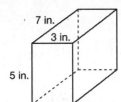

7 in.
3 in.
5 in.

Think: $V = lwh$
$V = 7 \times 3 \times 5 = 105$

_____ **105 in³** _____

4.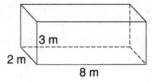

3 m
2 m
8 m

_____

For a school project, students have to build a pyramid of cubes.

5. Each cube will be like the one shown at the right. What are the dimensions of the cube?

   length: _____ mm   height: _____ mm

   width: _____ mm

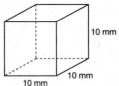

10 mm
10 mm
10 mm

6. What is the volume of the cube at the right?

   _____

The completed pyramid will look like the figure shown at the right.

7. How many cubes are in the pyramid?

   _____

8. What is the volume of the entire pyramid?

   _____

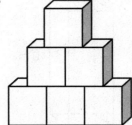

LESSON 9-5

Solving Volume Problems
Reteach

The **volume** of a solid figure is the number of cubic units inside the figure.

A prism is a solid figure that has length, width, and height.

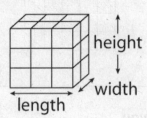

Each small cube represents one cubic unit.

one cubic unit

Volume is measured in cubic units, such as in^3, cm^3, ft^3, and m^3.

The volume of a solid figure is the product of the area of the base (*B*) and the height (*h*).

$$V = Bh$$

Rectangular Prism	**Triangular Prism**	**Trapezoidal Prism**
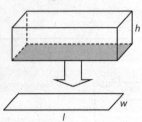	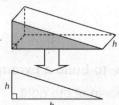	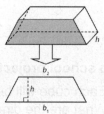
The base is a rectangle. To find the area of the base, use $B = lw$.	The base is a triangle. To find the area of the base, use $B = \frac{1}{2}bh$.	The base is a trapezoid. To find the area of the base, use $B = \frac{1}{2}(b_1 + b_2)h$.

Find the volume of each figure.

1.

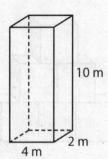

10 m
2 m
4 m

_____

2.

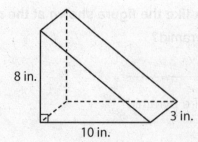

8 in.
10 in.
3 in.

_____

3.

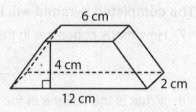

6 cm
4 cm
12 cm
2 cm

_____

Name _____ Date _____ Class_____

LESSON
9-5
Solving Volume Problems
Reading Strategies: Use a Graphic Organizer

You can use a graphic organizer to help when you are solving volume problems.

Volume of all Prisms	**Volume of a Rectangular Prism**
$$V = Bh$$ volume of a prism area of the base of prism height of the prism	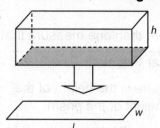 The base is a rectangle. To find the area of the base, use $B = lw$. $$V = Bh = lwh$$
Volume of a Triangular Prism	**Volume of a Trapezoidal Prism**
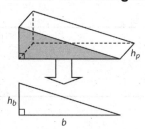 The base is a triangle. To find the area of the base, use $B = \frac{1}{2}bh$. $$V = Bh = \frac{1}{2}bh_bh_p$$	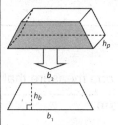 The base is a trapezoid. To find the area of the base, use $B = \frac{1}{2}(b_1 + b_2)h$. $$V = Bh = \frac{1}{2}(b_1 + b_2)h_bh_p$$

Find the volume of each figure.

1.

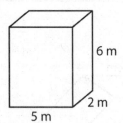

2.

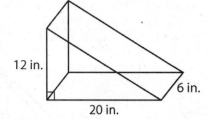

3.

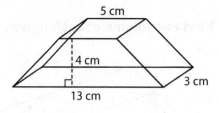

_____   _____   _____

LESSON 9-5

Solving Volume Problems

Success for English Learners

The volume of a prism is equal to the area of the base of the prism times the height of the prism.

Problem 1

Some prisms have more than one measure that is labeled "height."

Volume of a Triangular Prism	
In a triangular prism, there is the height of the base triangle and the height of the prism.	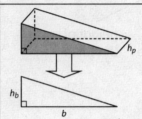
Sometimes subscripts (small letters to the right of a letter) can help you know which "height" to use.	
h_b is the height of the base. h_p is the height of the prism.	The base is a triangle. To find the area of the base, use $B = \frac{1}{2}bh_b$. $V = Bh = \frac{1}{2}bh_bh_p$

Problem 2

Some prisms have more than one measure that is labeled "base."

Volume of a Trapezoidal Prism	
In a trapezoidal prism, the area of the base is the average of the lengths of the two bases times the height.	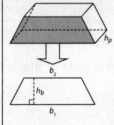
The subscripts tell you to use both bases (b_1 and b_2) when using this formula.	
The trapezoidal prism also has two "heights." h_b is the height of the base. h_p is the height of the prism.	The base is a trapezoid. To find the area of the base, use $B = \frac{1}{2}(b_1 + b_2)h_b$. $V = Bh = \frac{1}{2}(b_1 + b_2)h_bh_p$

Find the volume of each figure.

1.

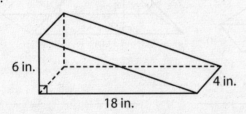

2.

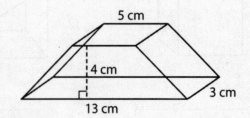

_____   _____

MODULE 9

Circumference, Area, and Volume

Challenge

The Schultz family is planning a garden for part of their back yard. The width of the garden will be 20 feet. Each family member has different requirements. The requirements are shown in the table below.

Name	Requirement
Mr. Schultz	The maximum length of fencing around the garden is 100 feet.
Mrs. Schultz	The area of the garden must be greater than 400 square feet.
Angelica	One-half of the garden will be flowers. At most, there will be 350 square feet for flowers.
Robert	At least 15% percent of the garden will be used to grow carrots and lettuce. At the least, there will be 45 square feet for carrots and lettuce.

Write and solve an inequality that represents the possible values for the widths of the garden for each family member. Then write an inequality that would satisfy everyone.

1. Mr. Schultz: _____   2. Mrs. Schultz: _____

3. Angelica: _____   4. Robert: _____

5. Dimensions for garden that satisfies all 4 people:

   width (*w*): _____   length (*l*): _____

The family also wants to put a circular fish pond in the backyard. The pond is to be at least 2 feet deep and have an area of at least $78\frac{4}{7}$ ft^2 and no greater than 154 ft^2. A 2-foot wide walkway will surround the pond. The family creates a pond that meets the requirements. Use $\pi = \frac{22}{7}$. Use that information to answer each question.

6. What are the possible dimensions of the radius (*r*) of the pond?   _____

7. What are the possible lengths of the circumference (C_p) of the pond?   _____

8. What are the possible lengths of the circumference (C_w) of the outside of the walkway?   _____

9. What are the possible values of the volume (*V*) of the pond?   _____

LESSON
10-1
Populations and Samples

Practice and Problem Solving: A/B

Name the *population* and the *sample* in each exercise. Explain your answer.

1. The number of roadrunners born within a 50-mile radius of Lubbock.

   _____

2. The cars traveling at 75 kilometers per hour between Beaumont and Lufkin.

   _____

Name the sampling method that will best represent the whole population in each situation. Explain your answer.

3. Student satisfaction with the middle school cafeteria.

   Method A: Survey 40 students in two seventh-grade math classes. 72 percent are satisfied with the food in the cafeteria.

   Method B: Survey 65 students from a list of all students in the school. 85 percent are satisfied with the food in the cafeteria.

   Method _____ best represents the whole population of the school.

   _____

4. Predicted winner in an election for town mayor.

   Method C: Telephone 100 randomly-chosen voters who live in the town. 54 percent plan to vote for the incumbent mayor.

   Method D: Telephone 70 people who have lived in the town for more than 25 years. 45 percent plan to vote for the incumbent mayor.

   Method _____ best represents the whole population of the town's voters.

   _____

Which of these may be biased samples? Explain your answer.

5. A town official surveys 50 people in a library to decide if town residents want the library services and facilities expanded.

   _____

6. A cable television company randomly calls 200 customers and asks them if they are satisfied with their service.

   _____

LESSON 10-1 **Populations and Samples**

Practice and Problem Solving: C

Answer the questions about each problem. Explain your answers.

1. A manufacturing plant would like to locate in a town. The plant will have openings for 125 new, full-time jobs. However, the plant will have an impact on the town's water system and other infrastructure systems. Describe each proposed sampling of the town's residents as random, non-random, biased, or some combination of the three. Justify your description.

   Sample A: Randomly survey residents in each of the town's 15 voting precincts.

   _____

   Sample B: Randomly survey all registered voters within the town's boundaries without regard to precinct.

   _____

   Sample C: Randomly survey all residents in the voting precinct in which the plant will be located and where it will have the greatest impact on the town's infrastructure systems, like electricity, sewer, and water systems.

   _____

2. Why is a telephone survey of 250 of a city's residents based on their home addresses not necessarily a random sample?

   _____

3. The owner of a scooter-rental business in the city center would like to know more about his customers' rental needs before buying more scooters. He decides to sample employees in the office buildings near his business. He also plans to sample residents of nearby apartment buildings in which some of his renters live. Answer the questions about his sampling plans.

   a. Are the scooter-rental owner's sampling plans random? Explain.

   _____

   b. In the sample questionnaires, the scooter-rental owner lists two different rental pricing arrangements, one of which favors weekend scooter rental with lower daily and mileage rates. Describe any bias in the questionnaires.

   _____

Name _____ Date _____ Class_____

Populations and Samples
Practice and Problem Solving: D

Identify the population and the sample in each exercise. The first one is done for you.

1. The number of home runs hit during one week in July of the 2014–2015 baseball season.

   Population:

   Home runs hit in 2014–2015.

   Sample:

   Home runs hit one week in July.

2. The amount of sap that is collected from six sugar maples from a 12-acre forest of sugar maples that are being tapped.

   Population:

   _____

   Sample:

   _____

Identify the best method of getting a random sample in Exercises 3 and 4. Explain your answer. The first one is done for you.

3. The school board wants to study how middle school teachers use computers and the Internet in their classes.

   Sample A: all middle-school math-science teachers

   Sample B: teachers whose last name begins with "N"

   Sample C: every eighth teacher on a list of the school's teachers

   Sample C is the best method of getting a random sample. _____

4. A lawn service wants to find out how satisfied its customers are with its lawn services and pricing.

   Sample X: the ten customers who spent the most money with the lawn service over the past year.

   Sample Y: ten customers who only used the lawn service one time over the past year

   Sample Z: ten customers who used the lawn service at any time during the past year

   _____

Answer the question.

5. Why does the following question show bias in a survey of a town's citizens about a new professional sports stadium?

   "What are your feelings about a new stadium that will bring in a professional sports teams and the possibility of more business development by hotels and restaurants in our town?"

   _____

   _____

LESSON
10-1

Populations and Samples
Reteach

Survey topic: number of books read by seventh-graders in Richmond

A **population** is the whole group that is being studied.	*Population*: all seventh-graders in Richmond
A **sample** is a part of the population.	*Sample*: all seventh graders at Jefferson Middle School
A **random sample** is a sample in which each member of the population has a random chance of being chosen. A random sample is a better representation of a population than a non-random sample.	*Random sample*: Have a computer select every tenth name from an alphabetical list of each seventh-grader in Richmond.
A **biased sample** is a sample that does not truly represent a population.	*Biased sample*: all of the seventh-graders in Richmond who are enrolled in honors English classes.

Tell if each sample is biased. Explain your answer.

1. An airline surveys passengers from a flight that is on time to determine if passengers on all flights are satisfied.

   _____

2. A newspaper randomly chooses 100 names from its subscriber database and then surveys those subscribers to find if they read the restaurant reviews.

   _____

3. The manager of a bookstore sends a survey to 150 customers who were randomly selected from a customer list.

   _____

4. A team of researchers surveys 200 people at a multiplex movie theater to find out how much money state residents spend on entertainment.

   _____

Populations and Samples

Reading Strategies: Compare and Contrast

To get information about issues, a survey is conducted. Surveys can be done in two different ways.

- **Population**   The entire group is surveyed.
- **Sample**   Part of the entire group is surveyed.

1. Compare the difference between collecting information from the population and collecting information from a sample.

_____

There are two different types of samples.

- **Unbiased sample**   The sample represents the population.
- **Biased sample**   The sample does not represent the population.

2. What is the difference between an unbiased sample and a biased sample?

_____

Mrs. Jones wants to know which sport 7th graders in the district like best. There are 7th graders in 6 different schools in the district. She can collect data in one of the following ways:

Population—Ask every 7th grade student at all 6 schools.
Unbiased sample—Ask every other 7th grader at 3 of the schools.
Biased sample—Ask 7th grade boys at 3 of the schools.

Write "unbiased sample" or "biased sample" to describe each survey.

3. A survey conducted at an ice cream store asked only mothers their favorite ice cream flavor.

_____

4. A reporter asked every tenth person coming out of a theater how well they liked the movie.

_____

5. A survey asked only girls to identify their favorite item on the school cafeteria menu.

_____

Name _____ Date _____ Class_____

 LESSON
10-1

Populations and Samples
Success for English Learners

Problem 1

You want to know how many hours members of your school track and field team train each week during the winter months.

⟶ Do you sample a few members of the track team, or do you ask all of the track team athletes?

Think:

> Who do you ask? Hurdlers, long-distance runners, sprinters? How many athletes?

If there are 15 athletes on the track team, how many do you sample?

Problem 2

A restaurant in your town wants to know the average size of families who eat at cafeterias across south Texas.

⟶ How do you sample the families?

Think:

> Where do you sample? Your town, towns within 30 miles of your town?

If there are no cafeterias in your town, how does the restaurant find a sample of families who eat at cafeterias?

1. In Problem 1, what is the population?

_____

2. What groups within the track team could you sample for Problem 1? Explain your choices.

_____

3. In Problem 2, how could the restaurant find a sample of families who eat at cafeterias without leaving town?

_____

LESSON 10-2

Making Inferences from a Random Sample

Practice and Problem Solving: A/B

What can you infer about the population from each data set represented below?

1.

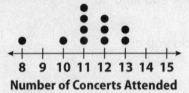

Number of Concerts Attended

2.

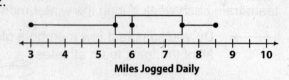

Miles Jogged Daily

_____   _____

The box plots show the distribution of grade-level test scores of 20 students in an elementary school. Use the box plots for Exercises 3–5.

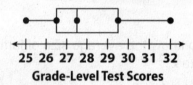

Grade-Level Test Scores

3. What were the high and low scores for the test?

_____

4. The middle fifty percent of students scored between what two values?

_____

5. Is 30 a typical test score? If so, explain your reasoning. If not, what is a typical test score?

_____

Solve.

6. A seventh-grade student chooses a random sample of 50 out of 400 students. He finds that 7 students have traveled outside the United States. The student claims that over 50 of the 400 students have likely traveled outside the United States. Is the student correct? Explain.

_____

7. A metal-fabricating company produces 150,000 souvenir tokens each year. In a random sample of 400 tokens, 3 have stamping errors. Predict the total number of coins that will have stamping errors in a year.

_____

Name _____ Date _____ Class_____

Making Inferences from a Random Sample
Practice and Problem Solving: C

A package-delivery business wants to improve its hourly delivery rate. The business collects the data shown from 12 of its delivery staff members on a Wednesday afternoon.

Number of Deliveries for 12 Staff Members

1. Describe the distribution of delivery data in the sample.

_____

2. Draw a box plot of the data on the number line below.

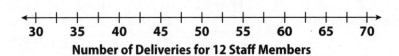

Number of Deliveries for 12 Staff Members

The delivery company would like to improve its hourly delivery so that it looks like the box plot shown.

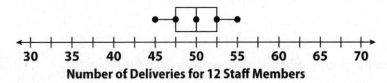

Number of Deliveries for 12 Staff Members

3. List possible delivery data for this box plot for 12 delivery staff members.

_____

4. If the delivery company achieves its improvement goal, by how much will the hourly delivery rate of the typical delivery staff member change? Explain.

_____

Name _____ Date _____ Class_____

Answer the questions about the dot plot. The first one is done for you.

1.

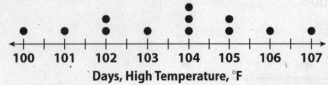

Days, High Temperature, °F

   a. What was the median high temperature? _____ **104 °F** _____

   b. What high temperatures occurred on more than one day?

   102 °F (twice), 104 °F (3 times), and 105 °F (twice)

2. The number of porpoises observed, in a one-hour period, by a random sample of people was recorded. The data are represented by the box plot below.

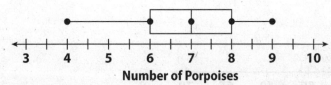

Number of Porpoises

   a. What was the median number of porpoises observed?

   _____

   b. Every observer saw at least how many porpoises?

   _____

   c. About what percent of the people observed anywhere from 6 to 8 porpoises?

   _____

   d. Use the graph to make an accurate observation about the data.

   _____

LESSON 10-2

Making Inferences from a Random Sample
Reteach

Once a **random sample** of a **population** has been selected, it can be used to make inferences about the population as a whole. **Dot plots** of the randomly selected data are useful in visualizing trends in a population.

Numerical results about the population can often be obtained from the random sample using **ratios** or **proportions** as these examples show.

Making inferences from a dot plot
The dot plot shows a random sample of 20 motorcycles. What will be the median number of motorcycle-tire blowouts in a population of 400 motorcycles?

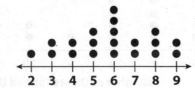

Motorcycle Tire Blowouts in a Road Race

Solution In this dot plot, the median number of blowouts is 6. Set up a proportion to find the median number of blowouts predicted for 400 motorcycles:

$$\frac{\text{sample}}{\text{population}} = \frac{20}{400}$$

$$\frac{20}{400} = \frac{6}{x}$$

$$\frac{1}{20} = \frac{6}{x}$$

$$x = 120$$

So, 120 blowouts is the median number of blowouts predicted for the population.

1. In a random sample, 3 of 400 computer chips are defective. Based on the sample, how many chips out of 100,000 would you expect to be defective?

_____

2. In a sample 5 of 800 T-shirts were defective. Based on this sample, in a production run of 250,000 T-shirts, how many would you expect to be defective?

_____

Making Inferences from a Random Sample

LESSON 10-2

Reading Strategies: Analyze Information

Sample data displayed in dot or box plots can provide a variety of information about the sample itself and also about the population from which it is taken.

Example

Make five statements about the sample data shown in the dot plot. Include one *inference* that can be made about the population from which the sample was taken.

Solution The statements should make use of terms used to describe a distribution of data: median, mode, number of data points, outliers, range, skew, etc. The inference about the general population should be based on the features of the sample that have the most certainty.

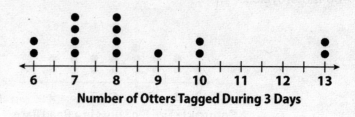

Number of Otters Tagged During 3 Days

1. The data is **skewed to the left** or lower end, of the distribution.

2. The **range** of the data is 13 – 6 or 7 otters tagged.

3. There are 15 data points, so the **median** is the middle or 8th data point, which is 8. Even if the **outlier** data points, 13 otters tagged twice are ignored, the median is still 8.

4. There are two **modes**, 7 and 8 otters.

5. Since over half of the data are represented by the eight data points representing 7 and 8 otters tagged, this information is probably the most reliable to use to make an inference about the entire population of otters tagged by the wildlife conservation department.

Use the box plot to make four statements about the sample data using the terms listed.

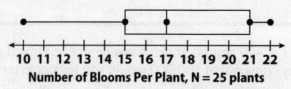

Number of Blooms Per Plant, N = 25 plants

1. Skew: _____

2. Outlier: _____

_____

_____

3. Median, with and without outlier: _____

4. Population inference: _____

_____

_____

LESSON 10-2
Making Inferences from a Random Sample
Success for English Learners

Problem 1

Birds at the birdbath between 9 A.M. and 10 A.M. on Monday:

⟶ 4 cardinals, 8 chickadees, 3 mockingbirds, and 2 thrashers

How many birds are at the birdbath between 9 A.M. on Monday and 9 A.M. on Tuesday?

Think: One hour on Monday;
24 hours before Tuesday

Problem 2

Think of a **proportion**:

⟶ If *six* cardinals visit in *one* hour, how many will visit in *24* hours?

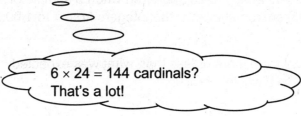

6 × 24 = 144 cardinals?
That's a lot!

Can this be right?

1. Suppose you have never seen more than *nine* cardinals at any one time in the yard near the birdbath. Why would this make you think your estimate in Problem 2 is too large?

   _____

   _____

   _____

2. How could you get a better estimate of the number of cardinals that are visiting the birdbath in a day?

   _____

   _____

   _____

Name _____ Date _____ Class _____

Use the description below to complete Exercises 1–3.

In a set of 1,000 integers from 1 to 1,000, an integer chosen at random on a single trial should be an integer from 1 to 25 about 25 out of every 1,000 trials, or one out of every 40 integers selected.

Trial 1	406
Trial 2	734
Trial 3	44
Trial 4	340
Trial 5	996

1. A sample of 5 integers selected is shown. Does this sample represent the general rule for picking an integer from 1 to 25 in the population of integers from 1 to 1,000? Explain.

   _____

2. How many integers between 1 and 25 would you expect to appear in a sample of 80 trials? Explain.

   _____

3. The following integers from 1 to 25 appeared when a sample of 50 integers was taken from the list of the integers from 1 to 1,000.

   12, 21, and 16

   Is this sample of 50 trials more or less than what was expected for the population as a whole? Explain.

   _____

Use the description below to complete Exercises 4–5.

A manufacturer of flea collars for animals that weigh less than 5 kilograms injects the collars with 15 milligrams of a biocide that only acts on fleas. The manufacturer will release a collar that has no less than 14 milligrams and no more than 16 milligrams of insecticide. The following list shows the result of sampling 36 collars from an actual production run of 720 collars.

   17, 14, 14, 16, 14, 15, 15, 15, 16, 14, 16, 14, 15, 15, 15, 16, 13, 13,

   13, 13, 13, 14, 14, 13, 17, 14, 15, 13, 14, 15, 16, 17, 14, 17, 14, 15

4. How many flea collars out of a production run of 720 collars would be acceptable to ship according to this sample? Explain your reasoning.

   _____

5. How many flea collars out of a production run of 720 flea collars would have too much biocide and could not be shipped? Explain your reasoning.

   _____

Generating Random Samples

Practice and Problem Solving: C

Use the situation below to complete Exercises 1–3.

A national conservation organization plans to award grants to fish hatcheries that produce populations of 1,000 or more individuals of endangered species during a seasonal breeding period. The number of fish born at each of the hatcheries that enter the grant competition is 12,000 fish. Three hatcheries sampled broods of 240 new-born fish and reported these results of the number of endangered species born.

Hatchery A	
Sample 1	3
Sample 2	19
Sample 3	2

Hatchery B	
Sample 1	10
Sample 2	12
Sample 3	9

Hatchery C	
Sample 1	4
Sample 2	3
Sample 3	1

1. How many individual endangered fish would need to be in each sample to qualify for the grant prize? Explain your reasoning.

   _____

2. Why do these samples imply that *none* of the three hatcheries have enough endangered species individuals to qualify for the grant?

   _____

3. What would be a reasonable guess for the number of endangered individuals in the whole population of each hatchery? Show the calculations that support your answers.

   _____

Solve.

4. The six-by-six grid shows 36 consecutive nightly samples of the sky and the number of galaxies that can be seen on each night with a small refracting telescope.

   What range of numbers would you give for the number of galaxies visible on any one of the 36 nights? Justify your answer.

30	17	20	24	23	30
16	27	13	3	30	25
3	25	16	28	9	11
2	6	29	27	1	27
6	21	7	8	13	19
2	21	7	5	30	13

   _____

Name _____ Date _____ Class_____

LESSON 10-3

Generating Random Samples

Practice and Problem Solving: D

Answer the questions below. Part of the first one is done for you.

1. A rancher's herd of 250 cattle grazes over a 40-acre pasture. He would like to find out how many cattle are grazing on each acre of the pasture at any given time, so he has some images of the pasture taken by the state department of agriculture's aerial photography division. Here are the number of cattle found in three one-acre sections.

Sample 1	4
Sample 2	1
Sample 3	9

   a. What can the rancher conclude from these samples about how many cattle graze on each acre of the 40-acre pasture?

   Sample answer: There could be as few as one or as many as 9 cattle

   grazing on an acre, or an average of about 5 cattle grazing per acre.

   b. If the cattle were equally "spread out" across all of the 40 acres, how many cattle would you expect to find on each acre?

   _____

   _____

   c. Why could the sample collected above differ from the number you would expect on each acre of pasture land?

   _____

   _____

2. The manager of a warehouse would like to know how many errors are made when a product's serial number is read by a bar-code reader. Six samples of 1,000 scans each are collected. The number of scanning errors in each sample of 1,000 scans is recorded:
36, 14, 21, 39, 11, and 2 errors

   a. Find the mean and the median number of errors per 1,000 scans based on these six samples.

   _____

   Just to be sure, the manager collects six more 1,000-scan samples with these results:

   33, 45, 34, 17, 1, and 29 errors

   b. Find the mean and the median number of errors based on all 12 samples. How do your answers compare to your answers in part **a**?

   _____

LESSON 10-3

Generating Random Samples

Reteach

A *random sample* of equally-likely *events* can be generated with random-number programs on computers or by reading random numbers from random-number tables in mathematics textbooks that are used in the study of statistics and probability.

In your math class, random samples can be modeled using coins or number cubes. For example, consider the random sample that consists of the sum of the numbers on two number cubes.

Example 1 ⟶

Generate 10 random samples of the sum of the numbers on the faces of two number cubes.

Solution

Rolling the number cubes gives these random samples:
2, 6, 6, 4, 3, 11, 11, 8, 7, and 10

Example 2 ⟶

What are the different *possible* outcomes from rolling the two number cubes in Example 1? Write the outcomes as sums.

Solution

List the outcomes as ordered pairs:
(1, 1), (1, 2), (1, 3), (1, 4), (1, 5), (1, 6),
(2, 1), (2, 2), (2, 3), (2, 4), (2, 5), (2, 6),
(3, 1), (3, 2), (3, 3), (3, 4), (3, 5), (3, 6),
(4, 1), (4, 2), (4, 3), (4, 4), (4, 5), (4, 6),
(5, 1), (5, 2), (5, 3), (5, 4), (5, 5), (5, 6),
(6, 1), (6, 2), (6, 3), (6, 4), (6, 5), (6, 6)

Then, write the sums of the ordered pairs:
2, 3, 4, 5, 6, 7, 3, 4, 5, 6, 7, 8, 4, 5, 6, 7, 8,
9, 5, 6, 7, 8, 9, 10, 6, 7, 8, 9, 10, 11, 7, 8, 9,
10, 11, and 12

Example 3 ⟶

How do the frequency of the outcomes of the 10 random samples in Example 1 compare with the frequency of their sums in Example 2?

Solution

In Example 1, there is one each of 2, 3, 4, 7, 8, and 10, two 6's, and two 11's. In Example 3, there is one 2, two 3's, three 4's, four 5's, five 6's, six 7's, five 8's, four 9's, three 10's, two 11's, and one 12.

Answer the questions about the examples.

1. How do the random samples compare with the predicted number of outcomes?

   _____

   _____

2. How do you think the outcomes in 100 random samples would compare with the expected results?

   _____

   _____

LESSON 10-3 Generating Random Samples
Reading Strategies: Read a Table

When you are generating or reading about random samples, you will often find the details about the sampling and its results in a table. This lesson presents two different uses of tables for random sampling.

Random Sampling Results

This type of table simply presents the sampling categories and the *results* of a random sampling activity.

Rose bushes, 1st sample	24
Rose bushes, 2nd sample	15
Rose bushes, 3rd sample	20
Rose bushes, 4th sample	11
Rose bushes, 5th sample	23

Random Sampling Grid

The random sampling grid is used as a means of *generating* random samples from a population. This grid shows a professional golfer's scores on each hole after playing 36 holes or two rounds of golf. A random sample of the golfer's scores on each hole can be estimated by taking a sample of the holes using a pair of number cubes.

First round:

4	3	5	3	3	2
4	4	5	3	3	4
5	6	3	3	2	2

Second round

4	3	4	5	3	3
3	4	2	3	4	3
3	3	3	4	5	3

Sample scores per round: 3, 5, 4 (first round); 4, 2, 5 (second round)

Answer the questions.

1. A farmer expects to harvest 600 apricots per tree this growing season. The table shows the results of three sample pickings. Will the farmer get the yield he wants?

Apricots, 1st sample	559
Apricots, 2nd sample	590
Apricots, 3rd sample	578

2. The table shows the number of female beagle puppies in 18 litters. A number cube is rolled three times to give samples of 1, 5, and 3 female puppies. Are these representative samples? Explain.

1	2	4	5	3	2
2	1	5	1	4	2
2	2	3	4	1	3

LESSON 10-3

Generating Random Samples

Success for English Learners

Problem 1

How many free throws are made out of 10 attempts by each eighth-grade physical education class team?

"Good" free throws by eighth-grade teams:

5	1	10	9	5	1	9
9	9	4	8	8	9	1
7	10	7	9	7	4	1
4	1	5	6	2	4	3
4	6	6	5	4	7	2
6	3	9	9	5	4	2

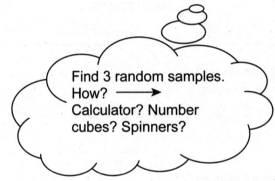

Find 3 random samples. How? ⟶ Calculator? Number cubes? Spinners?

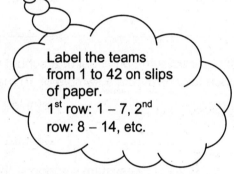

Label the teams from 1 to 42 on slips of paper. 1st row: 1 – 7, 2nd row: 8 – 14, etc.

Results of drawing three of the slips of paper: Teams 20, 29, and 12

Free throws by team in the samples:

Team 20 ⟶ 4 goals

Team 29 ⟶ 4 goals

Team 12 ⟶ 8 goals

1. How many teams got 4 goals?

_____

2. How many teams got 8 goals?

_____

3. What number of goals appears most?

_____

4. What number of goals appears least?

_____

Random Samples and Populations
Challenge

The director of technology in a large public school system would like to sample the teachers and schools in the system about their use of technology and ways to change school system policy to make technology use more effective. Identify the *sample* and the *population*, and comment on the *randomness* of the sampling described for each activity.

1. The director selects every third teacher from an alphabetical list in the school to take a survey.

   Population: Sample: Randomness:

   _____   _____   _____

2. The director selects all technology teachers from five randomly-selected schools in the system to take a survey.

   Population: Sample: Randomness:

   _____   _____   _____

3. The director asks the principal of a school to select 3 math and 3 science teachers from a sample of 10 math-science classes.

   Population: Sample: Randomness:

   _____   _____   _____

4. From across all of the system's schools, the director interviews 10 teachers with 12 or more years of teaching experience and 10 teachers with less than 12 years of teaching experience.

   Population: Sample: Randomness:

   _____   _____   _____

5. The director interviews all of the technology teachers in four randomly-selected schools across the system.

   Population: Sample: Randomness:

   _____   _____   _____

6. The director randomly selects 10 elementary, 5 middle, and 5 high school teachers to interview from all of the schools in the system.

   Population: Sample: Randomness:

   _____   _____   _____

Comparing Data Displayed in Dot Plots
Practice and Problem Solving: A/B

Find the values for each dot plot.

1.

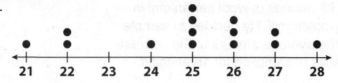

Range: _____   Median: _____   Mode: _____

2.

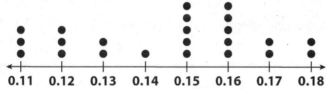

Range: _____   Median: _____   Mode: _____

Compare the dot plots by answering the questions.

Plot A

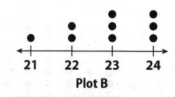

Plot B

3. How do the ranges compare?

_____

5. How do the modes compare?

_____

4. Compare the number of elements.

_____

6. How do the medians compare?

_____

7. Describe the distribution of the dots in each plot.

_____

LESSON 11-1 Comparing Data Displayed in Dot Plots

Practice and Problem Solving: C

Use the description and dot plots below to complete Exercises 1–4.

A rancher needs to shear an average of 25 pounds of wool per animal in order to meet the production quota of a woolen mill. He decides to sample part of his herd to get a first estimate of the average amount to the nearest whole pound. The dot plot shows the results of sampling for 15 animals.

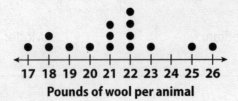

Pounds of wool per animal

1. Describe this dot set using median, mode, and range.

   _____

2. How should the rancher interpret this sample in terms of the average amount of wool needed?

   _____

3. Next, the rancher decides to look at a larger sample of animals.
   The dot plot shows the shearing results for 50 animals.

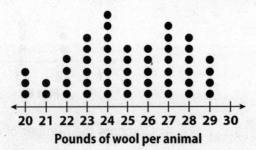

Pounds of wool per animal

   How do the central measures of this dot plot of 50 animals differ from the data you found in Exercise 1?

   _____

4. What would you recommend to the rancher in terms of reporting the results of the sampling to the woolen mill?

   _____

   _____

LESSON 11-1 **Comparing Data Displayed in Dot Plots**

Practice and Problem Solving: D

Answer the questions for each dot plot. The first one is done for you.

1. What is the range of the data? _____**15**_____

2. Since there is an even number of dots, the *median* is halfway between the values of the two middle data points. What is the median?

    _____

3. The *mode* is the value of the data point that appears the most often. What is the mode?

    _____

Answer the questions about the two dot plots.

Plot X

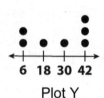

Plot Y

4. Which data set has the larger range? Explain.

    _____

5. Which data set has the mode with the most equivalent elements, or dots? Explain.

    _____

6. What is the median of Plot X?

    _____

7. What is the median of Plot Y?

    _____

LESSON 11-1
Comparing Data Displayed in Dot Plots
Reteach

A **dot plot** is a visual way to show the spread of data. A number line is used to show every data point in a set. You can describe a dot plot by examining the center, spread, and shape of the data.

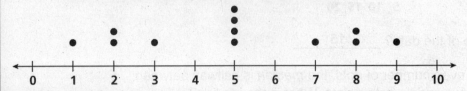

Paula: Goals Scored Per Game This Season

This dot plot shows a symmetric distribution of data. Recall that symmetric means that the two halves are mirror images. In a symmetric distribution, the mean and median are equal.

- The data are symmetric about the center, 5.
- The median has the greatest number of data.
- The mean and the median are both 5.

Some data sets may cluster more to the left or right. The mean and the median for data that are clustered this way are not necessarily equal.

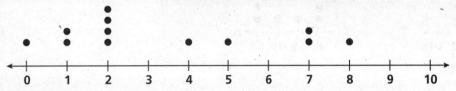

Paula: Goals Scored Per Game Last Season

This dot plot shows data that are clustered to the left.

- The data are not symmetric.
- The mean, about 3.4, is more than the median, 2.

Describe the shape of the data distribution for the dot plot.

1.

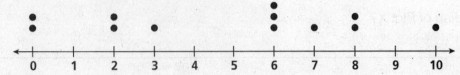

Jaime: Goals Scored Per Game This Season

_____

_____

Name _____ Date _____ Class_____

LESSON 11-1

Comparing Data Displayed in Dot Plots
Reading Strategies: Understanding Vocabulary

Central measures of a data set should be used that give the most accurate picture of how the data are distributed. This can have an effect on how one data set compares to another.

Mean, Median, and Mode

These three central measures are used most often in describing a data set. However, depending on how the data are distributed, one measure can be more accurate than another.

Example

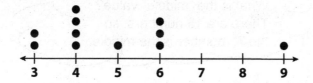

Mean ⟶ Add the values and divide by the *number* of values.

(2 × 3 + 4 × 4 + 1 × 5 + 3 × 6 + 1 × 9) ÷ 11 = **4.9**

Mode ⟶ Occurs most frequently: **4**

Median ⟶ The "middle" value: **4**

Two of the central measures have the same value, but the third is larger. This is often caused by an **outlier** data value that is much larger or smaller than most of the data values. The outlier also has an effect on the **range**, another measure of how widely data values are distributed. The outlier has an effect on the mean, too.

Outlier ⟶ **9**   **Range** ⟶ 9 – 3, or **6**

Without the outlier, the range would be 3 and the mean would be 4.5.

Find the central measures with and without the outlier.

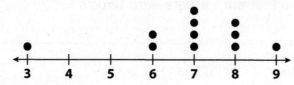

1. With the outlier

_____

2. Without the outlier

_____

LESSON 11-1

Comparing Data Displayed in Dot Plots
Success for English Learners

Problem 1

What is the **mode**?

11 12 13 14 15 16 17

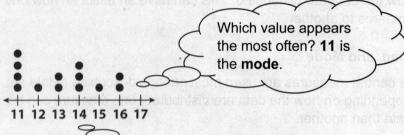

Which value appears the most often? **11** is the mode.

What is the **median**?

What is the "middle" value? There are 13 numbers, so the 7th number is the middle.

The **median** is **13**.

Problem 2

What is the **outlier**?

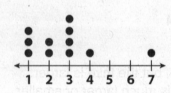

1 2 3 4 5 6 7

The outlier is much larger or smaller than the rest of the values.

The outlier is **7**.

What is the **mean** of *all* of the data? $(1 \times 3 + 2 \times 2 + 3 \times 4 + 1 \times 4 + 1 \times 7) \div 11$

The mean is about **2.7**.

What is the **mean** *without* the outlier? $(1 \times 3 + 2 \times 2 + 3 \times 4 + 1 \times 4) \div 10$

The mean is about **2.3**.

1. How would you find the median in Problem 1 if there were 12 dots?

_____

2. What would the mode be in Problem 2 if both "1" and "3" had four dots?

_____

LESSON 11-2

Comparing Data Displayed in Box Plots

Practice and Problem Solving: A/B

1. Use the data to make a box-and-whisker plot. 24, 32, 35, 18, 20, 36, 12

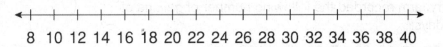

The box-and-whisker plot shows the test scores of two students. Use the box-and-whisker plot for Exercises 2–5.

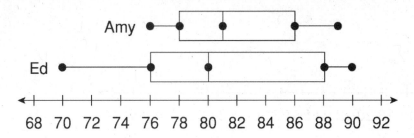

2. Which student has the greater median test score? _____

3. Which student has the greater interquartile range of test scores? _____

4. Which student has the greater range of test scores? _____

5. Which student appears to have more predictable test scores? Explain your answer.

_____

_____

The box-and-whisker plot shows prices of hotel rooms in two beach towns. Use the box-and-whisker plot for Exercises 6–8.

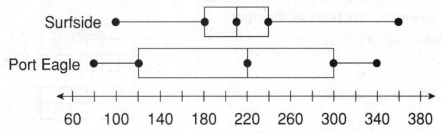

6. Which town has the greater median room price? _____

7. Which town has the greater interquartile range of room prices? _____

8. Which town appears to have more predictable room prices? Explain your answer.

_____

_____

LESSON 11-2

Comparing Data Displayed in Box Plots

Practice and Problem Solving: C

Use the situation and data given below to complete Exercises 1–4.

The owner of a blueberry farm recorded the following number of gallons of berries picked over 11 days:

38, 42, 26, 32, 40, 28, 36, 27, 29, 6, and 30 gallons

1. Construct two box plots in the space provided, one with the outlier data point and one without the outlier.

4 6 8 10 12 14 16 18 20 22 24 26 28 30 32 34 36 38 40 42 44

2. How does the outlier affect the interquartile range of the data? Explain using the data.

_____

3. Which is affected more by the outlier: the range or the interquartile range? Explain.

_____

4. Which box plot gives the more realistic picture of the blueberry farm's average production over the 11-day period? Explain your reasoning.

_____

Answer the questions about the box plots at the right.

5. Comment on the "skewness" of the data in each box plot.

_____

_____

6. Compare the ranges and the interquartile ranges of the two plots.

_____

_____

LESSON 11-2

Comparing Data Displayed in Box Plots

Practice and Problem Solving: D

Answer the questions about the box plot. The first one has been done for you.

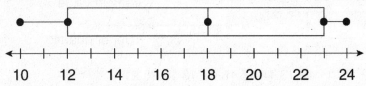

1. What are the least and greatest data points in the data set of the box plot?

   The least data point value is 10; the greatest data point value is 24.

2. What is the median of the data set? _____

3. What are the first and third quartiles of the data set?

   1st quartile: _____   3rd quartile: _____

4. What percent of the data is located between the first and third quartiles?

   _____

Use the description and data given below to complete Exercises 5–10. The first question after the drawing is done for you.

The points scored by a basketball player for eight games are:

   6, 10, 12, 14, 16, 18, 20, and 23.

5. Draw a box plot of the data in the space provided.

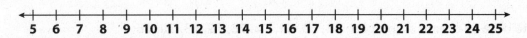

6. What is the range of the data? **17 points**

7. What is the median of the data? _____

8. What are the first and third quartiles?

   1st quartile: _____   3rd quartile: _____

9. What is the interquartile range? _____

10. Describe the distribution of the data.

    _____

LESSON 11-2

Comparing Data Displayed in Box Plots
Reteach

A **box plot** separates a set of data into four equal parts.

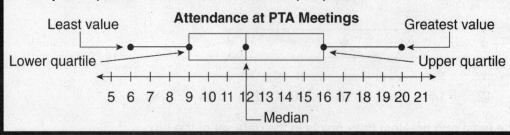

Attendance at PTA Meetings

Least value   Greatest value

Lower quartile   Upper quartile

5 6 7 8 9 10 11 12 13 14 15 16 17 18 19 20 21

Median

Use the data to create a box plot on the number line: 35, 24, 25, 38, 31, 20, 27

1. Order the data from least to greatest.

2. Find the least value, the greatest value, and the median.

_____   _____

3. The **lower quartile** is the median of the lower half of the data.
   The **upper quartile** is the median of the upper half of the data.
   Find the lower and upper quartiles.

   Lower quartile: _____   Upper quartile: _____

4. Above the number line, plot points for the numbers you found in
   Exercises 2 and 3. Draw a box around the quartiles and the median.
   Draw a line from the least value to the lower quartile. Draw a line from
   the upper quartile to the greatest value.

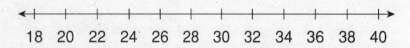

18   20   22   24   26   28   30   32   34   36   38   40

Use the data to create a box plot: 63, 69, 61, 74, 78, 72, 68, 70, 65

5. Order the data. _____

6. Find the least and greatest values, the median, the lower and
   upper quartiles.

_____

7. Draw the box plot above the number line.

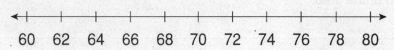

60   62   64   66   68   70   72   74   76   78   80

Comparing Data Displayed in Box Plots

LESSON 11-2

Reading Strategies: Use Graphic Aids

A **box plot** shows a set of data divided into four equal parts called **quartiles**. When you compare box plots, the quartiles are important features that sometimes allow for easier comparisons than central measures.

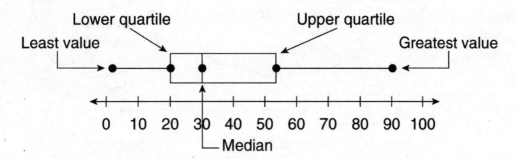

→ The **median** score divides the set of data in half.

→ The **box** shows the middle half of the data, or 50 percent of the data, from the lower to the upper quartile.

→ The lines, sometimes called "whiskers," extending from the lower and upper quartiles to the least and greatest data point values, identify the rest of the data.

→ Twenty-five percent of the data is below the lower quartile, and 25 percent of the data is above the upper quartile.

Answer the questions.

A crafts store offers two different knitting classes. The attendance for each class for 12 sessions is shown.

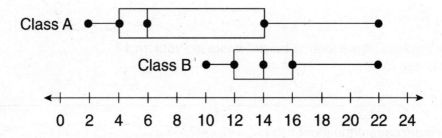

1. Which class has a greater median attendance? How much greater is it?

_____

2. Which class appears to have a more consistent attendance?

_____

3. Which class has an attendance of less than 14 people 75 percent of the time?

_____

4. What percent of the time does Class B have an attendance greater than 16?

_____

LESSON 11-2
Comparing Data Displayed in Box Plots
Success for English Learners

Problem 1

What are the parts of the diagram?

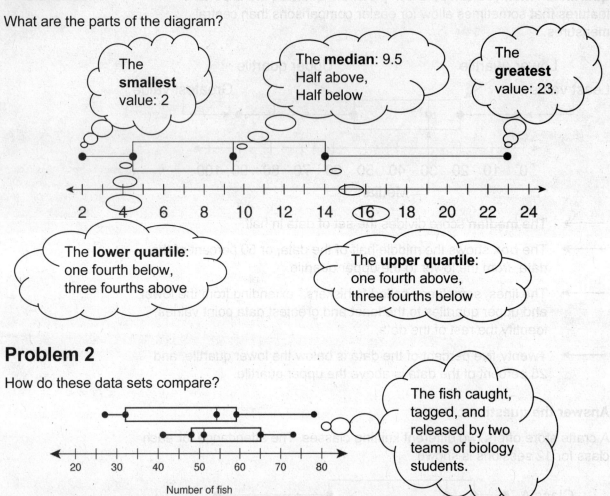

The **smallest** value: 2

The **median**: 9.5 Half above, Half below

The **greatest** value: 23.

The **lower quartile**: one fourth below, three fourths above

The **upper quartile**: one fourth above, three fourths below

Problem 2

How do these data sets compare?

Number of fish

The fish caught, tagged, and released by two teams of biology students.

1. What does "one fourth above, three fourths below" mean in Problem 1? (*Hint*: What percent is one fourth?)

_____

2. In Problem 2, which team caught the most fish *on average*?

_____

LESSON
11-3

Using Statistical Measures to Compare Populations

Practice and Problem Solving: A/B

The table shows the ages of random samples of 10 students at two different secondary schools.

Mountain View
11, 14, 13, 13, 19, 18, 15, 16, 16, 14

Ocean View
13, 14, 15, 14, 18, 17, 12, 18, 11, 14

1. What is the mean and the mean absolute deviation of the ages of the sample of students at Mountain View?

   Mean: _____ MAD: _____

2. What is the mean and the mean absolute deviation of the ages of the sample of students at Ocean View?

   Mean: _____ MAD: _____

3. What is the difference of the means?

   _____

4. What is the difference of the means as a multiple of the mean absolute deviations?

   _____

The box plots show the distributions of mean incomes of 10 samples of 10 adults from each of two cities, A and B.

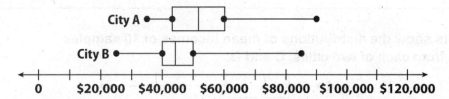

5. What can you say about any comparison of the incomes of the two populations? Explain.

   _____

   _____

   _____

   _____

   _____

LESSON 11-3 Using Statistical Measures to Compare Populations

Practice and Problem Solving: C

The table shows the scores students in a class earned on their last exam, and the final grades students earned in the class.

Scores on Last Exam	Grades Earned in Class
48, 82, 97, 29, 75, 89, 68	56, 88, 93, 35, 90, 78, 74

1. What is the mean and the mean absolute deviation for the scores on the last exam?

   Mean: _____ MAD: _____

2. What is the mean and the absolute deviation for the grades earned in class?

   Mean: _____ MAD: _____

3. What is the difference of the means?

   _____

4. What is the difference of the mean absolute deviations?

   _____

5. What is the difference of the means as a multiple of the difference of the mean absolute deviations?

   _____

The box plots show the distributions of mean incomes of 10 samples of 10 adults from each of two cities, C and D.

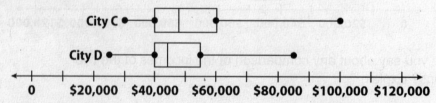

6. What can you say about any comparison of the incomes of the two populations? Explain.

   _____

   _____

   _____

Using Statistical Measures to Compare Populations

LESSON 11-3

Practice and Problem Solving: D

The tables show the weights of 10 Labradors and 10 standard poodles at a dog show.

Labradors	Standard Poodles
58, 62, 56, 74, 78, 63, 68, 72, 59, 60	67, 60, 51, 53, 57, 75, 60, 65, 50, 67

1. What is the mean and the mean absolute deviation of the weights of the Labradors?

   Mean: _____ MAD: _____

2. What is the mean and the mean absolute deviation of the weights of the standard poodles?

   Mean: _____ MAD: _____

3. What is the difference of the means?

   _____

4. What is the difference of the means as a multiple of the mean absolute deviations?

   _____

The box plots show the distributions of mean incomes of 10 samples of 10 adults from each of two cities, A and B.

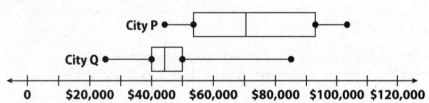

5. What can you say about any comparison of the incomes of the two populations? Explain.

   _____

   _____

   _____

Using Statistical Measures to Compare Populations

Reteach

The Thompson family of 5 has a mean weight of 150 pounds. The Wilson family of 5 has a mean weight of 154 pounds. Based on that information, you might think that the Thompson family members and the Wilson family members were about the same weight. The actual values are shown in the tables below.

Thompson Family
55, 95, 154, 196, 250

Wilson Family
132, 153, 155, 161, 169

By comparing the means to a measure of variability we can get a better sense of how the two families differ.

The Thompson family's mean absolute deviation is 60. The Wilson family's mean absolute deviation is 9.2.

The difference of the two means is 4. This is 0.07 times the mean absolute deviation for the Thompson family, but 0.4 times the mean absolute deviation for the Wilson family.

The tables show the number of pets owned by 10 students in a rural town and 10 students in a city.

Rural Town
3, 16, 3, 6, 4, 5, 0, 2, 12, 8

City
2, 0, 1, 2, 4, 0, 1, 0, 0, 1

1. What is the difference of the means as a multiple of each range?

_____

A survey of 10 random people in one town asked how many phone calls they received in one day. The results were 1, 5, 3, 2, 4, 0, 3, 6, 8 and 2. The mean was 3.4.

Taking 3 more surveys of 10 random people added more data. The means of the new surveys were 1.2, 2.8, and 2.2. Based on the new data, Ann's assumption that 3.4 calls was average seems to be incorrect.

---

2. Raul surveyed 4 groups of 10 random people in a second town to ask how many phone calls they receive. The means of the 4 groups were 3.2, 1.4, 1.2, and 2.1. What can you say about the number of phone calls received in the towns surveyed by Ann and Raul?

_____

_____

LESSON 11-3 Using Statistical Measures to Compare Populations

Reading Strategies: Focus on Vocabulary

The **mean** and **median** are often called *centers* of data.

Some *measures of variation* include the **mean absolute deviation** and the **range**. These measure how much difference, or variance, there is between the numbers in a data set.

Comparing the *centers* to the *measures of variation* can tell you more information about the data than just looking at the *centers* alone.

When you are taking **samples** of a population, you select part of a group to survey instead of surveying the whole group. Taking multiple samples makes your data more accurate.

Desirae surveyed her friends to ask their shoe sizes. Her survey results are shown in the tables below.

Girls
5, 7, 6.5, 8, 4.5, 9, 6, 7.5, 9.5, 5, 6

Boys
8, 8.5, 9, 9, 9.5, 10, 10.5, 11.5, 12, 13

Find the difference of the means as a **multiple** of the mean absolute deviation.

Mean of girls sizes: 6.7

Mean Absolute Deviation of girls' sizes: 1.3

Mean of boys sizes: 10.1

Mean Absolute Deviation of boys' sizes: 1.3

Difference of the means: $10.1 - 6.7 = 3.4$

Difference of the means as a multiple of the MAD:

1.3 times what equals 3.4?

$3.4 \div 1.3 = 2.6$

1. What could Desirae do to get a more accurate assessment of 7th grade shoe sizes?

_____

LESSON 11-3 Using Statistical Measures to Compare Populations
Success for English Learners

Problem 1

One week in January, a grocery store tracked the number of customers served between the hours of 3:00 P.M. and 4:00 P.M. Six months later, the store tracked the number of customers from 3:00 P.M. to 4:00 P.M. for another week. What is the difference of the means as a multiple of the range?

January	July
24, 21, 18, 15, 16, 27, 19	14, 18, 12, 13, 19, 22, 10

Difference of means

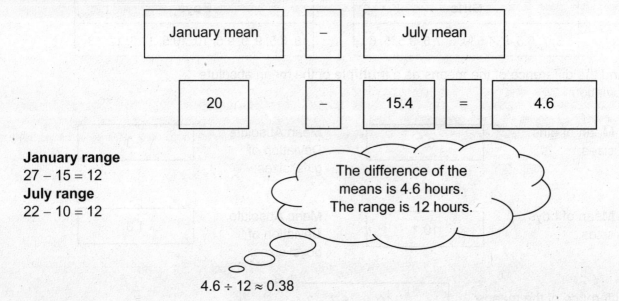

January mean	–	July mean

20	–	15.4	=	4.6

January range
27 – 15 = 12
July range
22 – 10 = 12

The difference of the means is 4.6 hours. The range is 12 hours.

4.6 ÷ 12 ≈ 0.38

The difference of the means is 0.38 times the range.

Answer the questions.

1. The grocery store tracked the number of customers served between the hours of 3:00 P.M. and 4:00 P.M. for one week in January of the following year. The mean was 26 and the range was 10. Is this enough information for the store to assume that their sales are increasing?

   _____

2. How could the store manager gather enough data to determine if the number of customers is increasing or decreasing?

   _____

Analyzing and Comparing Data

Challenge

Solve each puzzle.

1. There are 6 whole numbers in a set of numbers. The least number is 8, and the greatest number is 14. The mean, the median, and the mode are 11. What are the numbers?

   _____

2. There are 7 whole numbers in a set of numbers. The least number is 10, and the greatest number is 20. The median is 16, and the mode is 12. The mean is 15. What are the numbers?

   _____

3. There are 8 whole numbers in a set of numbers. The greatest number is 17, and the range is 9. The median and the mean are 12, but 12 is not in the data set. The modes are 9 and 14. What are the numbers?

   _____

4. The mean of a data set of 6 numbers is 8. The mean of a different data set of 6 numbers is 20. What is the mean of the combined data sets?

   _____

5. Find the mean of 7 numbers if the mean of the first 4 numbers is 5 and the mean of the last 3 numbers is 12. What is the mean of the combined data sets?

   _____

6. The mean of a data set of 3 numbers is 12. The mean of a data set of 9 numbers is 40. What is the mean of the combined data sets?

   _____

Probability

Practice and Problem Solving: A/B

LESSON 12-1

Determine the probability of each event. Write *impossible, unlikely, as likely as not, likely,* **or** *certain*. **Then, tell whether the probability is 0, close to 0, $\frac{1}{2}$, close to 1, or 1.**

1. randomly picking a blue card from a bag containing all blue cards

   _____

2. rolling an odd number on a number cube containing numbers 1 through 6

   _____

3. picking a red marble from 4 white marbles and 7 green marbles

   _____

Find each probability. Write your answer in simplest form.

4. A bag holds 6 tiles: 2 lettered and 4 numbered. Without looking, you choose a tile. What is the probability of drawing a number? _____

5. The names Phil, Angelica, Yolanda, Mimi, and Ed are on slips of paper in a hat. A name is drawn without looking. What is the probability of **not** drawing Ed? _____

6. A standard deck of cards contains 13 of each suit: red hearts, red diamonds, black clubs, and black spades. What is the probability of drawing a red card without looking? _____

A board game includes the 9 cards below.

| Move back 2. | Move up 1. | Move up 4. | Move back 3. | Move up 3. | Move up 6. | Move back 2. | Move up 5. | Move up 2. |

7. Mia says the probability of moving back is the same as the probability of moving up. Is she correct? What is the probability of moving back? Explain.

   _____

   _____

8. Gavin needs to move up more than 4 spaces to win the game. Is he likely to win on his next turn? What is the probability that he will **not** win on his next turn? Explain.

   _____

   _____

LESSON 12-1

Probability

Practice and Problem Solving: C

Find each probability. Write your answer in simplest form.

1. picking a blue shirt from a drawer with 8 blue shirts and 2 white shirts

    _____

2. drawing a vowel from letter tiles that spell out MATHEMATICS

    _____

3. A spinner is divided into 8 equal sections: 4 red, 2 white, 1 green, and 1 blue. What is the probability that the spinner lands on blue or white?

    _____

There are 6 cans of soup in a kitchen cabinet: 2 chicken noodle, 3 tomato, and 1 vegetable.

4. You select a can without looking. What is the probability that you will **not** choose chicken noodle soup?

    _____

5. Suppose you use a can of chicken noodle soup from the original 6 cans. Then your father adds 2 cans of vegetable soup and 1 can of tomato soup to those left in the kitchen cabinet. What is the probability that you will choose tomato soup now?

    _____

6. Later, your mother adds 7 more cans of soup to the cabinet, some chicken noodle and some vegetable. Now the probability of not choosing chicken noodle soup is $\frac{4}{5}$. How many cans of chicken noodle soup did your mother add to those already in the cabinet? Explain.

    _____

    _____

Use the picture at the right.

7. Write one number in each section of the spinner at right. Then write a probability problem about the spinner. The answer to your problem should be between $\frac{1}{2}$ and 1.

    _____

    _____

LESSON 12-1

Probability
Practice and Problem Solving: D

Match each event to its likelihood. The first one is done for you.

1. rolling a number less than 6 on a number
   cube labeled 1 through 6 _____**A**_____   A. likely

2. flipping a coin and getting heads _____   B. unlikely

3. spinning a number less than 3 on a spinner
   with 8 equal sections marked 1 through 8 _____   C. as likely as not

4. drawing a red or blue marble from a bag of
   red marbles and blue marbles _____   D. impossible

5. rolling a number greater than 6 on a number
   cube labeled 1 through 6 _____   E. certain

Solve. Write your answer in simplest form. The first one is done for you.

6. A bag contains 4 red marbles, 3 green marbles, and 2 yellow
   marbles. The probability of randomly picking a yellow marble is $\frac{2}{9}$.
   What is the probability of not picking a yellow marble? _____$\frac{7}{9}$_____

7. A number cube is labeled 1 through 6. The probability of randomly
   rolling a 5 is $\frac{1}{6}$. What is the probability of not rolling a 5? _____

**Tell whether the event is *impossible*, *unlikely*, *as likely as not*, *likely*,
or *certain*. Explain your choice. The first one is done for you.**

8. Tyrone rides his bicycle to school if he gets up by 7:15 A.M. Tyrone
   gets up by 7:15 about half the time. Estimate the probability that
   Tyrone will ride his bicycle to school.

   **as likely as not; Since he gets up by 7:15 about half the time, he will ride his**

   **bicycle about half the time. The probability is about $\frac{1}{2}$, or as likely as not.**

9. There are 10 shirts in a drawer. Eight of the shirts have short sleeves.
   Two shirts have long sleeves. Estimate the probability that you get a
   short-sleeved shirt if you select one out without looking.

   _____

   _____

LESSON 12-1 Probability
Reteach

Picturing a thermometer can help you rate probability.

At right are 8 letter tiles that spell AMERICAN.

If something will always happen, its probability is **certain**.
If you draw a tile, the letter will be in the word "American."

P(A, M, E, R, I, C, or N) = 1

If something will never happen, its probability is **impossible.**
If you draw a tile, you cannot draw a "Q."

P(Q) = 0

The probability of picking a vowel is **as likely as not** because there are 4 vowels and 4 consonants.

$$P(\text{a vowel}) = \frac{4 \text{ vowels}}{8 \text{ letters}} = \frac{1}{2}$$

Picking the letter "C" is **unlikely** because there is only one "C."

$$P(C) = \frac{1 \text{ "c"}}{8 \text{ letters}} = \frac{1}{8}$$

Picking a letter besides "A" is **likely** because there are 6 letters that are not "A".

$$P(\text{not A}) = \frac{6 \text{ letters}}{8 \text{ letters}} = \frac{3}{4}$$

Another way to find P(not A) is to subtract P(A) from 1.

$$P(\text{not A}) = 1 - P(A) = 1 - \frac{1}{4} = \frac{3}{4}$$

Certain —
Likely —
as likely as not —
Unlikely —
Impossible —

Tell whether each outcome is *impossible, unlikely, as likely as not, likely,* or *certain*. Then write the probability in simplest form.

1. choosing a red crayon from a box of 24 different colored crayons, including red crayons

_____

2. rolling an odd number on a number cube containing numbers 1 through 6

_____

3. randomly picking a white card from a bag containing all red cards

_____

Probability

Reading Strategies: Use a Table

Creating a table can help you solve probability problems.

You are to choose one of the cards at right without looking.

| M | A | T | H |

Consider the probability of three outcomes: 1) choosing a vowel, 2) choosing a B, or 3) choosing a letter in the word *MATH*.

Complete the table by writing whether each of the desired outcomes is *impossible, unlikely, as likely as not, likely,* or *certain*.

Possible Outcomes	Desired Outcomes		
	Vowel	**B**	**Letter in MATH**
M	no	no	yes
A	yes	no	yes
T	no	no	yes
H	no	no	yes
Results	1 out of 4	0 out of 4	4 out of 4
Probability	1. _____	2. _____	3. _____

4. You spin the spinner at the right. Complete the table. Tell whether each of the desired outcomes is *impossible, unlikely, as likely as not, likely,* or *certain*.

Possible Outcomes	Desired Outcomes		
	6	**Factor of 4**	**Greater than 0**
Results	_____ out of _____	_____ out of _____	_____ out of _____
Probability			

Name _____ Date _____ Class_____

Probability
Success for English Learners

Problem 1

A number cube can help you understand probability.

Possible outcomes:
1 2 3 4 5 6

Is it **likely** that you will roll a 1 every time?

This means the probability of rolling a 1 every time is low.

No. The cube has 6 sides. Only one side is a 1. It is **unlikely** that I will roll a 1 every time.

Problem 2

There are 16 marbles in a bag.

To find the probability of **not** drawing a red marble, first find the probability of drawing a red marble.

R = Red   G = Green   B = Blue

P(Red) means "the probability of drawing a red marble."
P(Not Red) means "the probability of drawing any marble that is NOT red."

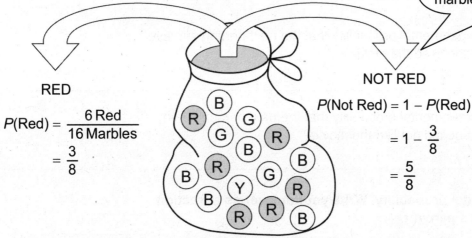

RED

$P(\text{Red}) = \dfrac{6\,\text{Red}}{16\,\text{Marbles}}$

$= \dfrac{3}{8}$

NOT RED

$P(\text{Not Red}) = 1 - P(\text{Red})$

$= 1 - \dfrac{3}{8}$

$= \dfrac{5}{8}$

1. In Problem 1, is it more likely, less likely, or as likely as not to roll an even number? Why?

_____

_____

2. In Problem 2, how likely is it that you will select a purple marble? Why?

_____

_____

**LESSON
12-2**
Experimental Probability of Simple Events
Practice and Problem Solving: A/B

Solve.

1. Jolene is playing basketball. She scored 11 baskets in 15 free throws.
   What is the experimental probability that she will score a basket on her
   next free throw?

   _____

2. Sarah has gone to work for 60 days. On 39 of those days, she arrived
   at work before 8:30 A.M. On the rest of the days she arrived after
   8:30 A.M. What is the experimental probability she will arrive after
   8:30 A.M. on the next day she goes to work?

   _____

3. For the past four weeks, Micah has been recording the daily high
   temperature. During that time, the high temperature has been greater
   than 45°F on 20 out of 28 days. What is the experimental probability
   that the high temperature will be below 45°F on the twenty-ninth day?

   _____

4. After the movie premiere 99 out of 130 people surveyed said they liked
   the movie.

   a. What is the experimental probability that the next person surveyed
      will say he or she liked the movie?

      _____

   b. What is the experimental probability that the next person surveyed
      will say he or she did not like the movie?

      _____

**Find each experimental probability. Write your answer as a fraction,
as a decimal, and as a percent.**

5. For the past 40 days, Naomi has been recording the number of
   customers at her restaurant between 10:00 A.M. and 11:00 A.M. During
   that hour, there have been fewer than 20 customers on 25 out of the
   40 days.

   a. What is the experimental probability there will be fewer than
      20 customers on the forty-first day?

      _____

   b. What is the experimental probability there will be 20 or more
      customers on the forty-first day?

      _____

LESSON 12-2

Experimental Probability of Simple Events

Practice and Problem Solving: C

1. A factory makes bicycles. Out of 300 bicycles, 2 were found to have defective brakes.

   a. What is the experimental probability that the next bike manufactured will have defective brakes?

   _____

   b. Predict how many bikes out of 2,100 will have defective brakes.

   _____

2. A factory makes light bulbs. Out of 400 light bulbs, 18 were found to have defective filaments.

   a. What is the experimental probability that the next light bulb manufactured will have a defective filament?

   _____

   b. Predict how many bulbs out of 6,000 will have defective filaments.

   _____

3. A factory makes ceramic bowls. Out of 200 bowls, 8 were chipped.

   a. What is the experimental probability that the next bowl made will **not** be chipped?

   _____

   b. Predict how many bowls out of 10,000 will be chipped

   _____

4. A manufacturer of sparkplugs has a goal of producing less than 2% defective ones. Of the last 8,000 sparkplugs, 13 were defective.

   a. What is the experimental probability that the next sparkplug will be defective?

   _____

   b. Did the manufacturer reach its goal? Explain.

   _____

5. A manufacturer of electric switches has a goal of producing less than 1.5% defective switches. Of the last 300 switches, 23 were defective.

   a. What is the experimental probability that the next switch made will be defective?

   _____

   b. Did the manufacturer reach its goal? Explain.

   _____

Experimental Probability of Simple Events

Practice and Problem Solving: D

Find each experimental probability. The first one is done for you.

1. Kathy played a game of darts. She threw 15 darts and hit the target 9 times. What is the experimental probability that Kathy will hit the target the next time she throws a dart?

   a. What is the number of favorable outcomes? _____9_____

   b. What is the total number of trials? _____15_____

   c. What is the experimental probability that Kathy will hit the target the next time she throws a dart?

   $$\frac{9}{15} = \frac{3}{5}$$

2. Between 10 A.M. and 11 A.M., 48 people came into Brad's store. 40 of them made a purchase. What is the experimental probability that the next person to come into the store will make a purchase?

   a. What is the number of favorable outcomes? _____

   b. What is the total number of trials? _____

   c. What is the experimental probability the next person to come into the store will make a purchase?

   _____

3. Sharona kept track of the colors of cars that passed her house one afternoon. She collected her data in the table below.

Car Color	Number	Car Color	Number
red	12	white	42
blue	9	silver	36
black	32	yellow	1

   What is the experimental probability that the next car will be silver?

   a. What is the number of favorable outcomes? _____

   b. What is the total number of trials? _____

   c. What is the experimental probability that the next car to pass Sharona's house will be silver?

   _____

   d. What is the experimental probability that the next car to pass Sharona's house will **not** be silver?

   _____

LESSON 12-2

Experimental Probability of Simple Events
Reteach

Experimental probability is an estimate of the probability that a particular event will happen.

It is called *experimental* because it is based on data collected from experiments or observations.

Experimental probability $\approx \dfrac{\text{number of times a particular event happens}}{\text{total number of trials}}$

JT is practicing his batting. The pitcher makes 12 pitches. JT hits 8 of the pitches. What is the experimental probability that JT will hit the next pitch?

- A favorable outcome is hitting the pitch.

- The number of favorable outcomes is the number JT hit: 8.

- The number of trials is the total number of pitches: 12.

- The experimental probability that JT will hit the next pitch is $\dfrac{8}{12} = \dfrac{2}{3}$.

1. Ramon plays outfield. In the last game, 15 balls were hit in his direction. He caught 12 of them. What is the experimental probability that he will catch the next ball hit in his direction?

   a. What is the number of favorable events? _____

   b. What is the total number of trials? _____

   c. What is the experimental probability that Ramon will catch the next ball hit in his direction?

   _____

2. In one inning Tori pitched 9 strikes and 5 balls. What is the experimental probability that the next pitch she throws will be a strike?

   a. What is the number of favorable events? _____

   b. What is the total number of trials? _____

   c. What is the experimental probability that the next pitch Tori throws will be a strike?

   _____

3. Tori threw 5 pitches for one batter. Kevin, the catcher, caught 4 of those pitches. What is the experimental probability that Kevin will **not** catch the next pitch? Show your work.

_____

Name _____ Date _____ Class_____

LESSON 12-2

Experimental Probability of Simple Events

Reading Strategies: Make Predictions

Experimental probability is a ratio. The ratio compares the number of times an event occurs to the total number of trials.

A trial is the number of times that an experiment is carried out or an observation is made.

$$\text{Experimental probability} \approx \frac{\text{number of times a favorable event happens}}{\text{total number of trials}}$$

The net of a number cube is shown below. Use the net to complete Exercises 1–2.

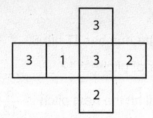

1. Predict which number you will land on most often. Explain.

   _____

2. Predict which number you will land on least often. Explain.

   _____

Actual events in an experiment may or may not match your prediction. The table shows the outcomes of tossing the above number cube 100 times

Outcome	1	2	3
Number of Tosses	39	28	33

Use the table to complete Exercises 3–4.

3. Did your prediction for landing on 1 match the outcome shown in the table? Explain.

   _____

4. Did your prediction for landing on 3 match the outcome shown in the table? Explain.

   _____

LESSON 12-2

Experimental Probability of Simple Events

Success for English Learners

Problem 1

Nikos flipped a coin 10 times. It landed heads up 6 times.

What is the experimental probability that the coin will land heads up on the next toss?

Experimental probability $\approx \dfrac{\text{number of times a favorable event happens}}{\text{total number of trials}}$

Experimental probability $\approx \dfrac{6}{10} \approx \dfrac{3}{5}$

> **favorable event:** the outcome you want
>
> **total number of trials:** how many times the coin was tossed

Problem 2

Nikos flipped the coin 20 times. It landed tails up 11 times.

What is the experimental probability that the coin will **not** land tails up on the next toss?

Experimental probability (tails) $\approx \dfrac{11}{20}$

Experimental probability (not tails) $\approx 1 - \dfrac{11}{20} \approx \dfrac{9}{20}$

1. Marco counted 40 cars in the parking lot. 28 were silver. What is the experimental probability that the next car in the lot will be silver?

   a. What is the number of events? _____

   b. What is the number of trials? _____

   c. What is the experimental probability that the next car in the parking lot will be silver?

   _____

2. Janine flipped a coin 52 times. The coin landed heads up 18 times. What is the experimental probability that the coin will land tails up on the next flip?

   _____

3. Write your own experimental probability problem. Give the answer.

   _____

   _____

   _____

Experimental Probability of Compound Events

LESSON 12-3

Practice and Problem Solving: A/B

Solve.

1. A coin was tossed and a spinner with three equal sections numbered 1 to 3 was spun. The results are shown in the table.

	Heads	Tails
1	53	65
2	49	71
3	54	62

What is the experimental probability that the next toss and spin will result in 3 and Tails?

_____

2. A receptionist recorded the number of people who took an elevator up from his floor and the number who took an elevator down. He also noted the number of men and women. The table shows the results.

	Elevator Up	Elevator Down
Men	36	43
Women	39	42

What is the experimental probability that the next person will be a woman taking the elevator up?

_____

3. Sandwich shop customers can choose the bread and meat they want. The table shows the sandwiches that were sold on a given day.

	White Bread	Wheat Bread
Ham	22	24
Turkey	21	22
Tuna	25	23

What is the experimental probability that the next sandwich sold will be tuna on wheat bread?

_____

4. A store sells a coat in three sizes: small, medium, and large. The coat comes in red, navy, and tan. Sales numbers are shown in the table.

	Small	Medium	Large
Red	18	21	19
Navy	24	22	20
Tan	19	25	22

What is the experimental probability that the next coat sold is **not** a large navy?

_____

LESSON 12-3

Experimental Probability of Compound Events

Practice and Problem Solving: C

Solve.

1. Two brands of paint—Durable and Forever—are each sold by the gallon in three different grades: good, better, and best quality. The sales manager at a hardware store tracks all the paint sales. She started making a table, but did not finish it.

	Good	Better	Best
Durable	48	45	35
Forever		39	33

The experimental probability that the next gallon of paint sold will be better-quality Durable paint is $\frac{9}{50}$.

a. How many gallons of good-quality Forever were sold?

_____

b. What is the experimental probability that the next gallon of paint sold will **not** be the best quality paint?

_____

2. A horseback riding club is sending one individual, one pair, and one team of vaulters to the championships. These performers will be judged against others in each class. They will be awarded 1 to 5 points for artistry, and 1 to 6 points for precision. Explain how to use a simulation to find the experimental probability that each of the club's entries will score 11 points.

_____

_____

_____

3. Give your own example of a compound event that could be tested through a simulation.

_____

_____

4. Give your own example of a compound event that could **not** be tested through a simulation.

_____

_____

Name _____ Date _____ Class_____

LESSON
12-3

Experimental Probability of Compound Events
Practice and Problem Solving: D

Solve each problem. The first one is done for you.

1. Peter tossed a dime and a quarter at the same time. He did this 100 times. The results are shown in the table.

		Quarter	
		Heads	**Tails**
Dime	**Heads**	18	30
	Tails	32	20

What is the experimental probability that the next time he tosses the coins he will get a tails on the dime and a heads on the quarter?

a. What is the number of favorable events? _____**32**_____

b. What is the total number of trials? **18 + 30 + 32 + 20 = 100**

c. What is the experimental probability that the next time Peter tosses both coins he will get a tails on the dime and a heads on the quarter?

$$\frac{32}{100} = \frac{8}{25}$$

2. Aimee tossed a coin and spun a spinner that is divided into 3 equal sections. She did this 50 times. The results are shown in the table.

		Spinner		
		1	**2**	**3**
Coin	**Heads**	4	7	8
	Tails	12	8	11

What is the experimental probability that the next time Aimee tosses the coin and spins the spinner she will get a Tails and a 2?

_____

3. The Reliable Car dealership sells cars and trucks. The cars and trucks come in red, white, and silver. Damon made this table to show the cars and trucks that are on the lot today.

	Red	**White**	**Silver**
Car	45	41	46
Truck	21	24	23

What is the experimental probability that the next vehicle that comes on the lot will be a red car?

_____

Original content Copyright © by Houghton Mifflin Harcourt. Additions and changes to the original content are the responsibility of the instructor.

LESSON 12-3

Experimental Probability of Compound Events
Reteach

A **compound event** includes two or more simple events.

The possible outcomes of flipping a coin are heads and tails.

A spinner is divided into 4 equal sections, each one a different color. The possible outcomes of spinning are red, yellow, blue, and green.

If you toss the coin and spin the spinner, there are 8 possible outcomes.

2 possible **coin outcomes**

4 possible **spinner outcomes**

8 possible **compound outcomes**

	Red	Yellow	Blue	Green
Heads	9	11	11	14
Tails	10	12	7	6

To find the experimental probability that the next trial will have an outcome of Tails and Blue:

a. Find the number of times Tails and Blue was the outcome: 7.

b. Find the total number of trials: $9 + 11 + 11 + 14 + 10 + 12 + 7 + 6 = 80$.

c. Write a ratio of the number of tails and blue outcomes to the number of trials: $\frac{7}{80}$.

A store hands out yogurt samples: peach, vanilla, and strawberry. Each flavor comes in regular or low-fat. By 2 P.M. the store has given out these samples:

	Peach	Vanilla	Strawberry
Regular	16	19	30
Low-fat	48	32	55

Use the table to answer the questions.

1. What is the total number of samples given out? _____

2. What is the experimental probability that the next sample will be regular vanilla?

   _____

3. What is the experimental probability that the next sample will be strawberry?

   _____

4. What is the experimental probability that the next sample will **not** be peach?

   _____

Name _____ Date _____ Class_____

LESSON 12-3 Experimental Probability of Compound Events

Reading Strategy: Make a Table

Making a table is often a good way to organize information.

If you are doing an experiment where you flip a coin and toss a number cube, recording the results in a list can be difficult to tabulate later. A table is much easier to read.

Tables work well for experiments that include one or two events.

> Ezekiel tosses a coin and rolls a number cube that has sides labeled 1 to 6. He does this 8 times. Using tick marks, he recorded his results in the table below.

	1	2	3	4	5	6
Heads			//	/		/
Tails			/		//	/

Complete.

1. Jalayne tosses a coin and spins a spinner divided into three equal sections (1, 2, and 3). She does this 20 times. The results of Jalayne's 20 trials are shown below. Make a table to display her results.

```
1H  3H  3T  2H  2T  1T  2H  1H  3H  1T
3H  2T  1T  3H  1H  2T  3T  3H  1T  3T
```

Use the data in your table to find each experimental probability.

2. The next trial will have the outcome Tails and 3. _____

3. The next trial will have the outcome Heads and 2. _____

4. The next trial will have the outcome **not** Heads and **not** 2. _____

5. The next trial will have the outcome **not** Tails. _____

LESSON 12-3

Experimental Probability of Compound Events

Success for English Learners

Problem

A **compound event** includes 2 or more simple events.

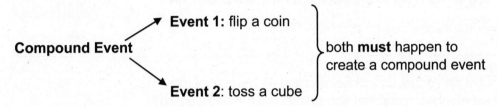

Compound Event

Event 1: flip a coin

Event 2: toss a cube

} both **must** happen to create a compound event

A coin is flipped **and** a number cube is tossed 50 times.

compound event   **number of trials**

The results are shown in the table below.

2 possible outcomes from the coin

This is an outcome for the number cube *and* the coin. The outcome was **Heads** *and* **2** a total of **3 times** out of 50.

6 possible outcomes from the number cube

	1	2	3	4	5	6
Heads	4	3	6	4	4	5
Tails	3	5	2	5	3	6

1. What is the experimental probability that the next outcome will be Tails *and* 4?

   a. Look in the table to find the number for Tails *and* 4. _____

   b. Write that number over the total number of trials: _____

2. What is the experimental probability that the next outcome will **not** be Heads?

   a. Look in the table to find all the outcomes for heads. Add the numbers to find the total.

   _____

   b. In a fraction, write that number over the total number of trials.

   _____

   c. Subtract that fraction from 1 to find the outcomes for "**not** heads."

   _____

Making Predictions with Experimental Probability

LESSON 12-4

Practice and Problem Solving: A/B

Make a prediction based on experimental probability.

1. A bowler knocks down at least 6 pins 70 percent of the time. Out of 200 rolls, how many times can you predict the bowler will knock down at least 6 pins?

   _____

2. A tennis player hits a serve that cannot be returned 45 percent of the time. Out of 300 serves, how many can you predict will not be returned?

   _____

3. West Palm Beach, Florida, gets rain about 16 percent of the time. On how many days out of 400 can residents of West Palm Beach predict they will get rain?

   _____

4. Rob notices that 55 percent of the people leaving the supermarket choose plastic bags instead of paper bags. Out of 600 people, how many can Rob predict will carry plastic bags?

   _____

5. A baseball player reaches base 35 percent of the time. How many times can he expect to reach base in 850 at-bats?

   _____

6. Fredericka can make 65 percent of her shots from the free-throw line. If she shoots 75 times, how many shots can she expect to make?

   _____

7. In a current-events class, a professor predicted that at least 78 percent of students prefer getting their news from a digital source rather than from a print source. He polled 3 classes. The results are shown in the table below.

	Class 1	Class 2	Class 3
Digital	20	14	30
Print	5	10	7

   In which class(es) did his prediction hold true? Explain.

   _____

LESSON 12-4

Making Predictions with Experimental Probability

Practice and Problem Solving: C

Solve each problem.

1. The Arno family is planning a 14-day April vacation. The location they've chosen has an average of 10 rainy days every April. The Arnos would like at least 7 days without rain. Should they keep their current plan? Explain.

   _____

   _____

2. Advertisements claim that the train is on-time 90 percent of the time. The bus has a record of being on-time 56 out of 64 days. Which form of transportation provides more reliable service? Explain.

   _____

   _____

3. During February and March, Jack is spending 7 days in the Yukon observing endangered species. Historically, the region has snowfall that blocks roads 20 days during these months. Can Jack expect to be able to get around at least 5 of the days? Explain.

   _____

   _____

4. ABC Airlines has had delays on 18 of 126 recent flights. DEF Airlines has had delays 13 percent of the time.

   a. Which airline would you expect to provide more reliable service? Why?

   _____

   b. Over the last 7 days at one airport, DEF Airlines maintained the record shown in this table.

	Mon	Tue	Wed	Thu	Fri	Sat	Sun
On Time	5	7	9	10	9	11	6
Delayed	2	6	3	1	1	2	2

   On which days, if any, did DEF do better than its average? Explain.

   _____

   _____

Name _____ Date _____ Class _____

LESSON 12-4

Making Predictions with Experimental Probability

Practice and Problem Solving: D

Solve each problem. The first one is done for you.

1. In 1951, Odessa, Texas had high temperatures of at least 95°F for 11 percent of the year. During that year, how many days could residents predict would have highs of at least 95°F? Show your work.

   Use the proportion to solve. Round to the nearest whole number.

   $\dfrac{11}{100} = \dfrac{x}{365}$ $x =$ __**40**__

   The residents of Odessa could predict highs of at least 95°F on

   __**40**__ days of the year.

2. A survey shows that 67 percent of peanut-butter lovers prefer chunky-style. Out of 850 people surveyed, how many can be predicted to say they prefer chunky-style peanut butter?

   Use the proportion to solve. Round to the nearest whole number.

   $\dfrac{67}{100} = \dfrac{x}{850}$ $x =$ _____

   _____ people can be expected to say they prefer chunky-style peanut butter.

3. A football player forces at least 1 turnover in 27.5 percent of the games he plays. If the player plays in 57 games, in how many games can he predict he will force a turnover? Show your work.

   Use the proportion to solve. Round to the nearest whole number.

   $\dfrac{27.5}{100} = \dfrac{x}{57}$ $x =$ _____

   He can expect to force a turnover in _____ games.

4. Sandy says she splits her time on her homework as follows: 45 percent on math, 20 percent on science, 18 percent on social studies, and 17 percent on language arts.
   a. If Sandy spends 100 hours on homework over a month, predict how much time she spend on each subject.

      Math: _____   Science: _____

      Social Studies: _____   Language Arts: _____

   b. If Sandy only spends 75 hours on homework over a month, predict how much time she spends on each subject to the nearest tenth of an hour.

      Math: _____   Science: _____

      Social Studies: _____   Language Arts: _____

Making Predictions with Experimental Probability
Reteach

When you have information about previous events, you can use that information to predict what will happen in the future.

If you can throw a basketball into the basket 3 out of 5 times, you can predict you will make 6 baskets in 10 tries. If you try 15 times, you will make 9 baskets. You can use a proportion or multiply to make predictions.

A. Use a proportion.

A survey found that 8 of 10 people chose apples as their favorite fruit. If you ask 100 people, how many can you predict will choose apples as their favorite fruit?

$$\frac{8}{10} = \frac{x}{100}$$ Write a proportion. *8 out of 10 is how many out of 100?*

$$\frac{8}{10} = \frac{x}{100}$$
$$\times 10$$

Since 10 times 10 is 100, multiply 8 times 10 to find the value of *x*.

$$x = 80$$

You can predict that 80 of the people will choose apples as their favorite fruit.

B. Multiply.

Eric's baseball coach calculated that Eric hits the ball 49 percent of the time. If Eric receives 300 pitches this season, how many times can Eric predict that he will hit the ball?

$$0.49 \times 300 = x$$
$$147 = x$$

Eric can predict that he will hit the ball 147 times.

Solve.

1. On average, 25 percent of the dogs who go to ABC Veterinarian need a rabies booster. If 120 dogs visit ABC Veterinarian, how many of them will likely need a rabies booster?

   Set up a proportion: $\dfrac{}{100} = \dfrac{x}{}$

   Solve for *x*: $x =$ _____

   _____ dogs will likely need a rabies booster.

2. About 90 percent of seventh graders prefer texting to emailing. In a sample of 550 seventh graders, how many do you predict will prefer texting?

   $0.9 \times 550 =$ _____

   _____ seventh graders will likely prefer texting.

LESSON 12-4
Making Predictions with Experimental Probability
Reading Strategies: Use Models

Predicting is making an educated guess about a future result.

You can use **experimental probability** to make a prediction.

Pat is able to flip a game disk into a cup
4 times in 10 tries. Out of 50 tries, how many
flips will Pat predict she can make?

Use a grid to model Pat's successful flips: $\frac{4}{10}$.

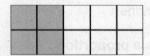

Then expand your grid to 50 squares to predict the
number of Pat's successful flips out of 50.

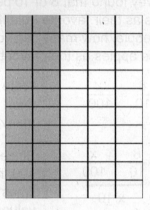

$$\frac{4}{10} \times 50 = \frac{200}{10} = 20$$

Pat will predict she can make 20 flips out of 50.

**Solve. On a separate sheet of paper, create grids to model the
situation and make your prediction.**

1. A tire manufacturer checks 5 tires and finds that 1 of them has a leak.
   If they produced 20 tires, how many of them would be likely to have a
   leak?

_____

Solve. You may use a model if you like.

2. Will has calculated that he usually makes 60 percent of his attempted
   free throws. How many throws out of 15 should Will predict he can
   make?

_____

3. An ad for the elevated train line states that it is on time 96 percent of
   the time. The subway, which Bob has been taking, has been on time
   75 times out of 83. Should Bob switch to the elevated train? Why or
   why not?

_____

_____

_____

Making Predictions with Experimental Probability

LESSON 12-4

Success for English Learners

Problem

The Marino family plans a trip to Florida. They will go for 2 weeks.
They hope to have *at least* 10 out of 14 days when it does **not** rain.

Weather Report for July through September

JULY						
Su	Mo	Tu	We	Th	Fr	Sa
						1
2	3	4	5	6	7	8
9	10	11	12	13	14	15
16	17	18	19	20	21	22
23	24	25	26	27	28	29
30	31					

AUGUST						
Su	Mo	Tu	We	Th	Fr	Sa
		1	2	3	4	5
6	7	8	9	10	11	12
13	14	15	16	17	18	19
20	21	22	23	24	25	26
27	28	29	30	31		

SEPTEMBER						
Su	Mo	Tu	We	Th	Fr	Sa
					1	2
3	4	5	6	7	8	9
10	11	12	13	14	15	16
17	18	19	20	21	22	23
24	25	26	27	28	29	30

All but 19 days
are **not** rainy

⟵ **92 days** ⟶

19 days
are rainy

Should the family go to Florida during those 3 months?

Write a proportion.

$$\frac{\text{rainy days}}{\text{total days}} = \frac{\text{predicted rainy days}}{\text{total vacation days}}$$

$$\frac{19}{92} = \frac{x}{14}$$

$x \approx 2.89$, or about 3 **rainy** days

> 14 vacation days – 3 rainy days
> = **11 days that are not rainy**
> The family should go!

Use the information above to answer the questions.

1. What if there were 32 rainy days? Would the family go to Florida?
   Explain.

   _____

2. What if there were 10 rainy days in July and August? Would the family
   go to Florida? Explain.

   _____

MODULE 12

Experimental Probability
Challenge

Shlomo is the manager of a toy company. He needs to select a factory to produce toys his company will sell. His company cannot sell defective toys. The probability that each factory produces defective toys and the maximum production for each factory are shown below.

Factory	Probability of Producing a Defective Toy	Maximum Daily Production
A	$\frac{2}{49}$	3,000
B	$\frac{17}{99}$	3,300
C	$\frac{13}{70}$	2,900
D	$\frac{11}{83}$	3,200

Solve. Show your work.

1. Calculate the expected number of defective toys produced daily in each factory. Which one produces the fewest defective toys each day?

   _____

   _____

   _____

   _____

2. Shlomo's company would like to sell at least 2,750 toys each day. Which factory should the company select to produce the toys?

   _____

   _____

3. Shlomo's company decides to produce toys at Factory A and Factory C. It costs $2.49 to manufacture each toy at Factory A and $1.89 to manufacture each toy at Factory C. The toys sell for $29.99 each. How much profit will the toy company generate in one day?

   _____

   _____

   _____

   _____

LESSON 13-1
Theoretical Probability of Simple Events
Practice and Problem Solving: A/B

Find the probability for each event.

1. tossing a number cube numbered from 1 to 6 and getting an even number that is greater than or equal to 2

_____

2. tossing a number cube numbered from 1 to 6 and getting an odd number that is less than or equal to 3

_____

3. randomly selecting a seventh grader from a school that has 250 sixth graders, 225 seventh graders, and 275 eighth graders

_____

4. without looking, **not** picking a red hat from a box that holds 20 red hats, 30 blue hats, 15 green hats, and 25 white hats

_____

Match each event to its likelihood.

5. rolling a number greater than 6 on a number cube labeled 1 through 6   _____   A. likely

6. flipping a coin and getting heads   _____   B. unlikely

7. drawing a red or blue marble from a bag of red marbles and blue marbles   _____   C. as likely as not

8. spinning a number less than 3 on a spinner with 8 equal sections labeled 1 through 8   _____   D. impossible

9. rolling a number less than 6 on a number cube labeled 1 through 6   _____   E. certain

Use the information to find probabilities in 10–13.

At a school health fair, individual pieces of fruit are placed in paper bags and distributed to students randomly. There are 20 apples, 15 apricots, 25 bananas, 25 pears, and 30 peaches.

10. the probability of getting an apple _____

11. the probability of **not** getting a pear _____

12. the probability of **not** getting an apple _____

13. the probability of getting an orange _____

LESSON 13-1

Theoretical Probability of Simple Events

Practice and Problem Solving: C

Use the information below to answer 1–3.

Three students are playing a video game. Each player is randomly assigned a character from a collection of characters that includes 5 blue, 6 green, and 3 red characters. After each character is picked, it is not replaced in the collection.

1. What is the probability that the first player does **not** get a blue character?

   _____

2. The first player gets a blue character. What is the probability that the second player also gets a blue character?

   _____

3. Both the first and second players get blue characters. What is the probability that the third player does **not** get a blue character?

   _____

Fill in the blank.

4. $P = 0.4$

   Total outcomes: 50

   Number of events: _____

5. Number of events: 75

   $P = 0.3$

   Total outcomes: _____

Use the information below to answer 6–9.

On its first day, a neighborhood pet show includes 5 rabbits, 7 cats, 8 dogs, and 4 hamsters. Each pet has its own petting station. Children who wish to pet the animals are randomly assigned to a station.

6. How many cats would need to be added on the second day to make the probability of picking a cat from the group at least one half?

   _____

7. Assume that the cats in question 6 were added on the second day. What is the probability of picking a dog from the new group?

   _____

8. On the third day, no more animals were added. What is the probability of picking a rabbit or a hamster on the third day of the show?

   _____

9. What is the probability of **not** picking a goldfish on the third day of the show? Explain.

   _____

Name _____ Date _____ Class_____

 # Theoretical Probability of Simple Events
Practice and Problem Solving: D

Solve each problem. The first one is done for you.

1. The kitchen-tile installer has 20 green, 14 beige, and 16 white tiles in a box. What is the probability of picking a beige tile from the box without looking?

$$\frac{14}{20 + 14 + 16} = \frac{14}{50} = \frac{7}{25}$$

2. There are 25 spools each of blue, green, red, white, and yellow thread in the sewing basket. Without looking, what is the probability of picking a spool of blue thread from the basket?

_____

Find the probability. The first one is done for you.

3. A gardener has a bag of flower seeds. Half of the seeds are roses, one fourth are gardenias, and one fourth are irises.

P(gardenias)   *P*(not gardenias)

$\frac{1}{4}$ $1 - \frac{1}{4} = \frac{3}{4}$
_____   _____

4. The traffic-control monitor on the freeway shows 200 vehicles per minute passing the camera in 5 minutes. Of those vehicles, on average, 125 have one passenger, 60 have four or fewer passengers, and 15 have more than four passengers.

P(vehicle with more than four people)   *P*(vehicle with four or fewer people)

_____   _____

Use the information below to complete the table. The first row is done for you.

Tina has 3 quarters, 1 dime, and 6 nickels in her pocket. Find the probability of randomly drawing each of the following coins.

	Probability		
	Fraction	**Decimal**	**Percent**
5. quarter	$\frac{3}{10}$	0.3	30%
6. dime			
7. nickel			

LESSON 13-1

Theoretical Probability of Simple Events

Reteach

The probability, P, of an event is a ratio.
It can be written as a fraction, decimal, or percent.

$$P(\text{probability of an event}) = \frac{\text{the number of outcomes of an event}}{\text{the total number of all events}}$$

Example 1

There are 20 red apples and green apples in a bag. The probability of randomly picking a red apple is 0.4. How many red apples are in the bag? How many green apples?

Total number of events ⟶ 2

Probability, P: $0.4 = \dfrac{\text{number of red apples}}{20}$

So:

number of red apples $= 0.4 \times 20 = 8$

number of green apples $= 20 - 8 = 12$

There are 8 red apples and 12 green apples.

Example 2

A bag contains 1 red marble, 2 blue marbles, and 3 green marbles.

The probability of picking a red marble is $\dfrac{1}{6}$.

To find the probability of **not** picking a red marble, subtract the probability of picking a red marble from 1.

$$P = 1 - \frac{1}{6} = \frac{5}{6}$$

The probability of not picking a red marble from the bag is $\dfrac{5}{6}$.

Solve.

1. A model builder has 30 pieces of balsa wood in a box. Four pieces are 15 inches long, 10 pieces are 12 inches long, and the rest are 8 inches long. What is the probability the builder will pull an 8-inch piece from the box without looking?

   _____

2. There are 30 bottles of fruit juice in a cooler. Some are orange juice, others are cranberry juice, and the rest are other juices. The probability of randomly grabbing one of the other juices is 0.6. How many bottles of orange juice and cranberry juice are in the cooler?

   _____

3. There are 13 dimes and 7 pennies in a cup.

   a. What is the probability of drawing a penny out without looking?

      _____

   b. What is the probability of **not** drawing a penny? _____

4. If $P(\text{event A}) = 0.25$, what is $P(\textbf{not}\ \text{event A})$? _____

5. If $P(\textbf{not}\ \text{event B}) = 0.95$, what is $P(\text{event B})$? _____

LESSON 13-1 **Theoretical Probability of Simple Events**

Reading Strategies: Building Vocabulary

The study of probability introduces new words and words used in ways with which you may not be familiar.

- probability ←——— the likelihood of an event occurring

- event ←——— an outcome of a calculation or an experiment

- outcome ←——— the result of an action or a calculation

- experimental probability ←——— based on experimental data; outcomes may not be equally likely to occur

- theoretical probability ←——— based on equally-likely outcomes

Several of these terms are combined in the definition of probability, *P*, of Event A occurring.

$$P(\text{event A}) = \frac{\text{number of event A outcomes}}{\text{number of all outcomes}}$$

Event A is an outcome of a calculation or an experiment.

In each situation, identify the outcomes and event. Find the probability.

1. A coin is tossed. What is the probability that a head will occur?

    a. Outcomes: _____

    b. Event: _____

    c. Probability of the event: _____

2. A softball team has a catcher, a pitcher, 4 infielders, and 3 outfielders. One player is chosen at random. What is the probability that the player is an outfielder?

    a. Outcomes: _____

    b. Event: _____

    c. Probability of the event: _____

Label the items.

3. A cube numbered 1 to 6 is rolled. What is the probability of a 4 being rolled?

    1, 2, 3, 4, 5, 6 ←——— a. _____

    4 ←——— b. _____

    $\frac{1}{6}$ ←——— c. _____

LESSON 13-1 Theoretical Probability of Simple Events
Success for English Learners

Problem 1

What is the probability of picking a B from the bag?

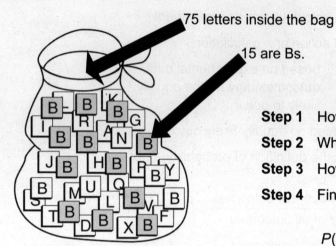

75 letters inside the bag

15 are Bs.

Step 1 How many possible outcomes? 75

Step 2 What event do you want? B

Step 3 How many of that event? 15

Step 4 Find the probability.

$$P(B) = \frac{\text{number of Bs}}{\text{number of tiles}} = \frac{15}{75} = \frac{1}{5}$$

Problem 2

Math class has 25 students. 14 are boys.

How many are girls?

25 students − 14 boys = 11 girls

What is the probability of choosing a girl at random?

$$P(\text{girl}) = \frac{\text{event (girl)}}{\text{outcomes (boys + girls)}} = \frac{11}{25}$$

What is the probability of choosing a boy at random?

So, $P(\text{boy}) = 1 - P(\text{girl})$

$$P(\text{boy}) = 1 - \frac{11}{25} = \frac{14}{25}$$

THINK: Only 2 possible outcomes

boy OR girl

Find the probability.

1. 12 dogs and 6 cats being given away

   $P(\text{cat}) =$ _____

2. 8 pencils and 5 pens in a bag

   $P(\text{pen}) =$ _____

Theoretical Probability of Compound Events

Practice and Problem Solving: A/B

Use the table of probabilities to answer questions 1–3.

	Burrito	**Taco**	**Wrap**
Cheese	$P = \frac{1}{9}$	$P = \frac{1}{9}$	$P = \frac{1}{9}$
Salsa	$P = \frac{1}{9}$	$P = \frac{1}{9}$	$P = \frac{1}{9}$
Veggie	$P = \frac{1}{9}$	$P = \frac{1}{9}$	$P = \frac{1}{9}$

1. List the members of the sample space that include a taco.
   Use parentheses.

   _____

2. List the members of the sample space that include cheese.
   Use parentheses.

   _____

3. What is the probability of choosing a burrito with cheese and a taco or
   a wrap with salsa? Explain.

   _____

   _____

Use the information below to answer questions 4–6.

A basket of 40 pairs of pliers at a discount hardware store includes 5 pairs
of 6-inch pliers. A second basket contains 20 hammers, including 3 large
hammers.

4. What is the probability of drawing a 6-inch pair of pliers from the first

   basket without looking?_____

5. What is the probability of **not** drawing a large hammer from the second

   basket without looking?_____

6. What is the probability of drawing a pair of 6-inch pliers and

   not drawing a large hammer?_____

7. What is the probability of drawing a pair of 6-inch pliers from the

   second basket? Explain. _____

LESSON 13-2

Theoretical Probability of Compound Events

Practice and Problem Solving: C

The table below lists 3 brands of outdoor lights and 2 colors of lighting. It also identifies some of the probabilities of picking one brand and one color at random. Use the table to answer 1–5.
(Hint: The probability in each cell is the product of two probabilities, one for the brand and one for the color.)

	Brand X	Brand Y	Brand Z
blue	0.18		0.3
white	0.12	0.08	

1. What is the probability of picking blue lighting or white lighting?

   _____

2. How can you find the probability of picking blue lighting or the probability of picking white lighting made by Brand X?

   _____

   _____

3. What is the probability of picking Brand X, Y, or Z?

   _____

4. What is the probability of picking blue lighting made by Brand Y?

   _____

5. What is the probability of picking white lighting made by Brand Z?

   _____

Solve.

6. Based on earlier expeditions to a dig site, a geologist expects to find igneous, metamorphic, and sedimentary rocks in the percentages by weight of 25%, 60%, and 15%, respectively. The rock sizes to be found and their percentages of appearance are pebbles (60%), small rocks (20%), medium rocks (15%), and boulders (5%).

   a. What is the most likely combination of rock type and weight the geologist will find? Use compound probability to prove your answer.

   _____

   b. Compute the probabilities for finding the four weights of igneous rock.

   _____

LESSON 13-2 **Theoretical Probability of Compound Events**

Practice and Problem Solving: D

Solve.

1. Each student receives one of 4 calculator models and one of 3 types of ruler. Fill in the tree diagram to show the probabilities of receiving each type of calculator and ruler. The first one in each row is done for you.

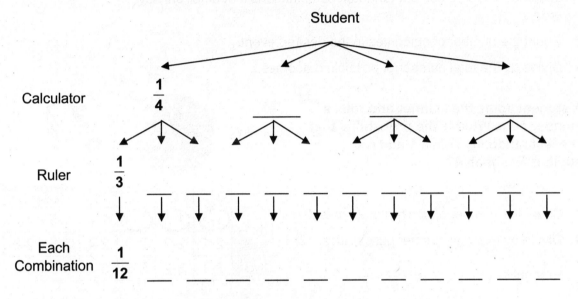

Use the tree diagram to complete Exercises 2–4.

2. What is the probability of receiving each calculator? _____

3. What is the probability of receiving each ruler? _____

4. What is the probability of receiving a certain combination of calculator and ruler? Show how this probability is calculated.

_____

Solve. The first one is done for you.

5. Two students are playing a game with a quarter and a spinner that is divided into equal sixths, with the sections numbered 1 to 6. Each player tosses the coin and spins the spinner.

   a. How many outcomes are possible for the coin toss? List them.

      two: (heads, tails)
      _____

   b. How many outcomes are possible for the spin? List them.

      _____

   c. How many outcomes are possible for the toss and spin? List them.

      _____

LESSON 13-2

Theoretical Probability of Compound Events
Reteach

Compound probability is the likelihood of two or more events occurring.

1. To identify the sample space, use a list, tree diagram, or table. If order does not matter, cross out repeated combinations that differ only by order.

2. Count the number of outcomes in the desired event.

3. Divide by the total number of possible outcomes.

A student spins the spinner and rolls a number cube What is the probability that she will randomly spin a 1 and roll a number less than 4?

1. Identify the sample space.

2. Count the number of desired outcomes: 3.

3. Divide by the total number possibilities: 18.

Probability (1 and < 4) = $\frac{3}{18}$ = $\frac{1}{6}$

	1	2	3	4	5	6
1	1-1	1-2	1-3	1-4	1-5	1-6
2	2-1	2-2	2-3	2-4	2-5	2-6
3	3-1	3-2	3-3	3-4	3-5	3-6

At a party, sandwiches are served on 5 types of bread: multi-grain, pita, rye, sourdough, and whole wheat. Sam and Ellen each randomly grab a sandwich. What is the probability that Ellen gets a sandwich on pita or rye and Sam gets a sandwich on multi-grain or sourdough?

1. The table shows the sample space. Draw an X in each cell in which Ellen gets a sandwich on pita or rye.

2. Draw a circle in each cell in which Sam gets a sandwich on multi-grain or sourdough.

3. Count the number of possibilities that have both an oval and a rectangle.

_____

4. Divide the number you counted in Step 4 by the total number of possibilities in the sample space.

_____

This is the probability that Ellen gets a pita or a rye sandwich *and* that Sam gets a multi-grain or a sourdough sandwich.

		Ellen				
		M	P	R	S	W
Sam	M					
	P					
	R					
	S					
	W					

Name _____ Date _____ Class_____

 LESSON 13-2

Theoretical Probability of Compound Events
Reading Strategies: Choose a Strategy

Probability is a measure of how likely an event is to occur. To find probability, you must identify the number of possible outcomes.

- A **simple** *event* is an event with a single outcome.

- A **compound event** combines two or more simple events.

To find the number of possible outcomes for a compound event, you must find all the combinations of each of the outcomes of the simple events.

To keep track of the combinations of outcomes, you can create an organized list, table, or tree diagram.

Consider the following guidelines when choosing an organizer.

- A tree diagram will have a branch for each choice of each event. When there are more than three branches or three events, a tree diagram may not be the best choice.

	Organized List	**Tree Diagram**	**Table**
2 events	✓	✓	✗
3 events	✓	✓	✗
More than 3 events	✗	✗	✓

- When an event includes computation, a table can provide both a system for doing the mental math and a place to store the results.

- No matter which organizer you choose, if the possible outcomes involve long words, consider using a code for each choice.

Identify the number of events and choices in each situation. Tell which method you would choose to find all possible outcomes.

1. During an early-morning power outage, Sara must get dressed in the dark. Her clothing options include black or blue pants, a white or yellow shirt, and a solid red or a striped scarf.

   _____

2. Hector can go to the movies with either Eddie or Miguel. He will see either a comedy or a drama.

   _____

3. Ben rolls two six-sided number cubes. If the product of the numbers is an even number, he gets 5 points. If the sum of the numbers is an even number, he gets 2 points.

   _____

LESSON
13-2
Theoretical Probability of Compound Events
Success for English Learners

Problem 1

Sal's pizza sells 6 toppings.

extra cheese (C)   onion (O)

green olives (GO)   peppers (P)

mushrooms (M)   tomato (T)

Find the total number of 2-topping combinations.

	C	GO	M	O	P	T
C	C-C	C-GO	C-M	C-O	C-P	C-T
GO	GO-C	GO-GO	GO-M	GO-O	GO-P	GO-T
M	M-C	M-GO	M-M	M-O	M-P	M-T
O	O-C	O-GO	O-M	O-O	O-P	O-T
P	P-C	P-GO	P-M	P-O	P-P	P-T
T	T-C	T-GO	T-M	T-O	T-P	T-T

The pizza must have 2 different toppings. Cross out doubles.

Order does not matter. Cross out duplicates.

There are 15 unique combinations of 2-topping pizzas.

Look at the highlighted cell for T-GO above.

$$P(\text{tomato} + \text{green olive}) = \frac{1}{15}$$

1 combo out of 15 is tomato + green olive.

1. Why are more than half of the combinations crossed out?

_____

_____

2. What pattern do you see in the table?

_____

_____

3. What other ways could you have used to find the combinations?

_____

LESSON 13-3
Making Predictions with Theoretical Probability
Practice and Problem Solving: A/B

In each odd-numbered question, find the theoretical probability. Then use that probability to make a prediction in the even-numbered question that follows it.

1. Martin flips a coin. What is the probability that the coin will land on heads?

   _____

2. Martin flips the coin 64 times. How many times can Martin expect the coin to land on heads?

   _____

3. A spinner is divided into five equal sections labeled 1 to 5. What is the probability that the spinner will land on 3?

   _____

4. If the spinner is spun 60 times, how many times can you expect the spinner to land on 3?

   _____

5. Harriet rolls a number cube. What is the probability that the number cube will land on 3 or 4?

   _____

6. If Harriet rolls the number cube 39 times, how many times can she expect to roll a 3 or 4?

   _____

7. A bag contains 6 red and 10 black marbles. If you pick a marble from the bag, what is the probability that the marble will be black?

   _____

8. If you pick a marble, record its color, and return it to the bag 200 times, how many times can you expect to pick a black marble?

   _____

Make a prediction based on the theoretical probability.

9. Gill rolls a number cube 78 times. How many times can he expect to roll an odd number greater than 1?

   _____

10. Jenna flips two pennies 105 times. How many times can she expect both coins to come up heads?

    _____

11. A shoebox holds a number of disks of the same size. There are 5 red, 6 white, and 7 blue disks. You pick out a disk, record its color, and return it to the box. If you repeat this process 250 times, how many times can you expect to pick either a red or white disk?

    _____

12. Ron draws 16 cards from a deck of 52 cards. The deck is made up of cards of four different colors—red, blue, yellow, and green. How many of the cards drawn can Ron expect to be green?

    _____

Making Predictions with Theoretical Probability

LESSON 13-3

Practice and Problem Solving: C

1. Kamila has two number cubes each labeled 1 to 6. She is going to conduct an experiment by tossing both cubes a total of 150 times. She will find the sum of the two numbers in each roll.

    a. How many possible outcomes are there? _____

    b. What is the probability of tossing a sum of 6? _____

    c. How many times should Kamila toss a sum of 7? _____

    d. How many times should Kamila toss a sum of 10 or greater?

       _____

2. Eric has two number cubes each labeled 1 to 6. Eric is going to conduct an experiment by tossing the cubes a total of 180 times. He will find the product of the two numbers in each roll.

    a. How many possible outcomes are there? _____

    b. How many times should Eric toss a product of 12? _____

    c. How many times should Eric toss a product greater than 20?

       _____

    d. How many times should Eric toss a product less than 10?

       _____

3. Natalie has two number pyramids each labeled 1 to 4. Natalie is going to conduct an experiment by tossing both pyramids a total of 96 times. She will find the difference of each pair of numbers rolled by subtracting the lesser number from the greater number.

    a. How many possible outcomes are there? _____

    b. How many times should Natalie toss a difference of 1? _____

    c. How many times should Natalie toss a difference of 0? _____

LESSON 13-3

Making Predictions with Theoretical Probability

Practice and Problem Solving D

Find the probability of each event. The first one is done for you.

1. Arjan flips a quarter. What is the probability of the quarter landing tails up?

$$\frac{1}{2}$$

2. Stephanie rolls a number cube that has sides numbered from 1 to 6. What is the probability of the cube landing on either 2 or 5?

_____

3. What is the probability of spinning this spinner and having it land on B?

_____

4. Jonathan has a bag that has 2 red marbles and 3 blue marbles inside of it. If you were to pick one marble from the bag without looking, what is the probability of picking a red marble?

_____

Make a prediction based on a theoretical probability. Show your work. The first one is done for you.

5. The probability of flipping a coin and having it land on heads is $\frac{1}{2}$. If a coin is tossed 4 times, how many times can you expect it to land on heads?

$$\frac{1}{2} \times 4 = \frac{1}{2} \times \frac{4}{1} = \frac{4}{2} = 2$$

6. A spinner is divided into 4 equal sections. The probability of landing on A is $\frac{1}{4}$.

Norma spins the spinner 16 times. How many times can she expect the spinner to land on A?

_____

7. The probability of a number cube landing on 4 is $\frac{1}{6}$. If a number cube is tossed 12 times, how many times can it be expected to land on 4?

_____

8. The probability of picking a blue pen from a cup of pens is $\frac{1}{3}$. Tim picks one pen from the cup without looking, records the color, and puts the pen back. He does this 15 times. How many times can he expect to pick a blue pen?

_____

LESSON 13-3	**Making Predictions with Theoretical Probability**

Reteach

Predictions are thoughtful guesses about what will happen.
You can create an "outcome tree" to keep track of outcomes.

> Sally is going to roll a number cube 21 times.
> She wants to know how many times she can expect to roll a 1 or 4.

There are a total of 6 **outcomes**.
Of these, *two* outcomes (1 and 4) are desirable.

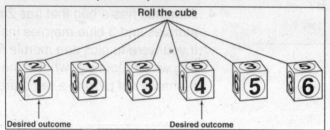

Use probability to predict the number of times Sally would roll a 1 or 4.

$$P(1 \text{ or } 4) = \frac{\text{number of desirable outcomes}}{\text{number of possible outcomes}} = \frac{2}{6} = \frac{1}{3}$$

Set up a proportion relating the probability to the number of tries.

$$\frac{1}{3} = \frac{x}{21}$$

$3x = 21$ Cross-multiply.

$x = 7$ Simplify.

In 21 tries, Sally can expect to roll seven 1s or 4s.

**For each odd-numbered question, find the theoretical probability.
Use that probability to make a prediction in the even-numbered
question that follows it.**

1. Sandra flips a coin. What is the probability that the coin will land on tails?

_____

2. Sandra flips the coin 20 times. How many times can Sandra expect the coin to land on tails?

_____

3. A spinner is divided into four equal sections labeled 1 to 4. What is the probability that the spinner will land on 2?

_____

4. If the spinner is spun 80 times, how often can you expect it to land on 2?

_____

Name _____ Date _____ Class_____

Making Predictions with Theoretical Probability
Reading Strategies: Use a Model

Predicting is making a thoughtful guess about a future result. You can use theoretical probability to make a prediction.

Al flips a coin 28 times. How many times can he expect to flip heads?

Make a bar model to help make a prediction.

Step 1 Find the theoretical probability of the coin landing on heads.

⬛ ←——— The shaded part represents heads.
⬜ ←——— The white part represents tails.

The probability of the coin landing on heads is $\frac{1}{2}$.

Step 2 Extend the model to show 28 tries.

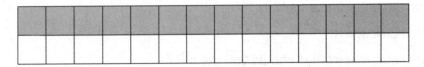

$$\frac{1}{2} \times \frac{28}{1} = \frac{28}{2} = 14$$

Al can expect the coin to land on heads 14 times in 28 tries.

Use the probability to make a prediction.

1. Li rolls a number cube labeled 1 to 6 a total of 24 times. How many times can she expect to roll a 1?

   _____

2. The theoretical probability of rolling a 1 or 2 is $\frac{1}{3}$. Out of 15 rolls,

   how many can you expect to be a 1 or 2?

   _____

3. The theoretical probability of spinning green on a spinner is $\frac{1}{4}$.

   How many spins in 32 tries can you expect to land on green?

   _____

4. The theoretical probability of drawing a red marble is $\frac{1}{9}$. How many

   red marbles can you expect to get in 72 draws?

   _____

Making Predictions with Theoretical Probability

LESSON 13-3

Success for English Learners

Problem 1

What is the theoretical probability of choosing a B from the bag?

15 Bs

75 tiles in all

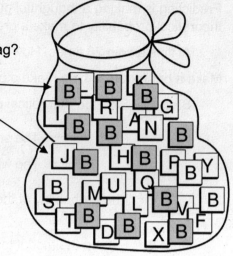

Theoretical probability $= \dfrac{\text{number of desirable outcomes}}{\text{number of possible outcomes}}$

$= \dfrac{15}{75} = \dfrac{1}{5}$

Problem 2

You pick a tile from the bag without looking.

You put it back. You pick again.

If you pick 30 times, how many times should you get a B?

Step 1 Write a proportion. $\dfrac{1}{5} = \dfrac{x}{30}$

Step 2 Cross-multiply. $5 \cdot x = 1 \cdot 30$

$5x = 30$

Step 3 Divide each side by 5. $\dfrac{5x}{5} = \dfrac{30}{5}$

$x = 6$

> In 30 picks, you can expect to get 6 Bs.

1. Explain the difference between theoretical probability and experimental probability.

   _____

   _____

2. Explain how to use the theoretical probability to make a prediction.

   _____

   _____

3. Write your own word problem about using theoretical probability to make a prediction.

   _____

   _____

Name _____ Date _____ Class_____

LESSON 13-4 Using Technology to Conduct a Simulation

Practice and Problem Solving: A/B

Answer the questions below.

1. A marine biologist has historical records to show that the chance of finding shrimp in a catch of ocean animals is 20 percent. The simulation below models the experimental probability of finding shrimp in at least one of the next 5 catches. The numbers 1 and 2 represent catches with shrimp. The numbers 3–10 represent catches without shrimp.

   a. What does the marine biologist do?

   _____

   _____

   b. Here is the table the marine biologist created. Fill in the missing data.

Trial	Numbers Generated	Shrimp Caught	Trial	Numbers Generated	Shrimp Caught
1	7, 3, 2, 7, 10		6	8, 4, 7, 6, 5	
2	2, 4, 5, 3, 10		7	6, 10, 1, 7, 6	
3	9, 9, 7, 6, 6		8	7, 9, 8, 3, 8	
4	7, 9, 6, 6, 4		9	1, 4, 4, 8, 9	
5	10, 6, 4, 6, 4		10	7, 8, 9, 5, 3	

2. According to the simulation above, what is the experimental probability that shrimp will be caught in at least one of the next 5 catches?

   _____

3. At a television game show, prizes are placed under 10 percent of the seats in the studio audience. What is the experimental probability that you have to reserve exactly 4 seats before you win a prize?

   a. Describe a model to use for this simulation.

   _____

   _____

   _____

   b. Give an example of a trial that would result in winning a prize for exactly 4 seats.

   _____

LESSON
13-4

Using Technology to Conduct a Simulation
Practice and Problem Solving: C

Answer the questions below.

1. During the regular season, a soccer team has a 30 percent chance of scoring more than 4 goals in a match. Use a calculator and the table to find the experimental probability that the team will score exactly 4 goals in a match.

Trial	Numbers Generated	Result
1		
2		
3		
4		
5		

2. What is the experimental probability based on these 5 trials?

_____

3. What do you think will happen to the *total* experimental probability if 5 more trials are run?

_____

4. Complete the table below for 5 more trials.

Trial	Numbers Generated	Result
6		
7		
8		
9		
10		

5. What is the experimental probability based on all 10 trials?

_____

Name _____ Date _____ Class_____

Using Technology to Conduct a Simulation
Practice and Problem Solving: D

Use the information below to complete Exercises 1–3. The first parts of 1 and 2 are done for you.

A pizza parlor puts coupons in 25 percent of its pizza boxes. Answer the questions to find the experimental probability that a customer would need to buy exactly 4 pizzas before finding a coupon.

1. Choose a model.

   a. What is the probability of finding a coupon?

   $$25\% = \frac{25}{100} = \frac{1}{4}$$

   b. If you use the whole numbers 1–4 to represent getting or not getting a winning number, what would the winning number(s) be?

   _____

   c. What would the non-winning number(s) be?

   _____

2. Use your calculator to generate some random numbers for 10 trials. Remember, you are looking for exactly 4 pizzas, at least 1 of which has a coupon. Two trials are done for you. Fill in the rest of the table with your randomly generated numbers.

Trial	Numbers Generated	Pizzas Bought	Trial	Numbers Generated	Pizzas Bought
1	3, 1, 1, 3	4	6		
2	3, 2, 4, 2	4	7		
3			8		
4			9		
5			10		

Why is Trial 1 a winner but Trial 2 is not? (Hint: Is there any limit on how many of the 4 boxes in a trial can have a coupon?)

_____

3. Find the experimental probability of needing to buy exactly 4 pizzas before finding a coupon in the 10 trials.

   The experimental probability = ____ trials ÷ 10 trials = ____.

LESSON 13-4

Using Technology to Conduct a Simulation
Reteach

Use a graphing calculator to help you conduct a probability simulation.

There is a 20 percent possibility of rain during the week of the school fair. What is the experimental probability that it will rain on at least one of the days of the festival, Monday through Friday?

Step 1 Choose a model.

Probability of rain: $20\% = \dfrac{20}{100} = \dfrac{1}{5}$

Use whole numbers 1–5 for the days.
　Rain: 1　　　　No rain: 2–5

Step 2 Generate random numbers from 1 to 5 until you get a 1.

Example: 1, 2, 2, 5, 2
This trial counts as an outcome that it will rain on at least one of the days of a week.

Step 3 Perform multiple trials by repeating Step 2:

Trial	Numbers Generated	Rain	Trial	Numbers Generated	Rain
1	1, 2, 2, 5, 2	1	6	1, 4, 5, 5, 3	1
2	5, 2, 2, 2, 3	0	7	3, 4, 5, 2, 2	0
3	5, 2, 3, 1, 5	1	8	4, 1, 2, 2, 2	1
4	3, 2, 3, 2, 2	0	9	2, 2, 2, 4, 2	0
5	3, 2, 2, 2, 2	0	10	2, 2, 4, 3, 3	0

Step 4 In 10 trials, the experimental probability that it will rain on 1 of the school days is 4 out of 10 or 40 percent, 0.4, or $\dfrac{2}{5}$ (two-fifths).

Find the experimental probability. Draw a table on a separate sheet of paper and use 10 trials.

1. An event has 5 outcomes. Each outcome: 50-50 chance or more.

_____

_____

2. An event has a 40 percent probability. Each outcome: exactly 3-in-5 chance.

_____

_____

Using Technology to Conduct a Simulation

Reading Strategies: Read a Table

A table that contains data from a simulation includes several types of information that must be interpreted.

The *Theoretical* Probability of an Event

Suppose there is a 1-in-6 chance that an event will occur. This can be represented with the numbers 1 through 6.

$$1 \longrightarrow \text{The event occurs.}$$

$$2\text{–}6 \longrightarrow \text{The event does } not \text{ occur.}$$

These numbers are found in the columns labeled "Numbers Generated."

Trial	Numbers Generated	Result	Trial	Numbers Generated	Result
1	1, 4, 4, 5, 6, 1	2	6	2, 5, 2, 2, 5, 2	0
2	6, 5, 6, 1, 1, 5	2	7	1, 1, 6, 1, 5, 1	4
3	2, 4, 1, 3, 5, 6	1	8	1, 1, 5, 1, 6, 5	3
4	2, 6, 1, 3, 1, 4	2	9	6, 6, 3, 1, 3, 5	1
5	2, 1, 4, 2, 1, 1	3	10	3, 6, 5, 1, 6, 6	1

The *Experimental* Probability of an Event

Next, suppose you are asked to find the probability that the event occurs no more than 2 times in 10 trials. The event is a "1". In which trials does a "1" occur once or twice? Those outcomes are in bold above.

• To calculate the experimental probability, count the results 1 or 2 in the "Result" columns. There are 6 results of 1 or 2.

• The experimental probability is 6 out of 10, 0.6, 60 percent, or $\frac{3}{5}$.

Give the theoretical probability. Then, give the numbers for the random-number generation. Finally, find the experimental probability.

1. The chance of drawing a blue pen is 25 percent. What is the experimental probability for exactly 2 chances out of 10?

_____

_____

2. The chance of snow during the month of January is 7 out of 8. What is the experimental probability for at most 1 chance out of 10?

_____

_____

Using Technology to Conduct a Simulation

LESSON 13-4

Success for English Learners

Problem

The six sides of a cube are numbered 1 to 6.

What is the chance of rolling a 5?

1 out of 6. That is about 17%.

Method 1

To find the **experimental probability**, you could roll the cube 60 times and record the results.

Method 2

There is another way to find the **experimental probability**. You could generate random numbers from 1 to 6.

- 5 is your desired outcome.

- So, 1, 2, 3, 4, and 6 are the other possible outcomes.

- Now, run 10 trials. Randomly generate 6 numbers in each trial.

- Record the results of your 10 trials in the chart. The first trial has been done for you.

Trial	Numbers	Desired Outcome?	Trial	Numbers	Desired Outcome?
1	4, 3, 2, 2, 5	1	6		
2			7		
3			8		
4			9		
5			10		

1. Use the data in your simulation. What is the experimental probability of rolling a 5?

   _____

2. Look at your data. What is the experimental probability of rolling an odd number (the outcomes 1, 3, 5)?

   _____

3. Choose your own outcome. Use the data in the chart to find its experimental probability. What is the experimental probability of your chosen outcome?

   _____

Theoretical Probability and Simulations
Challenge

1. Julia is shooting arrows at a target. The shape of the target is a square with a circle inscribed, as shown at right.

   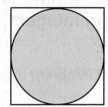

   Julia shoots an arrow and randomly hits a point within the target. What is the probability that the arrow lands inside the circle? Show your work. (Hint: *Area of a circle* $= \pi r^2$)

   _____

   _____

   _____

   _____

2. Tobias used a simulation to predict the number of rainy days in his town in a given week. In the simulation a "0" or "1" represents a rainy day. The numbers "2" through "9" represent sunny days. The results of the simulation are shown in the table below.

Trial	Simulation	Trial	Simulation
1	1, 2, 3, 2, 1, 0, 9	6	6, 5, 3, 9, 9, 8, 3
2	7, 8, 1, 9, 8, 5, 4	7	4, 3, 5, 6, 9, 2, 3
3	4, 5, 9, 9, 0, 2, 4	8	5, 5, 1, 8, 9, 0, 0
4	4, 3, 5, 2, 6, 9, 3	9	4, 5, 2, 8, 9, 0, 3
5	5, 5, 3, 2, 5, 1, 9	10	5, 0, 0, 9, 1, 8, 1

   Tobias claims that the probability of two or more rainy days in a week is greater than the probability of no rainy days in a week.

   a. According to the simulation model is Tobias correct? Explain.

   _____

   _____

   _____

   b. Use the simulation to calculate the probability of 0, 1, 2, 3, 4, 5, 6, and 7 rainy days in a week. Show your work. Which number of rainy days is most likely?

   _____

   _____

   _____

   _____

UNIT 1: The Number System

MODULE 1 Adding and Subtracting Integers

LESSON 1-1

Practice and Problem Solving: A/B

1. a. 8

   b. negative

   c. –8

2. a. 11

   b. negative

   c. –11

3. –6

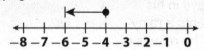

4. –10

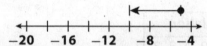

5. –9

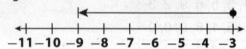

6. –12

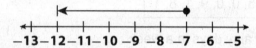

7. –8

8. –9

9. –53

10. –93

11. 224

12. –95

13. –600

14. –1310

15. $-3+(-2)+(-4)=-9$; –9 feet. The hole is 9 feet deep.

Practice and Problem Solving: C

1. a. $-42+(-87)+(-29)=-158$

   b. $-57+(-75)+(-38)=-170$

   c. The store had more red apples left over. The store started with the same number of red apples and green apples. It sold more green apples than red apples, so it had more red apples left.

2. a. $-2+(-3)+(-13)=-18$

   b. The hotel guest got off on the 14th floor. The manager started on the 19th floor and rode 2 floors down to the 17th floor when the hotel guest got on. They rode the elevator down 3 floors. $17 - 3 = 14$, so the hotel guest got off on the 14th floor.

Practice and Problem Solving: D

1. a. 7

   b. positive

   c. +7

2. a. 10

   b. negative

   c. –10

3. –5

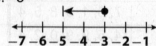

4. –6

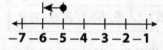

5. –7

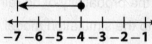

6. –7

7. –4

8. –8

9. –19

10. –35

11. –$8

Reteach

1. a. positive

   b. $3+6=9$

   c. 9

2. a. negative

   b. $7 + 1 = 8$

   c. -8

3. a. negative

   b. $5 + 2 = 7$

   c. -7

4. a. positive

   b. $6 + 4 = 10$

   c. 10

5. -13

6. -16

7. 37

8. -41

9. -24

10. 52

Reading Strategies

1. Each counter represents -1.

2. Each counter represents a dollar that Sarah withdrew. The counters make it is easier to see how many dollars Sarah withdrew each day.

3. You can simply count the counters to find the sum.

4. $-3 + (-5) + (-4) + (-1) = -13$

Success for English Learners

1. positive counters

2. because you are adding a negative number

3. Answers will vary. Sample answer: Erica bought stamps three times this week. She bought 5 stamps on Monday, 3 stamps on Wednesday, and 4 stamps on Friday. How many stamps did Erica buy this week? $(5 + 3 + 4 + 12)$

LESSON 1-2

Practice and Problem Solving: A/B

1. -1

2. 1

3. 5

4. -1

5. -1

6. -3

7. -2

8. 4

9. 8

10. 2

11. 43

12. 21

13. -29

14. -10

15. $11°F$

16. 3 yards

17. -9 points

18. a. negative

   b. loss of 6, or -6

Practice and Problem Solving: C

1. negative; -10

2. positive; 5

3. negative; -7

4. positive; 5

5. positive; 6

6. positive; 15

7. negative; -1

8. positive; 1

9. the same sign as the integers

10. It is the sign of the integer whose absolute value is greater.

11. -15

12. -24

13. 13

14. -30

15. 0

16. -18

17. $-5°F$

18. $150

19. Rita; 11 points

Practice and Problem Solving: D

1. -1

2. -7

3. -5

4. -1

5. -1

6. 12

7. 4

8. 8

9. −5

10. −10

11. −6

12. 5°F

13. −22°F

14. −97 ft

15. 17,500 ft

Reteach

1. subtract; the numbers have different signs

2. negative

3. 4

4. −5

5. −1

6. −4

7. 2

8. −5

9. 9

10. −10

11. −16

12. Sample answer: I look at 3 and 9 and see that 9 > 3. Since the sign on 9 is negative, the answer is negative.

Reading Strategies

1. 0

2. right; 6

3. left; 4

4. 2

5. 0

6. left; 5

7. left; 3

8. −8

Success for English Learners

1. negative number

2. No, the sum can be positive or negative.

3. negative

4. positive

LESSON 1-3

Practice and Problem Solving: A/B

1. −5

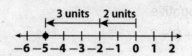

2. 6

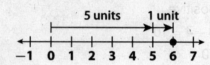

3. −10

4. 5

5. −4

6. 24

7. 0

8. 46

9. −1

10. 42

11. −6

12. −26

13. 30

14. −5

15. 9°C

16. 14°F

17. 4°C

18. 7°C

19. 240°C

Practice and Problem Solving: C

1. 16

2. −22

3. 7

4. 0

5. 29

6. 9

7. −2

8. 0

9. −10

10. when $x < y$

11. when $x > y$

12. 12°F, −2°F

13. Pacific; 2,400 m

14. 11,560; –185; –185 is closer to sea level; 11,375 ft
15. Saturday
16. 1°

Practice and Problem Solving: D

1. –5
2. –4
3. –7
4. –5
5. 6
6. –16
7. 0
8. 1
9. 7
10. 16
11. –11
12. 610°C
13. $35,000
14. 9°F

Reteach

1. a. 5
   b. –1
   c. 20
2. a. negative
   b. 2
   c. –2
3. 40
4. –3
5. –26
6. 0
7. 31
8. –5

Reading Strategies

1. left
2. 7
3. right
4. 3
5. –4
6. right; 2
7. left; 6
8. –4

Success for English Learners

1. positive
2. negative

LESSON 1-4

Practice and Problem Solving: A/B

1. $-2 - 19 + 7 = -14$; 14 feet below the surface of the water
2. $45 - 8 + 53 - 6 = 84$; 84 points
3. 20
4. –27
5. 18
6. 110
7. 52
8. 34
9. <
10. >
11. a. $225 + 75 - 30 = 270$; 270 points
    b. Maya

Practice and Problem Solving: C

1. $-35 - 29 + 7 - 10 = -67$; Jana is 67 ft from the end of the fishing line.
2. a. $500 + 225 - 105 + 445 = 1065$; 1065 ft above the ground
   b. Kirsten is closer to the ground; Gigi's balloon position is $500 + 240 - 120 + 460 = 1080$ ft, which is greater than 1065 ft.
3. a. $20 + 20 + 30 + 30 - 10 - 10 - 10 = 100$; 100 points
   b. David and Jon tied. Jon scored $20 + 20 + 20 + 30 + 30 - 10 - 10 = 100$, or 100 points, which is the same number of points that David scored.

Practice and Problem Solving: D

1. $-2 - 9 + 3 = -8$; 8 ft below the surface of the water
2. $20 - 5 + 10 = 25$; 25 points
3. –1
4. –24
5. 20
6. –9

7. 8

8. 100

9. <

10. >

11. $200 - 30 + 70 = 240$; 240 points

Reteach

1. a. $10 + 5 - 19$

   b. $15 - 19 = -4$

   c. -4

2. a. $14 - 15 - 3$

   b. $14 - 18 = -4$

   c. -4

3. a. $10 - 80 - 6$

   b. $10 - 86 = -76$

   c. -76

4. a. $7 + 13 - 21$

   b. $20 - 21 = -1$

   c. -1

5. a. $13 + 2 - 5 - 6$

   b. $15 - 11 = 4$

   c. 4

6. a. $18 + 6 - 4 - 30$

   b. $24 - 34 = -10$

   c. -10

Reading Strategies

1. +700; above

2. when the balloon rises; rise

3. when the balloon drops; drop

4. $700 - 200 + 500 - 100 = 900$

5. 900 ft above the ground

6. Angelo is higher than where he started because 900 is greater than 700.

Success for English Learners

1. When money is withdrawn, it is taken out of the bank account. So, you subtract.

2. When money is deposited, it is put into the bank account. So, you add.

3. Answers may vary. Sample answer: Jose has $25. He spends $5, and then earns $15. How much money does Jose have at the end? $(25 - 5 + 15 = 35; $35)$

MODULE 1 Challenge

1. Calculate the difficulty using the method shown in the example.

Trail	Mile 1	Mile 2	Mile 3	Mile 4	Mile 5	Total
Breakneck	$100 - (-2) = 102$	$-2 - 100 = -102$	$150 - (-2) = 152$	$-8 - 150 = -158$	$250 - (-8) = 258$	252
Lake Shore	$0 - (-10) = 10$	$6 - 0 = 6$	$55 - 6 = 49$	$-1 - 55 = -56$	$60 - (-1) = 61$	70
Mountain View	$-2 - 40 = -42$	$120 - (-2) = 122$	$35 - 120 = -85$	$200 - 35 = 165$	$180 - 200 = -20$	140

The most difficult trail is Breakneck.

2. The greatest possible value is obtained by filling the boxes as follows.

   $-3 \boxed{+} 5 \boxed{-} -4 \boxed{-} -10 \boxed{+} 18 = 34$

MODULE 2 Multiplying and Dividing Integers

LESSON 2-1

Practice and Problem Solving: A/B

1. −80
2. −72
3. 40
4. −39
5. 0
6. −80
7. 189
8. −11
9. −72
10. 80
11. −54
12. 49
13. 4(−6) = −24; −24 points
14. 5(−3) = −15; −15°
15. 8(−18) = −144; 200 + (−144) = 56; $56
16. 3(−5) = −15; 8 + (−15) = −7; −7°
17. 6(−25) = −150; 325 + (−150) = 175; $175

Practice and Problem Solving: C

1. −98
2. 120
3. −144
4. 135
5. −24
6. −36
7. 0
8. −1,440
9. 1,176
10. 3(−4) = −12; −12 + 9 = −3; −3 yd
11. 4(−35) = −140; −140 + 220 = 80; $80
12. 3(−50) = −150; −125 + (−150) = −275; −275 ft
13. 1
14. −1
15. 1
16. −1
17. 1
18. negative; positive

Practice and Problem Solving: D

1. −6
2. 0
3. 8
4. −28
5. 12
6. −36
7. −50
8. −18
9. −70
10. 1
11. −12
12. 4
13. 5(−3) = −15; −15 points
14. 3(−1) = −3; −3°
15. 2(−4) = −8; −8 yd
16. 7(−9) = −63; −$63
17. 5(−5) = −25; −$25

Reteach

1. −2
2. 18
3. −5
4. 54
5. 44
6. 4(−8) = −32; −32 points
7. 5(−500) = −2,500; −2,500 ft

Reading Strategies

1. gaining 10 points
2. losing 17 points
3. left
4. 4
5. left
6. 4
7. left
8. 4
9. The score decreased by 12.
10. −12 points
11. −16 points

Success for English Learners

1. –20
2. 3
3. (–20) × (3)
4. –$60
5. Sample answer: You know the product will be either 400 or –400. It will be 400 because both factors are negative, so the product is positive.
6. Yes. The product of both will be negative because there is one positive factor and one negative factor. Since 4 × 8 = 32, each product will be –32.

LESSON 2-2

Practice and Problem Solving: A/B

1. –12
2. 19
3. –3
4. –4
5. 11
6. –8.75
7. –5
8. –10
9. –1
10. 32 ÷ (–4)
11. $\frac{-30}{6} + (-8)$
12. 12 ÷ (–3) + (–14)4
13. $3,000 ÷ 40 = $75; $75 – $40 = $35
14. a. –240 ÷ (–15) = 16; 16 weeks
    b. 20 × $15 = $300; $300 – $245 = $55

Practice and Problem Solving: C

1. –16
2. 2
3. $3\frac{2}{3}$
4. +2 produces +2; +3 produces +6.
5. +2 produces +2.
6. None of the integers from –3 to 3 produces a positive, even integer.

7. +1 produces +2.
8. –16 ÷ 4 = –4; –4 points for each penalty
9. a. 58°F; 70°F – (6 yd)(2°F/yd) = 70°F – 12°F = 58°F; from 6 yd to 15 yd deep, the temperature is constant, so at 10 yd deep, the temperature is 58°F.

    b. 73°F; 50 ft = $16\frac{2}{3}$ yd below the surface; at 15 yd below the surface, the temperature is 58°F. But, from 15 yd to 20 yd the temperature increases 3°F per ft. $16\frac{2}{3}$ yd is $16\frac{2}{3}$ – 15 or $1\frac{2}{3}$ yd, which is 5 ft, so the temperature there is 58°F + (5 ft)(3°F/ft) or 58°F + 15°F = 73°F.

    c. 70°F – (6 yd)(2°F/yd) + (5)(3 ft)(3°F) = 103°F at the spring source

Practice and Problem Solving: D

1. 5
2. –9
3. –4
4. >
5. <
6. =
7. –45 ÷ 5 = –9
8. $\frac{55}{-11} = -5$
9. –38 ÷ 19 = –2
10. –4 ÷ –2 = 2
11. –24 ÷ 4 = –6; On average, each investor lost 6%.
12. –760 ÷ 4 = –190; On average, the temperature dropped 190°/h.
13. –5,100 ÷ 3 = –1,700; On average, the car's value decreased $1,700/yr.

Reteach

1. right; negative; negative
2. left; negative; positive
3. left; positive; negative

4.

Divisor	Dividend	Quotient
+	+	+
−	+	−
+	−	−
−	−	+

Reading Strategies

1. 3,600 km; 225 kmh; 16 hours
2. 35 degrees; 7 hours; 5 degrees per hour
3. 1,600 liters; 2-liters/bottle; 800 bottles
4. Answers will vary. Sample answers: "102 divided by negative 6." "Negative 6 goes into 102 how many times?."
5. Answers will vary. Sample answers: "The opposite of 17 divided into negative 221." "Negative 221 divided by negative 17."

Success for English Learners

1. $\dfrac{-210}{70} = -3$
2. $300\overline{)-4200} = -14$
3. $-50 \div 10 = -5$
4. $27\overline{)54} = 2$
5. +; 1
6. −; −32
7. −; −4
8. +; 5

LESSON 2-3

Practice and Problem Solving: A/B

1. 14
2. −16
3. −27
4. 15
5. −29
6. −40
7. >
8. >
9. 15(2 − 5) = −45; $45 less

10. (−12) + (−11) + (−8) = −31; falls by 31 ft
11. 5(3) + 2(−12) = −9; 9-yd loss
12. 7(−3) + (−12) + 5 = −28; $28 less

Practice and Problem Solving: C

1. +10
2. −18
3. +104
4. −28
5. 8(−2 + 9 + 6)
6. gained $68
7. 4(−45) + 112 = −68; 68 ft lower
8. 17(5) + 5(−2) + 8 = 83; She got an 83.
9. 3(−20) + 2(−12) + (−42) + 57 − 15 = −84; $84 less
10. a. Positive, because there is an even number of negative factors.

    b. 2,880

Practice and Problem Solving: D

1. 15 + (−12); 3
2. 15 + 18; 33
3. −7 + 23; 16
4. 52 + (−5); 47
5. (−50) + (−112) + (−46) = −208; He has $208 less.
6. 8 + (−4) + 7 + 3 + (−11) = 3; They had a 3-yd gain.
7. 4(−2) + 2(−1) + 3 = −7; She had $7 less.
8. 3(−4) + 4(−2) = −20; The water was 20 in. lower.

Reteach

1. multiplication
2. addition
3. division
4. addition
5. multiplication
6. division
7. multiplication
8. subtraction
9. −1
10. −31

11. –31

12. 33

13. –62

14. –48

Reading Strategies

1. paid; gave; $4(-3) + 7 = -12 + 7 = -5$; $5 less

2. below; $-48 \div 4 = -12$; 12 feet below the surface

3. lost; gained; $3(-5) + 32 = -15 + 32 = 17$; gained 17 yards

Success for English Learners

1. 39

2. –5

3. 6

4. a. Sample answer: Tom bought 3 DVDs for $20 each. He had a coupon for $5 off one DVD. After his purchase, what is the change in the amount of money Tom has?

   b. $-3(20) + 5 = -60 + 5 = -55$; Tom has $55 less now.

MODULE 2 Challenge

1. Sample answer:

   $81 \div (-9) + (-4) - 17 + (4)(3) + 1$

   $-9 + (-4) - 17 + 12 + 1$

   $-13 - 17 + 12 + 1$

   $-30 + 12 + 1$

   $-18 + 1$

   -17

2. Sample answer: Play with 2–4 players. Shuffle the integer cards and deal them out. Place the operations card face-up on the table. One player starts making an expression by placing one card on the table. The next player can choose an operation card and an integer card from his/her hand and extend the expression. Each player does the same until the cards are gone or one player wins. To win, a player makes the expression equal to 0.

3. Sample answer:

   First find multiplication and division signs and do these operations first.

   1. Multiply $(-4)(7) = -28$. The product is negative because one of the factors is negative.

      $(-8) + (-3) + (-28) \div 14 + 9(-2)$

   2. Divide $(-28) \div 14 = -2$. The quotient is negative because the dividend is negative and the divisor is positive.

      $(-8) + (-3) + (-2) + 9(-2)$

   3. Multiply $(9)(-2) = -18$. Same reason as step 1.

      $(-8) + (-3) + (-2) + (-18)$

      Now go back and add and subtract from left to right.

   4. $(-8) + (-3) = (-11)$ because you are adding two negative numbers.

      $(-11) + (-2) + (-18)$

   5. $(-11) + (-2) = (-13)$, for the same reason. $(-13) + (-18)$

   6. $(-13) + (-18) = (-31)$

MODULE 3 Rational Numbers

LESSON 3-1

Practice and Problem Solving: A/B

1. 0.95

2. –0.125

3. 3.4

4. –0.777... or $0.\overline{7}$

5. 0.7333... or $0.7\overline{3}$

6. 2.666... or $2.\overline{6}$

7. $\frac{29}{9}$; 3.222...; repeating or $3.\overline{2}$

8. $\frac{301}{20}$; 15.05; terminating

9. $-\frac{53}{10}$; –5.3; terminating

10. a. Answers may vary. Sample answer:
$2\frac{3}{4}$, 2.75; $3\frac{2}{4}$, 3.5

    b. Answers may vary. Sample answer:
$4\frac{2}{3}$, 4.666... or $4.\overline{6}$

11. They all convert to terminating decimals.

Practice and Problem Solving: C

1. $\frac{25}{18}$; 1.3888... or $1.3\overline{8}$; repeating

2. $\frac{200}{15}$; 13.333... or $13.\overline{3}$; repeating

3. Possible answer: $\frac{5}{20}$, $\frac{18}{20}$, $\frac{3}{20}$; the decimals are 0.25, 0.9, 0.15. They terminate because a rational number with 20 in the denominator is equivalent to a rational number with 100 in the denominator, which always terminates.

4. Possible answer: $\frac{30}{15} = 2.0$; $\frac{5}{15} = 0.333...$ or $0.\overline{3}$; To find a repeating decimal, select a multiple of 5 that is less than 15. To find a terminating decimal, select a numerator that is a multiple of 15.

5. Possible answer: Yes; $\frac{1.5}{7.5} = \frac{15}{75}$, which is written as a ratio of two integers; $\frac{15}{75} = 0.2$

Practice and Problem Solving: D

1. 0.65; terminating

2. 4.666... or $4.\overline{6}$; repeating

3. 0.555... or $0.\overline{5}$; repeating

4. 3.833... or $3.8\overline{3}$; repeating

5. 8.75; terminating

6. 10.625; terminating

7. 1.3125

8. 7.3125

9. 26.3125

10. 1.266... or $1.2\overline{6}$

11. 17.266... or $17.2\overline{6}$

12. 23.266... or $23.2\overline{6}$

Reteach

1. $\frac{3}{4} = 0.75$ so $7\frac{3}{4} = 7.75$

2. $\frac{5}{6} = 0.833...$ or $0.8\overline{3}$ so $11\frac{5}{6} = 11.833...$ or $11.8\overline{3}$

3. $\frac{3}{10} = 0.3$ so $12\frac{3}{10} = 12.3$

4. $\frac{5}{18} = 0.277...$ or $0.2\overline{7}$ so $8\frac{5}{18} = 8.277...$ or $8.2\overline{7}$

5. Sample answer:
Method 1: Start with the fraction part.
$\frac{2}{9} = 0.222...$ or $0.\overline{2}$ so $9\frac{2}{9} = 9.222...$ or $9.\overline{2}$

Method 2: $9\frac{2}{9} = \frac{83}{9}$. Using long division, $\frac{83}{9} = 9.222...$ or $9.\overline{2}$; the results agree.

6. Sample answer:
Method 1: Start with the fraction part.
$\frac{5}{8} = 0.625$ so $21\frac{5}{8} = 21.625$.

Method 2: $21\frac{5}{8} = \frac{173}{8}$. Using long division, $\frac{173}{8} = 21.625$; the results agree.

Reading Strategies

1. Both −3 and 5 are integers.

2. 2 is an integer but 1.17 is not an integer (but that does not mean that $\frac{2}{1.17}$ is not a rational number).

3. 1 is an integer but $\frac{1}{3}$ is not an integer (but that does not mean that $\frac{1}{\frac{1}{3}}$ is not a rational number).

4. $\sqrt{2}$ is not an integer and $\sqrt{4}$ is not an integer (but $\sqrt{4}$ can be written as the integer 2).

5. $\dfrac{\sqrt{3}}{\sqrt{6}}$ cannot be written as a ratio of two integers.

6. $\dfrac{\sqrt{2}}{\sqrt{2}} = 1$, so it can be written as the ratio of two integers such as $\dfrac{1}{1}$ or $\dfrac{-3}{-3}$.

7. $\dfrac{\sqrt{4}}{\sqrt{25}} = \dfrac{2}{5}$, so it can be written as the ratio of two integers.

8. $\dfrac{\sqrt{1}}{2} = \dfrac{1}{2}$, so it can be written as the ratio of two integers.

Success for English Learners
1. D
2. B
3. Answers may vary. Sample answer:
   4.616161...; $4.\overline{61}$

LESSON 3-2

Practice and Problem Solving: A/B
1. 1
2. −7
3. 9
4. $-2\dfrac{1}{2}$
5. $\dfrac{1}{9}$
6. −8.4
7. $-5\dfrac{1}{2}$
8. −3.1
9. $-\dfrac{11}{20}$
10. −3.3
11. 2.46
12. −1.85
13. −6.85
14. $-3\dfrac{1}{8}$
15. $3.75

16. gain of 6
17. $6.85
18. 3.8 mi from his house

Practice and Problem Solving: C
1. 4
2. $2\dfrac{16}{45}$
3. $8\dfrac{19}{45}$
4. −7.6
5. $-2\dfrac{1}{8}$
6. −1.13
7. $-\dfrac{59}{180}$
8. 0
9. 9.929
10. −2.278
11. −1.75
12. $1\dfrac{3}{23}$
13. $8.07
14. $5.57
15. 5 in.

Practice and Problem Solving: D
1. 5
2. −1
3. −8
4. 3
5. 8
6. −6
7. 0.5
8. −2.0
9. 2
10. $-\dfrac{1}{2}$
11. 2
12. 0
13. 4

14. $2\dfrac{1}{3}$

15. $\dfrac{3}{4}$

16. −3.4

17. −3.2

18. −0.5

19. $-1\dfrac{1}{2}$

20. −3

21. −0.9

Reteach

1. 2

2. −5

3. −7

4. 0.6

5. 4.7

6. −6

7. $\dfrac{3}{5}$

8. $-1\dfrac{2}{3}$

9. $-\dfrac{1}{2}$

Reading Strategies

1. 0

2. to the right; 6

3. to the left; 4

4. 0

5. to the left; 5.5

6. to the left; 3

Success for English Learners

1. Answers will vary. Sample answer: so the digits of the same place value get added together

2. the total number of slices of pizza

LESSON 3-3

Practice and Problem Solving: A/B

1. −9

2. 9

3. 9

4. $-5\dfrac{1}{2}$

5. $-\dfrac{2}{7}$

6. 1.2

7. $\dfrac{3}{4}$

8. −3.7

9. $-5\dfrac{1}{2}$

10. 8.3

11. −9.08

12. 3.75

13. −6.2

14. $-1\dfrac{3}{5}$

15. −4.1°C

16. $1\dfrac{3}{5}$ m

Practice and Problem Solving: C

1. $-6\dfrac{2}{3}$

2. $1\dfrac{1}{21}$

3. −10

4. −7.2

5. $-2\dfrac{1}{8}$

6. −12.179

7. $-1\dfrac{5}{9}$

8. 0.36

9. −13.19

10. −4.35

11. −1.05

12. −7

13. 3.55

14. Alex by 7.1 points

15. 7°C

Practice and Problem Solving: D

1. 2

2. 6

3. −3

4. −7

5. −3

6. 8

7. 1.5

8. −3

9. −1.5

10. $1\frac{1}{2}$

11. −1

12. $-1\frac{1}{2}$

13. 7

14. $-\frac{4}{3}$ or $-1\frac{1}{3}$

15. $-\frac{1}{2}$

16. 1.4

17. −2.2

18. −7.8

19. −2

20. −6.5

21. −1

Reteach

1. a. 5

   b. −1

   c. 20

2. a. negative

   b. 2

   c. −2

3. 40

4. −3

5. −26

6. 4.2

7. 2

8. −3.25

9. 1

10. −2

11. $-\frac{5}{4}$

Reading Strategies

1. Sample answer: One number is placed in each square.

2. as a placeholder to show that there is no number in that place

3.

4	0	•	3	
−	6	•	5	4

4. yes; in the hundredths place of the first number

5. 33.76

Success for English Learners

1. −9

2. You are not adding or subtracting −4, you are subtracting 3 from −4.

3. No, in 3 − 5 you are subtracting 5 (or adding −5) to 3. In 5 − 3 you are subtracting 3 from 5.

4. Find a common denominator

5. $\frac{2}{15}$

LESSON 3-4

Practice and Problem Solving: A/B

1. −2

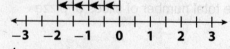

2. $3\frac{1}{3}$

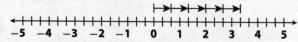

3. –6.2

4. –21.6

5. –19.8

6. 16.8

7. 36

8. –2.1

9. –8.2

10. 31.5

11. –20

12. $-\dfrac{4}{9}$

13. 9

14. $\dfrac{1}{2}$

15. $12\left(\dfrac{3}{4}\right) = 9$; 9 yards

16. $\left(\dfrac{1}{4}\right)\left(\dfrac{2}{3}\right)\left(\dfrac{3}{5}\right) = \dfrac{1}{10}$; $\dfrac{1}{10}$ m³

17. (–3 °F/half hour) × (2 half hours/hour) × 4 hours = –24 °F; 75 °F – 24 °F = 51 °F

Practice and Problem Solving: C

1. <; The product of 3 positive numbers, each of which is less than 1, is less than 1.

2. <; The product of 3 negative numbers is a negative number.

3. >; The product of 3 positive numbers is greater than the product of the opposite of each of the positive numbers.

4. <; the product of a positive and a negative number is less than 0.

5. False; A negative number raised to an even power is a positive number.

6. True; A number that is greater than 1 raised to a positive power is greater than 1.

7. False; A positive number that is less than one raised to a power is less than 1.

8. $V_1 = \dfrac{4}{3}\pi\left(\dfrac{1}{2}\right)^3 = \dfrac{4\pi}{24} = \dfrac{\pi}{6}$ ft³;

   $V_2 = \dfrac{4}{3}\pi\left(\dfrac{3}{4}\right)^3 = \dfrac{108\pi}{192} = \dfrac{9\pi}{16}$ ft³; $V_2 > V_1$,

   since $\dfrac{9\pi}{16} = 0.5625\pi$ and $\dfrac{\pi}{6} = 0.1\overline{6}\pi$.

9. $V = \dfrac{4}{3}\pi r^3$. If r becomes $\dfrac{2r}{3}$, then

   $V_2 = \dfrac{4}{3}\pi\left(\dfrac{2r}{3}\right)^3 = \dfrac{8}{27}\left(\dfrac{4}{3}\pi r^3\right)$. Therefore, if

   the radius is reduced to one third of its

   original value, the volume is $\dfrac{8}{27}$ or 0.296

   of the original volume.

Practice and Problem Solving: D

1. $\left(-\dfrac{1}{2}\right); \left(-\dfrac{1}{2}\right); \left(-\dfrac{1}{2}\right); \left(-\dfrac{1}{2}\right); \left(-\dfrac{1}{2}\right);$

   $\left(-\dfrac{1}{2}\right); -\dfrac{6}{2}$ or –3

2. $\left(-\dfrac{2}{3}\right); \left(-\dfrac{2}{3}\right); \left(-\dfrac{2}{3}\right); \dfrac{6}{3}$ or 2

3. Answers may vary. Sample answer:

   $4\left(-\dfrac{5}{8}\right); \dfrac{20}{8}$ or $\dfrac{5}{2}$ or $-2\dfrac{1}{2}$

4. Answers may vary. Sample answer:
   2(–2.5); –5

5. Answers may vary. Sample answer:

   $3\left(-\dfrac{2}{9}\right); -\dfrac{2}{3}$

6. $-\dfrac{1}{4} \times \left(\dfrac{-6}{25}\right) = \dfrac{6}{100} = \dfrac{3}{50}$ or 0.06

7. $4 \times 2.5 \times 0.8 = 10 \times 0.8 = 8$

8. a. (–3.5) + (–3.5) + (–3.5) + (–3.5) + (–3.5) = –17.5 m; –17.5 m

   b. 5 × (–3.5) = –17.5; –17.5 m

Reteach

1. 6; right; $\dfrac{6}{4}$; $1\dfrac{1}{2}$

2. 8 times; 26.4; 26.4

3. 5 times; 23; 23

Reading Strategies

1. 4
2. −5.25
3. $-2\dfrac{2}{5}$

Success for English Learners

1. −8.8
2. −3
3. −9.9
4. −9.9
5. 12
6. $\dfrac{12}{7}$ or $1\dfrac{5}{7}$
7. 4

LESSON 3-5

Practice and Problem Solving: A/B

1. $-\dfrac{1}{6}$
2. 8
3. $\dfrac{1}{12}$
4. 0.35
5. −7.5
6. 0.25
7. $\dfrac{2}{3}$
8. $-\dfrac{4}{3}$
9. $-\dfrac{9}{20}$
10. 6
11. −1.75
12. 2
13. −1
14. $\dfrac{3}{14}$
15. $\dfrac{1}{98}$
16. $8 \div \dfrac{1}{4}$; 32 packets

17. $\dfrac{3}{4} \div 12$; $\dfrac{1}{16}$ h
18. $\dfrac{35}{1.25}$; 28 pieces
19. $4\dfrac{1}{8} \div 2\dfrac{1}{6} = \dfrac{99}{52}$ or $1\dfrac{47}{52}$ tons per acre

Practice and Problem Solving: C

1. $\dfrac{1}{-5}$ and $-\dfrac{1}{5}$
2. $\dfrac{-7}{30}$ and $\dfrac{7}{-30}$
3. $\dfrac{-1}{2}$ and $-\dfrac{1}{2}$
4. =; $\dfrac{10}{3}$; $\dfrac{10}{3}$
5. <; $(4.5 \div 0.5) \div 3 = 3$; $4.5 \div (0.5 \div 3) = 27$
6. >; $\left(6 \div -\dfrac{1}{5}\right) \times -\dfrac{4}{3} = 40$;

   $6 \div \left(-\dfrac{1}{5} \times -\dfrac{4}{3}\right) = 22.5$
7. =; −123.75; −123.75
8. $\dfrac{0.4}{-0.625} = -0.64$
9. $\dfrac{-5.4}{-0.3125} = 17.28$
10. $\dfrac{0.25}{0.6} = 0.41\overline{6}$
11. $\dfrac{\left(1\dfrac{3}{4}\right)}{\dfrac{1}{4}} = 7$; $\dfrac{1.75}{0.25} = 7$
12. $\dfrac{\left(1\dfrac{1}{2}\right)}{\dfrac{1}{2}} = 3$; $\dfrac{1.5}{0.5} = 3$
13. $\dfrac{\left(1\dfrac{3}{8}\right)}{\dfrac{5}{8}} = 2\dfrac{1}{5}$; $\dfrac{1.375}{0.625} = 2.2$
14. The quotient will be less than 7, 3, and 2.2 but greater than 1. It decreases as the denominators of the fractions increase.

Practice and Problem Solving: D

1. $\frac{4}{3}$; -8

2. $\frac{1}{8}$; $\frac{1}{10}$

3. $\frac{-4}{7}$; $\frac{1}{2}$

4. $\frac{8}{7}$; $\frac{-40}{21} = -1\frac{19}{20}$

5. $\frac{9}{4}$; $\frac{-9}{2}$

6. $\frac{1}{4}$; $-1\frac{3}{16}$

7. $\frac{1}{40}$

8. $\frac{-21}{8} = -2\frac{5}{8}$

9. $\frac{7}{2} = 3\frac{1}{2}$

10. 0.40; 0.16

11. 0.30; -15.83

12. 8.0; 3.2

13. a. $6\frac{3}{4} \div \frac{1}{8}$

   b. 54 markers

   c. The town spaced the markers every eighth of a mile. They used 54 markers. Since $6\frac{3}{4}$ is evenly divisible by $\frac{1}{8}$, they used a whole number of markers.

Reteach

1. +

2. –

3. –

4. +

5. $-\frac{1}{7} \div -\frac{5}{9} = -\frac{1}{7} \times -\frac{9}{5}$; $-\frac{1}{7} \times -\frac{9}{5} = \frac{-9}{-35}$; $\frac{-9}{-35} = \frac{9}{35}$.

   A negative divided by a negative is positive.

6. $\frac{7}{8} \div \frac{8}{9} = \frac{7}{8} \times \frac{9}{8}$; $\frac{7}{8} \times \frac{9}{8} = \frac{63}{64}$; $\frac{63}{64}$ is positive since a positive divided by a positive is positive.

Reading Strategies

1. +
2. –
3. +
4. –
5. –
6. +
7. –
8. +
9. +
10. –
11. +
12. –
13. –
14. –
15. +

Success for English Learners

1. $2\frac{7}{88}$

2. 2

LESSON 3-6
Practice and Problem Solving: A/B

1. Answers may vary. Sample answer: One estimate would be 4 times 6 or 24 feet long. The actual answer is greater than 24 feet.

2. Answers may vary. Sample answer: 3 liters divided by a third of a liter makes about 9 servings. The actual answer is more than 9 servings.

3. Answers may vary. Sample answer: The perimeter is greater than 15 inches.

4. Answers may vary. Sample answer: 3-gram eggs would be 36 grams, but 4 gram eggs would be 48 grams, so a dozen 3.5-gram eggs should be about 42 grams.

5. Answers may vary. Sample answer:
8 divided by one half is 16, so the number of peas is greater than 16.

6. These numbers can be used as they are since there would be 8 drops in a milliliter, or 240 drops in 30 milliliters.

7. The second strip is 0.25 longer than 3.5, or 3.5 + 0.875, or 4.375 yards. The length of the third strip can be written as 6.25, so the total length is 3.5 + 4.375 + 6.25, or 14.125 yards. 0.125 yards is one eighth of a yard, so the answer might be written as $14\frac{1}{8}$ yd.

Practice and Problem Solving: C

1. $29\frac{37}{50}$ m/s $\times$ 3,600 s/h = 107,064 mi

2. $29\frac{37}{50} - 8\frac{3}{25} = 29\frac{37}{50} - 8\frac{6}{50} = 21\frac{31}{50}$ mi/s

3. 32,508 mi $\div$ $6\frac{2}{100}$ mi/s = 5,400 s

4. $21\frac{19}{25}$ mi/s $\times$ 60 s/min = $1,305\frac{3}{5}$ mi/min

Practice and Problem Solving: D

1. Bottles, paper, and cardboard boxes were $\frac{11}{20}$ of the total amount of recycled material collected by the middle school.

2. $\frac{1}{2} = \frac{3}{6}$, $\frac{1}{3} = \frac{2}{6}$; $\frac{3}{6} + \frac{2}{6} = \frac{5}{6}$; $\frac{5}{6}$ of the family budget

3. $\frac{1}{6} = \frac{4}{24}$, $\frac{3}{8} = \frac{9}{24}$; $\frac{4}{24} + \frac{9}{24} = \frac{13}{24}$; $1 = \frac{24}{24}$; $\frac{24}{24} - \frac{13}{24} = \frac{11}{24}$ of the budget

Reteach

1. $11\frac{2}{5}$ oz

2. 8 h

3. $15\frac{2}{5}$ t

4. $1\frac{1}{16}$ lb

Reading Strategies

1. $2\frac{1}{2}$ feet

2. $\frac{1}{2}$ foot

3. 5 servings

4. 5

5. 5 ft

6. 5

7. Answers may vary, but students should observe that the answers are the same, and divisor is the reciprocal of the factor 2.

Success for English Learners

1. the number of pieces of pizza

2. Find the common denominator.

3. Add the numerators, and write the sum over the common denominator.

MODULE 3 Challenge

1. Calculate the daily temperature change as shown.

Daily Temperature Change (°C)

City	Monday to Tuesday	Tuesday to Wednesday	Wednesday to Thursday	Thursday to Friday
City A	$2\frac{1}{4} - \left(-\frac{1}{8}\right) = 2\frac{3}{8}$	$-3\frac{1}{2} - 2\frac{1}{4} = -5\frac{3}{4}$	$5\frac{4}{5} - \left(-3\frac{1}{2}\right) = 9\frac{3}{10}$	$-12\frac{1}{2} - 5\frac{4}{5} = -18\frac{3}{10}$
City B	$-1\frac{3}{5} - 4\frac{1}{5} = -5\frac{4}{5}$	$-8\frac{1}{10} - 1\frac{3}{5} = -6\frac{1}{2}$	$11\frac{1}{5} - \left(-8\frac{1}{10}\right) = 19\frac{3}{10}$	$3\frac{3}{10} - 11\frac{1}{5} = -7\frac{9}{10}$
City C	$2\frac{5}{6} - 11\frac{1}{3} = -8\frac{1}{2}$	$-3\frac{2}{3} - 2\frac{5}{6} = -6\frac{1}{2}$	$-9\frac{1}{6} - \left(-3\frac{2}{3}\right) = -5\frac{1}{2}$	$2\frac{1}{3} - \left(-9\frac{1}{6}\right) = 11\frac{1}{2}$

Find the sum of the daily temperature changes for each city.

City A: $2\dfrac{3}{8} + -5\dfrac{3}{4} + 9\dfrac{3}{10} - 18\dfrac{3}{10} = -12\dfrac{3}{8}$

City B: $-5\dfrac{4}{5} + \left(-6\dfrac{1}{2}\right) + 19\dfrac{3}{10} + \left(-7\dfrac{9}{10}\right) = -\dfrac{9}{10}$

City C: $-8\dfrac{1}{2} + -6\dfrac{1}{2} + -5\dfrac{1}{2} + 11\dfrac{1}{2} = -9$

The greatest temperature volatility is in City B.

2. There are 24 ways to place the four operations in the three different boxes:

$2 \boxed{+} -\dfrac{1}{8} \boxed{-} -10 \boxed{\times} 16 = 161.875$; $2 \boxed{+} -\dfrac{1}{8} \boxed{-} -10 \boxed{\div} 16 = 2.5$;

$2 \boxed{+} -\dfrac{1}{8} \boxed{\times} -10 \boxed{-} 16 = -12.75$; $2 \boxed{+} -\dfrac{1}{8} \boxed{\times} -10 \boxed{\div} 16 = 2.078125$;

$2 \boxed{+} -\dfrac{1}{8} \boxed{\div} -10 \boxed{-} 16 = -13.9875$; $2 \boxed{+} -\dfrac{1}{8} \boxed{\div} -10 \boxed{\times} 16 = 2.2$;

$2 \boxed{-} -\dfrac{1}{8} \boxed{+} -10 \boxed{\times} 16 = -157.875$; $2 \boxed{-} -\dfrac{1}{8} \boxed{+} -10 \boxed{\div} 16 = 1.5$;

$2 \boxed{-} -\dfrac{1}{8} \boxed{\times} -10 \boxed{+} 16 = 16.75$; $2 \boxed{-} -\dfrac{1}{8} \boxed{\times} -10 \boxed{\div} 16 = 1.921875$;

$2 \boxed{-} -\dfrac{1}{8} \boxed{\div} -10 \boxed{+} 16 = 17.9875$; $2 \boxed{-} -\dfrac{1}{8} \boxed{\div} -10 \boxed{\times} 16 = 1.8$;

$2 \boxed{\times} -\dfrac{1}{8} \boxed{+} -10 \boxed{-} 16 = -26.25$; $2 \boxed{\times} -\dfrac{1}{8} \boxed{+} -10 \boxed{\div} 16 = -0.875$;

$2 \boxed{\times} -\dfrac{1}{8} \boxed{-} -10 \boxed{+} 16 = 25.75$; $2 \boxed{\times} -\dfrac{1}{8} \boxed{-} -10 \boxed{\div} 16 = 0.375$;

$2 \boxed{\times} -\dfrac{1}{8} \boxed{\div} -10 \boxed{+} 16 = 16.025$; $2 \boxed{\times} -\dfrac{1}{8} \boxed{\div} -10 \boxed{-} 16 = -15.975$;

$2 \boxed{\div} -\dfrac{1}{8} \boxed{+} -10 \boxed{-} 16 = -26.25$; $2 \boxed{\div} -\dfrac{1}{8} \boxed{+} -10 \boxed{\times} 16 = -176$;

$2 \boxed{\div} -\dfrac{1}{8} \boxed{-} -10 \boxed{+} 16 = 10$; $2 \boxed{\div} -\dfrac{1}{8} \boxed{-} -10 \boxed{\times} 16 = 144$;

$2 \boxed{\div} -\dfrac{1}{8} \boxed{\times} -10 \boxed{+} 16 = 176$; $2 \boxed{\div} -\dfrac{1}{8} \boxed{\times} -10 \boxed{-} 16 = 144$.

$2 \boxed{\div} -\dfrac{1}{8} \boxed{\times} -10 \boxed{+} 16 = 176$ is the greatest possible value of the expression. To obtain the answer without writing out all 24 possibilities, students can notice that dividing by a fraction will increase the value of the expression and that multiplying two negatives will create a positive.

UNIT 2: Rates and Proportional Relationships

MODULE 4 Rates and Proportionality

LESSON 4-1

Practice and Problem Solving: A/B

1. 2 eggs per batch
2. 53 mph
3. $8/h
4. 14 points per game
5. $0.20/oz
6. $1\frac{3}{4}$ gal/h
7. $\frac{1}{2}$ ft/min
8. Food A: 200 cal/serving; Food B: 375 cal/serving; Food A has fewer calories per serving.

Practice and Problem Solving: C

1. $\frac{1}{2}$ ac/h
2. $2\frac{1}{5}$ mph
3. $\frac{1}{80}$ of a wall
4. $\frac{2}{9}$ oz
5. $\dfrac{5\frac{1}{2}\text{ c}}{1\frac{9}{16}\text{ lb}} = \dfrac{88}{25} = \dfrac{3.52\text{ c}}{1\text{ lb}} = \dfrac{35.2\text{ c}}{10\text{ lb}}$; 35.2 > 35, so there are more than 35 cups of flour in 10 lb of flour.
6. Tank #1 is filling at a rate of 0.892857... gallons per hour while tank #2 is filling at a rate of $0.8\overline{3}$ gallons per hour. Since $0.892857... > 0.8\overline{3}$, tank #1 is filling faster.

Practice and Problem Solving: D

1. 3; 3
2. 45; 45
3. $9/h
4. $0.09/oz
5. $\dfrac{\frac{3}{4}\text{ oz}}{3\text{h}} = \dfrac{3}{4} \div \dfrac{3}{1} = \dfrac{3}{4} \times \dfrac{1}{3} = \dfrac{\frac{1}{4}\text{ oz}}{1\text{ h}}$; $\frac{1}{4}$ oz/h
6. $\frac{3}{10}$ mi/min
7. $\dfrac{150\text{ cal}}{\frac{3}{4}\text{ serving}} = \dfrac{150}{1} \div \dfrac{3}{4}$

   $= \dfrac{150}{1} \times \dfrac{4}{3} = \dfrac{200\text{ cal}}{1\text{ serving}}$;

   200 cal/serving

Reteach

1. $\dfrac{70\text{ students}}{2\text{ teachers}}$
2. $\dfrac{3\text{ books}}{2\text{ mo}}$
3. $\dfrac{\$52}{4\text{ h}}$
4. $\dfrac{28\text{ patients}}{2\text{ nurses}} = \dfrac{28 \div 2}{2 \div 2} = \dfrac{14\text{ patients}}{1\text{ nurse}}$
5. $\dfrac{5\text{ qt}}{2\text{ lb}} = \dfrac{5 \div 2}{2 \div 2} = \dfrac{2.5\text{ qt}}{1\text{ lb}}$
6. $\dfrac{3\text{ oz}}{\frac{3}{4}\text{ c}} = 3 \div \dfrac{3}{4} = \dfrac{3}{1} \times \dfrac{4}{3} = \dfrac{4\text{ oz}}{1\text{ c}}$
7. $\dfrac{3\frac{2}{3}\text{ ft}}{\frac{11}{60}\text{ h}} = 3\dfrac{2}{3} \div \dfrac{11}{60} = \dfrac{11}{3} \times \dfrac{60}{11} = \dfrac{20\text{ ft}}{1\text{ h}}$

Reading Strategies

1. No; It does not compare values that have different units.
2. Yes; It compares a number of yards to a number of seconds.

3. It compares miles to gallons.

4. Yes

5. No; $\dfrac{25 \text{ mi}}{1 \text{ gal}}$

6. No; $\dfrac{800 \text{ ft}^2}{1 \text{ h}}$

7. No; $\dfrac{\frac{2}{45} \text{ lb}}{1 \text{ min}}$ or $\dfrac{\frac{8}{3} \text{ lb}}{1 \text{ h}}$

Success for English Learners

1. 3 miles per hour or $\dfrac{3 \text{ mi}}{1 \text{ h}}$

2. $3\dfrac{3}{4}$ miles per hour or $\dfrac{3\frac{3}{4} \text{ mi}}{1 \text{ h}}$

3. Briana has the faster speed per hour.

LESSON 4-2

Practice and Problem Solving: A/B

1. a. yes

  b. Sample answer: $c = 27t$

  c. t

  d. c

2. a. yes

  b. Sample answer: $c = 4.35w$

  c. w

  d. c

3. not proportional

4. yes; Sample answers: $d = 40t$; d = distance; t = time

5. $k = \dfrac{1}{3}$; Sample answers: $b = \dfrac{1}{3}p$; b = boxes; p = pens

6. $k = 6$; Sample answers: $m = 6p$; m = muffins; p = packs

7. a.

Days	1	2	3	4	5
Hours	24	48	72	96	120

  b. yes

  c. Sample answer: $h = 24d$ where is d is the number of days and h is the number of hours

Practice and Problem Solving: C

1. a.

Number of Tickets	1	2	3	4	5
Total Cost ($)	27	54	81	108	135

  b. 27

  c. Sample answer: $c = 27t$

2. 32

3. yes; Sample answers: $p = 35h$; h is number of hours; p is pages read

4. yes; Sample answers: $y = 6x$; x is number of ounces; y is grams of protein

5. yes; Sample answers: $c = 4.5w$; w is weight; c is total cost

6. no; You cannot write an equation for the pairs in the table as they are not proportional.

Practice and Problem Solving: D

1. a. yes

  b. $y = 6x$

  c. x

  d. y

2. a. yes

  b. $c = 3h$

  c. h

  d. c

3. yes; Sample answer: $c = 0.75w$; w = weight (oz); c = total cost

4. not proportional

5. $k = \dfrac{1}{5}$; Sample answer: $b = \dfrac{1}{5}a$; a = apples; b = bags

6. $k = 12$; Sample answer: $e = 12c$; c = cartons; e = eggs

Reteach

1. yes

2. $\dfrac{3}{1} = 3$; $\dfrac{6}{2} = 3$; $\dfrac{9}{3} = 3$; $\dfrac{12}{4} = 3$

3. Sample answer: $y = 3x$

4. 3

5. $y = 35x$

6. $y = 7x$

Reading Strategies

1. $\dfrac{3}{1} = 3$; $\dfrac{6}{2} = 3$; $\dfrac{9}{3} = 3$; $\dfrac{12}{4} = 3$

2. 3

3. yes

4. $\dfrac{35}{1}$

5. $\dfrac{4.35}{1}$

Success for English Learners

1.

◯	6	3	9	12	15
⬭	2	1	3	4	5

2. 3

LESSON 4-3

Practice and Problem Solving: A/B

1.

Time (h)	2	4	5	9
Pay ($)	16	32	40	72

Earnings are always 8 times the number of hours.

2.

Weight (lb)	2	3	6	8
Price ($)	1.40	2.10	4.20	5.60

Cost is always 0.7 times the number of pounds.

3. Not proportional; The line will not pass through the origin.

4. Proportional; The line will pass through the origin.

5. The car uses 2 gal of fuel to travel 40 mi.

6. $y = 20x$, where x is the gallons of fuel used, y is the distance traveled (in miles), and k is the constant of proportionality

7. The graph for the compact car would be steeper.

Practice and Problem Solving: C

1. Employee B; Answers may vary. Sample answer: Employee A earns $7.50 per hour, and employee B earns $10 per hour, so employee B earns more money.

2. Employee A: 15 × $7.50 = $112.50; employee B: 15 × $10.00 = $150.00

3. Sample answer: $y = 8x$

4. Company A: proportional because a graph comparing months of service and total cost will form a line passing through the origin; Company B: not proportional because the line formed will not pass through the origin

5. Yes; $y = 2x$

6. Sample answer: Graph the points and analyze the graph. The graph of a proportional relationship is a line that passes through the origin.

Practice and Problem Solving: D

1. proportional; The cost is always 10 times the number of shirts.

2. proportional; The number of crayons is always 50 times the number of boxes.

3. proportional; The line will pass through the origin.

4. not proportional; The line will not pass through the origin.

5. $y = 6x$

6. $y = 4x$

7. $y = \dfrac{1}{3}x$

8. Use the point (1, 8) to find the constant of proportionality, 8 or $\dfrac{8}{1}$

Reteach

1. hours worked; pay (in dollars); Sample answer: (2, 14), $\dfrac{14}{2} = 7$; $y = 7x$

2. number of students; cost of admission (in dollars); Sample answer: (12, 24), $\dfrac{24}{12} = 2$; $y = 2x$

Reading Strategies

1. number of glasses filled and ounces of juice needed

2. The ounces of juice needed is 8 times the number of glasses filled.

3. the number of glasses filled

4. the ounces of juice needed

5. 16 ounces of juice are needed to fill 2 glasses.

6. (3, 24)

Success for English Learners

1. Constant of proportionality = $\dfrac{\text{change in } y\text{-values}}{\text{change in } x\text{-values}}$; The constant of proportionality is the ratio of the change in y-values to the change in x-values.

2. No; only lines that pass through (0, 0) represent proportional relationships.

MODULE 4 Challenge

Sample answers are given. You may also wish to have students make sketches to show their graphing explorations.

1. direct: straight line through (0, 0), makes 45° angle

   quadratic: curved line, starts at (0, 0), increases quickly as x increases

   indirect: y starts really large, decreases to (1, 1), continues getting smaller and smaller

2. direct: quadrants I and III

   quadratic: quadrants I and II

   indirect: quadrants I and III; $y = \dfrac{k}{x}$ does not include the value $x = 0$, since this is undefined.

3. direct: slope of the line increases, it gets steeper

   quadratic: the parabola gets skinnier

   indirect: the curves pull away from the origin

4. direct: quadrants II and IV

   quadratic: quadrants III and IV

   indirect: quadrants II and IV; $y = \dfrac{k}{x}$ does not include the value $x = 0$, since this is undefined.

MODULE 5 Proportions and Percent

LESSON 5-1

Practice and Problem Solving: A/B

1. 25%
2. 150%
3. 200%
4. 122%
5. 71%
6. 53%
7. 45%
8. 75%
9. 62%
10. 90%
11. 17%
12. 19%
13. $100
14. 128 bananas
15. 14 books
16. 65 companies
17. 12,600 miles
18. 639 points
19. 399 students
20. $12.87; $26.13
21. $40.80
22. $12,750

Practice and Problem Solving: C

1. a. 289

   b. 332

2. a. 47% increase, 28% decrease, 50% increase

   b. 20% increase, 17% increase, 10% increase

   c. Rodrigo received a bonus in weeks 2 and 4. Samantha received a bonus in week 3.

d. Neither Rodrigo nor Samantha met the goal of increasing sales by 15% each week.

3. 2.7%

Practice and Problem Solving: D

1. 40%
2. 300%
3. 90%
4. 75%
5. 81%
6. 75%
7. 33%
8. 67%
9. $27.50
10. 128 bananas
11. 50 books
12. 65 companies
13. 420 students
14. $27.30

Reteach

1. 14; 8; $\frac{14}{8}$; 175%
2. 9; 90; $\frac{9}{90}$; 10%
3. 75; 125; $\frac{75}{125}$; 60%
4. 340; 400; $\frac{340}{400}$; 85%
5. 25%
6. 95%
7. 80%
8. 40%
9. 200%
10. 5%

Reading Strategies

1. $50
2. decrease
3. in the denominator (or bottom part) of the fraction

4. 25
5. 20
6. $\frac{20}{25}$ = 0.8 × 100 = 80%; percent increase

Success for English Learners

1. A percent increase is when the amount increases or goes up. A percent decrease is when the amount decreases or goes down.
2. Sample answer: The height of a child from one year to the next.
3. Retail is the price for the customer. Wholesale is the amount that the store bought the item for.
4. wholesale price
5. Answers will vary. Sample answer: Mr. Jiro buys a pack of T-shirts for $4.95. He plans to sell them at an 80 percent increase. What is the selling price of each pack of T-shirts? ($4.95 • 80 = $3.96; selling price: $4.95 + $3.96 = $8.91.)

LESSON 5-2

Practice and Problem Solving: A/B

1. $0.30; $1.80
2. $1.30; $4.55
3. $2.40; $12.00
4. $9.75; $22.25
5. $42.90; $120.90
6. $4.49; $7.48
7. $57.20
8. $19.99
9. $35.70
10. $276.68
11. 0.57c or 0.57
12. 1 + 0.57c or 1.57c
13. $70.65
14. $25.65

Practice and Problem Solving: C

1. $89.99
2. $30

3. 50%

4. $90.75

5. $113.44

6. $76.00

7. 1.07*c*

8. 1.02*c*

9. Store B

Practice and Problem Solving: D

1. a. 0.40*p*

   b. *p* + 0.4*p*

   c. $78.40

   d. $22.40

2. $6; $36

3. $3.50; $13.50

4. $10; $50

5. $58.50

6. $21.35

7. $26.25

8. $276.25

9. *c* + 0.4*c*

Reteach

1. $45.00 + $9.00 = $54.00

2. $7.50 + $3.75 = $11.25

3. $1.25 + $1.00 = $2.25

4. $21.70 + $62.00 =$83.70

5. $150.00 – $60.00 = $90.00

6. $18.99 – $4.75 = $14.24

7. $95.00 – $9.50 = $85.50

8. $75.00 – $11.25 = $63.75

9. a. $3.15

   b. $2.52

Reading Strategies

1–4.

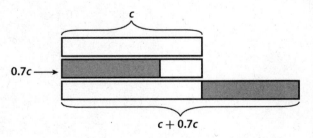

Retail price = Original cost + markup

$$= c + 07c$$

$$= 1.7c = 1.7(\$80) = \$136$$

1. the bar for the cost of a camera, *c*

2. the bar that shows the markup, 70% of *c*, or 0.7*c*

3. the original cost plus the markup, *c* + 0.7*c*.

4. $136

Success for English Learners

1. A markup is when the price increases or goes up. A markdown is when the price decreases or goes down.

2. The retail price is the original cost of an item plus a markup. The sales price is the original price of an item minus a markdown.

3. Answers will vary. Sample answer: A store buys shirts for $15. The store's markup is 50%. What is the retail price? ($22.50)

LESSON 5-3

Practice and Problem Solving: A/B

1.

Sale Amount	5% Sales Tax	Total Amount Paid
$67.50	$3.38	$70.88
$98.75	$4.94	$103.69
$399.79	$19.99	$419.78
$1250.00	$62.50	$1,312.50
$12,500.00	$625.00	$13,125.00

2.

Principal	Rate	Time	Interest Earned	New Balance
$300	3%	4 years	$36.00	$336.00
$450	5%	3 years	$67.50	$517.50
$500	4.5%	5 years	$112.50	$612.50
$675	8%	2 years	$108.00	$783.00

3. $1,250

4. salesperson A; $7,428.30

5. 18%

6. a. $780

   b. $900

   c. $450

   d. $300

   e. $570

Practice and Problem Solving: C

1.

Sale Amount	Tax	Amount of Tax	Total Cost
$49.95	8%	$4.00	$53.95
$128.60	5%	$6.43	$135.03
$499.99	7.5%	$37.50	$537.49
$2,599	4%	$103.96	$2,702.96
$12,499	7%	$874.93	$13,373.93

2.

Principal	Rate	Time	Interest Earned	New Balance
$2,400	3.5%	6 months	$42.00	$2,442.00
$45.00	4.9%	2 years	$4.41	$49.41
$9,460.12	5.5%	5 years	$2,601.51	$12,061.65
$3,923.87	2.2%	9 months	$64.74	$3,988.61

3. Jorge earned $8,046. Harris earned $8,493. Harris' commission rate is 9.5%.

4. The total at Big Box store comes to $47.88. The total online comes to $48.95. It is cheaper at the Big Box store.

5. The first item is full price: $100. The second item is half off: $50. The total comes to $150. A 50% discount on $200 would be $100.

Practice and Problem Solving: D

1.

Sale Amount	5% Sales Tax
$50	0.05 × $50 = 2.5 = $2.50
$120	0.05 × $120 = $6
$480	0.05 × $480 = $24
$2,240	0.05 × $2,240 = $112
$12,500	0.05 × $12,500 = $625

2.

Principal	Rate	Time	Interest Earned
$400	5%	2 years	$40
$950	10%	5 years	$475
$50	4%	1 year	$2
$1,000	8%	2 years	$160

3. 0.5 × 32 = 16; Karl is 16 years old.

4. 0.10 × 20 = 2.0; Jacquie saves $2 for referring a friend.

5. 0.15 × 8.40 = 1.26; Tyler's tip should be $1.26.

Reteach

1. $14.95

2. 6.5%

3. amount = $14.95 × 6.5% = $0.97

4. $14.95 + $0.97 = $15.92

Reading Strategies

1. $756

2. $68.06

3. $1,160.34

4. a. $800

   b. 4%

   c. 5 years

5. principal, rate, and time

Success for English Learners

1. $1,116

MODULE 5 Challenge

Possible solution steps are shown.

1. $\dfrac{30 \times 5{,}280 \times 12 \text{ m}}{39.37 \times 60 \times 60 \text{ s}} = 13.41 \text{ m/s}$

2. $2.3 \text{ km} \times \dfrac{1{,}000 \text{ m}}{1 \text{ km}} \times \dfrac{100 \text{ cm}}{1 \text{ m}} \times \dfrac{1 \text{ in.}}{2.54 \text{ cm}} = 90{,}551.2 \text{ in.}$

3. $\dfrac{67.3 \text{ ft}}{1 \text{ s}} \times \dfrac{12 \text{ in.}}{1 \text{ ft}} \times \dfrac{2.54 \text{ cm}}{1 \text{ in.}} \times \dfrac{1 \text{ m}}{100 \text{ cm}} \times \dfrac{1 \text{ km}}{1{,}000 \text{ m}} \times \dfrac{60 \text{ s}}{1 \text{ min}} \times \dfrac{60 \text{ min}}{1 \text{ h}} = 73.85 \text{ km/h}$

4. $\dfrac{750 \text{ ft}^3}{1 \text{ min}} \times \dfrac{1 \text{ gal}}{0.134 \text{ ft}^3} \times \dfrac{60 \text{ min}}{1 \text{ h}} = 335{,}820.9 \text{ gal/h}$

5. $130 \text{ ft} \times 274 \text{ ft} = 35{,}620 \text{ ft}^2$; $35{,}620 \text{ ft}^2 \times \dfrac{(12)^2 \text{ in.}^2}{1 \text{ ft}^2} \times \dfrac{(2.54)^2 \text{ cm}^2}{1 \text{ in.}^2} \times \dfrac{1 \text{ m}^2}{(100)^2 \text{ cm}^2} = 3{,}309.2 \text{ m}^2$

6. $9.6 \times 4.2 \times 15.6 = 628.992 \text{ m}^3$; $628.992 \text{ m}^3 \times \dfrac{(39.37)^3 \text{ in.}^3}{1 \text{ m}^3} \times \dfrac{1 \text{ ft}^3}{(12)^3 \text{ in.}^3} \times \dfrac{1 \text{ yd}^3}{(3)^3 \text{ ft}^3} = 822.69 \text{ yd}^3$

UNIT 3: Expressions, Equations, and Inequalities

MODULE 6 Expressions and Equations

LESSON 6-1

Practice and Problem Solving: A/B

1. $p + 4$
2. $3L - 5$
3. Answers will vary. Sample answer: $25 minus six-tenths of x
4. Answers will vary. Sample answer: four more than two thirds of y.
5. $2,000 + 80z$
6. $2.625a - 4.5b$
7. $5(9c + 2d)$
8. $3(9 - 3x + 5y)$
9. $20 - 3j$
10. $5 + 18y$

Practice and Problem Solving: C

1. $4a + 5b$
2. $4a + 5b = 120$
3. a. 20
   b. 20
   c. $100
   d. 10
   e. $40
   f. $80
   g. $60
   h. 12
   i. $60
   j. 20
   k. $80
   l. 8
   m. $40
4. The total price of the high-energy lamp is a whole-number multiple of 4. The total price of the low-energy lamp is a whole-number multiple of 5.
5. 20 high-energy lamps at $5 = $100; $120 - $100 = 20; $20 ÷ 4 = 5; 5 low-energy lamps can be bought

Practice and Problem Solving: D

1. $50 -$; 2; 2; 2; 2; $50 -$; $0.2m$; $50 - 0.20m$
2. $10 -$; 3; 3; 3; $10 - 0.3n$
3. $\frac{1}{4}$; $6x$; $\frac{1}{4}$; $14y$; $\frac{6}{4}x$; $\frac{14}{4}y$; $\frac{3}{2}x$; $\frac{7}{2}y$
4. $\frac{1}{6}$; $15a$; $\frac{1}{6}$; $20b$; $\frac{15}{6}a$; $\frac{20}{6}b$; $\frac{5}{2}a$; $\frac{10}{3}b$
5. 5; 5; 2; 3; 5; 5; 6
6. 7; 7; 2; 3; 7; 7; 6
7. $4(x + 3)$
8. $3(2s + 6t + w)$

Reteach

1. Answers will vary. Sample answer: one hundred minus five times the number of cars.
2. Answers will vary. Sample answer: twenty-five hundredths of the apartments and six tenths of the condos.
3. Answers will vary. Sample answer: one thirteenth of the difference between three times the number of hammers and eight times the number of pliers.
4. $\frac{1}{10}\left(\frac{1}{2}s + \frac{1}{3}e\right)$
5. $0.3f + 25$
6. $(3e - 4) + (6 + 2w)$

Reading Strategies

Problem 1

a. $0.35(50m + 75a)$

b. $0.35(50m + 75a) = 17.5m + 26.25a$

c. The original expression shows how much was contributed to the charity and to pay for the others costs of the event. The simplified expression might be easier to use to directly calculate the amount going to the charity.

Problem 2

a. $20d + 12c$, where d is the drill price and c is the charger price

b. $4(5d + 3c)$; Answers will vary.

Sample answer: The factor $5d + 3c$ shows that for every 5 drills purchased, 3 chargers were purchased.

c. The un-factored expression, $20d + 12c$, gives the total amount paid for both drills and chargers. The factored form of $20d + 12c$ which is $4(5d + 3c)$ gives a quick way to see how many chargers (3) are sold when a certain number of drills (5) are sold.

Success for English Learners

1. $10 + 3n$

2. Three times the price of a pizza and two drinks shows factoring, since it can be represented as the product of two factors—3 and $p + 2d$. Sample answers: $3p + 6d$; $3(p + 2d)$

3. $3(p + 2d) = 3p + 6d$

LESSON 6-2

Practice and Problem Solving: A/B

1. $n = 13\frac{1}{3}$

2. $y = 1.6$

3. $a = 24$

4. $v = -3$

5. $\dfrac{15.5z}{15.5} = \dfrac{-77.5}{15.5}$; $z = -5$

6. $-11\left(\dfrac{t}{-11}\right) = -11(11)$; $t = -121$

7. $\dfrac{0.5m}{0.5} = \dfrac{0.75}{0.5}$; $m = 1.5$

8. $4\left(\dfrac{r}{4}\right) = 4(250)$; $r = 1,000$

9. $\dfrac{1}{3}n - 8 = -13$

10. $-12.3f = -73.8$

11. $10 = T + 12$; $T = -1°C$

12. $3.2d = 48$; $d = 15$ days

13. $15t = 193.75$; $t = \$12.92$ (to the nearest cent)

14. $\dfrac{1}{3}d = \dfrac{1}{4}$; $d = \dfrac{3}{4}$ mi

Practice and Problem Solving: C

1. $x = 5\frac{1}{3}$

2. $m = 7.1$

3. $y = 2.76$

4. $z = 2.76$

5. $s = 5\frac{4}{7}$

6. $r = 5\frac{13}{25}$

7. $f = 2\frac{1}{4}$

8. $m = 1\frac{5}{9}$

9. a. $5h = 37.5$, $h = 7.5$; She worked 7.5 h on average per day.

   b. $\$118.125$; She made $\$118.13$ per day.

10. $3\frac{2}{3} \bullet x = 7\frac{1}{3}$; $x = 2$; He doubled the recipe.

11. $3\frac{2}{3} + 3\frac{2}{3} = 6\frac{4}{3} = 7\frac{1}{3}$, addition;

    $3\frac{2}{3} \bullet 2 = 6\frac{4}{3} = 7\frac{1}{3}$; multiplication

12. $1.89x \approx 6$; $x \approx 3$; She bought 3 bottles.

13. 38.4 in = 3.2 ft; $15.3 - x = 3.2$, $x = 12.1$; The piece he cut was 12.1 feet long.

Practice and Problem Solving: D

1. 8; 8; 19

2. 3; 3; 1

3. 5; 5; 3

4. 7; 7; −21

5. $3 \times \dfrac{a}{3} = 3 \times 5$; 15

6. 4.5; 4.5; 6

7. 5; 5; 30

8. 7.35; 7.35; 4

9. 110°; x; 180°; $110 + x = 180$; $x = 70°$

10. miles; gallon; 72.9, 2.7, 27; 27

Reteach

1. $m = 6\frac{7}{8}$

2. $t = -0.6$

3. $j = 13.1$

4. $y = 12$

5. $w = -20$

6. $a = -6$

Reading Strategies

1. $8 \times \dfrac{p}{8} = -2 \times 8$; -16

2. $1.5 - 1.5 + q = -0.6 - 1.5$; -2.1

3. $\dfrac{-9.5a}{-9.5} = \dfrac{-38}{-9.5}$; 4

4. $14v = 269.50$; $\dfrac{14v}{14} = \dfrac{269.50}{14}$; $v = \$19.25$

5. $\dfrac{3}{4}g = 18$; $\dfrac{4}{3} \times \dfrac{3}{4}g = \dfrac{4}{3} \times 18$; $g = 24$ games

Success for English Learners

1. The "7.2" has to be written as "7.20" so it will have the same number of decimal places as "3.84."

2. $\dfrac{a}{-3}$ can be written as $-\dfrac{1}{3}a$, so $-\dfrac{1}{3}$ is a rational number coefficient.

3. $\dfrac{1}{4}x$ could be written as $\dfrac{x}{4}$ or as $0.25x$.

LESSON 6-3

Practice and Problem Solving: A/B

1.
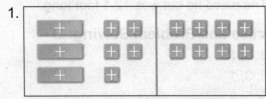

2.

3. $6t + 15 = 81$

4. $40 + 55h = 190$

5. $1.75 + 0.75m = 4.75$

Practice and Problem Solving: C

1. $\dfrac{p+7}{12} = 3$

2. $\dfrac{16}{q+1} = 4$

3. $\dfrac{7-s}{3} = 2$

4. $12.3 + 5.013d = 15.302$

5. $\dfrac{z+22}{z} = 12$

6. $75 + 255c = 1{,}605$

Practice and Problem Solving: D

1.
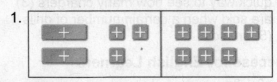

2.
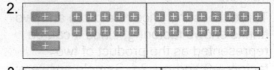

3.
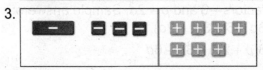

4. $3d + 5 = 17$

5. $40 + 25m = 240$

6. $10 + 7r = 45$

Reteach

1. $21 + 5f = 61$

2. $7j + 17 = 87$

3. $18 + 0.05n = 50.50$

4. $40 + 30s = 220$

Reading Strategies

1. Equation: $50 - 5n = 15$

   Number of steps and description:

   Two steps: Multiply a number n by 5, and subtract the result from 50.

2. Equation: $m + 8 = 27$

   Number of steps and description:

   One step: Add 8 to a number m.

3. Equation: $4b + 3 = 23$

   Number of steps and description:

   Two steps: Multiply a number b by 4, then add 3.

4. Equation: $15f = 90$

   Number of steps and description:

   One step: Multiply a number f by 15.

1. Sample answer: Eighteen less three times a number equals three.

2. $5x - 7 = -11$

LESSON 6-4

Practice and Problem Solving: A/B

1. $x = 3$
2. $p = -3$
3. $a = 4$
4. $n = -2$
5. $g = 2$
6. $k = -18$
7. $s = 18$
8. $c = -8$
9. $a = -6$
10. $v = 9$
11. $x = -2$
12. $d = 24$
13. $24s + 85 = 685$; $s = \$25$
14. $x + x + 1 = 73$; 36 and 37

Practice and Problem Solving: C

1. $2x - 17 = 3$; $x = 10$
2. $\dfrac{5x - 1}{3} = 4$; $x = 2.6$
3. $\dfrac{3 - 4x}{5} = -7$, $x = 9.5$
4. $8 + 5x = -12$ or $5x + 6 = -14$; $x = -4$
5. $-4x + 7 = -9$ or $7 = 4x - 9$; $x = 4$
6. $\dfrac{x + 11}{3} = 6$; $x = 7$
7. $s = \dfrac{u - t}{r}$; Subtract t from both sides, then divide both sides by r.
8. $t = \dfrac{u}{r} - s$; Divide both sides by r, then subtract s from both sides.
9. $n = pq - m$; Multiply both sides by p, then subtract m from both sides.
10. $p = \dfrac{m + n}{q}$; Multiply both sides by p, then divide both sides by q.

Practice and Problem Solving: D

1. Subtract 3 from both sides; $5x = 30$. Then divide both sides by 5; $x = 6$.
2. Add 1 to both sides; $8y = 32$. Then divide both sides by 8; $y = 4$.
3. Subtract 5 from both sides; $\dfrac{1}{2}z = 6$. Then multiply both sides by 2; $z = 12$.
4. Subtract 15 from both sides; $-4t = -12$. Then divide both sides by -4; $t = 3$.
5. Multiply both sides by 3; $q + 3 = 15$. Then subtract 3 from both sides; $q = 12$.
6. $m = 1$
7. $p = 8$
8. $2n - 3 = 17$; $n = 10$
9. $\dfrac{1}{2}x + 5 = 9$; $x = 8$
10. $15 + 2y = 29$; $y = 7$

Reteach

1. Subtract 11 from both sides. Then divide both sides by 4. $x = 2$
2. Subtract 10 from both sides. Then divide both sides by -3. $y = 8$
3. Multiply both sides by 3. Then add 11 to each side. $r = -10$
4. Subtract 5 from each side. Then divide both sides by -2. $p = -3$
5. Subtract 1 from each side. Then multiply both sides by $\dfrac{3}{2}$ $\left(\text{or divide both sides by } \dfrac{2}{3}\right)$. $z = 18$
6. Multiply both sides by 9. Then add 17 to each side. $w = 35$

Reading Strategies

1. Multiply by -2, then subtract 3.

   Add 3 to each side, then divide each side by -2.

   $x = 11$

2. Add 1, then divide the result by 3.

   Multiply both sides by 3, then subtract 1 from each side.

   $x = -16$

3. Multiply by –4, then add 5.

Subtract 5 from each side, then divide each side by –4.

$x = -3$

4. Subtract 7, then multiply the result by $\frac{1}{3}$.

Multiply both sides by 3

$\left(\text{or divide both sides by } \frac{1}{3}\right)$, then add 7

to both sides.

$x = 10$

Success for English Learners

1. a. Multiply a variable by 13, then add 2 to the result.

   b. Subtract 2 from both sides, then divide both sides by 13; $x = 3$

2. a. Subtract 3 from a variable, then divide the result by 5.

   b. Multiply both sides by 5, then add 3 to both sides; $x = -2$

MODULE 6 Challenge

1. Translate each brother's requirement into an inequality, then solve.

   Adam: $2x + 250 < 2{,}000 \rightarrow x < 875$

   Benny: $100 + 3x > 2{,}250 \rightarrow x > 700$

   Christopher: $700 < 0.25x + 500 \rightarrow 800 < x$ and $0.25x + 500 < 775 \rightarrow x < 900$

   Desmond: $0.35x + 1{,}000 > 1{,}275 \rightarrow x > 785.7$

   Eddie: $3x - 1{,}000 > 1{,}650 \rightarrow x > 850$

   The fence must be between 850 and 875 feet long; $850 < x < 875$.

2. The builder only needs requirements from Adam and Eddie.

   The other brother's requirements do not restrict the length of the fence any further.

MODULE 7 Inequalities

LESSON 7-1

Practice and Problem Solving: A/B

1. $e < 6$

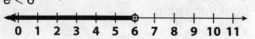

2. $n > 4$

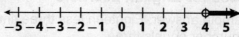

3. $2 < w$

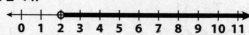

4. $4 \le m$

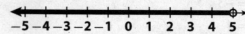

5. $r < 5$

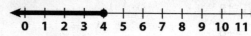

6. $-2 \ge t$

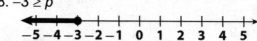

7. $4 \ge s$

8. $-3 \ge p$

9. $x \ge 3$

10. $r > -9$

11. $b < 5$

12. $a \le 45$

13. $136 + x \ge 189$; $x \ge 53$; Arthur must earn at least \$53.

14. $-5x < -80$; $5x > 80$, $x > 16$; Marna needs more than 16 correct answers.

Practice and Problem Solving: C

1. $a \ge -2.5$

2. $1.2 > n$

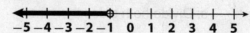

3. $b \ge -0.8$

4. $e < -1$

5. $r \le 0.1$

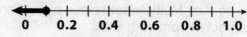

6. $0.8 \ge y$

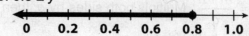

7. $-20a \le -250$; $a \ge 12.5$; 13 or more weeks ago

8. $s^3 > 125$; $s > 5$; greater than 5 cm

9. $-20t \le -4{,}200$; $t \ge 210$; No, 3 minutes is 180 seconds. The time needs to be at least 210 seconds.

Practice and Problem Solving: D

1. $a \le -3$;

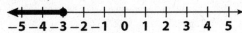

2. $-3 > n$

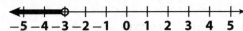

3. $b \ge 0$

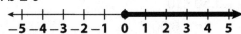

4. $e < -2$

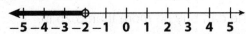

5. $t \ge 1$

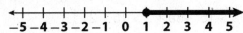

6. $c > 4$

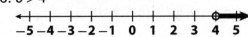

Reteach

1. $n \ge -9$

2. $n > 6$

3. $n \le -63$

4. $n \ge 4$

5. $n < 7$

6. $n > -2$

7. $n < -3$

8. $n < 12$

Reading Strategies

1. add 5; no

2. multiply by -6; yes

3. divide by 3; no

Success for English Learners

1. $\ge$

2. $>$

3. $\le$

4. $\ge$

5. $<$

6. $>$

7. When you multiply or divide by a negative number, the inequality sign reverses.

LESSON 7-2

Practice and Problem Solving: A/B

1. $10n + 4 \le 25$

2. $4n - 30 > -10$

3. $-\dfrac{1}{4}(5 - n) < 20$

4. Answers will vary. Sample answer: "The opposite of 5 times a number increased by 3 is greater than 1."

5. Answers will vary. Sample answer: "Twenty-seven less two times a number is less than or equal to the opposite of 6."

6. Answers will vary. Sample answer: "Half of the sum of 1 and a number is 5 or greater."

7. a. $10p$;

   b. $10p - 75$;

   c. $10p - 75 \ge 50$

Practice and Problem Solving: C

1. $24 + 4n \le 400$, or $n \le 94$

2. $120 \le 24 + 4n$, or $n \ge 24$

3. $24 \le n \le 94$

4. Answers will vary. Sample answer: $2x + 7 < 17$

5. Answers will vary. Sample answer: $\dfrac{1}{2}(x + 2) \ge 7$

6. Answers will vary. Sample answer: $2x - 5 > -55$

7. Each of the parts of the compound inequality, $-5 < 3x$ and $3x < 10$, is a one-step inequality. The only operation needed to simplify the compound inequality is to divide each term by 3.

Practice and Problem Solving: D

1. $4x \ge 2$

2. $-\dfrac{1}{3}x < 12$

3. $x + 5 < 7$

4. $n - 10 > 30$

5. $5n + 2 \geq 3$

6. $2n - 6 \leq 17$

7. Twelve times the number of cars she washes minus $50 for her savings must be greater than or equal to $100. Twelve times the number of cars, n, is $12n$. Subtract $50 for her savings: $12n - 50$. This has to be at least $100, so $12n - 50 \geq 100$.

8. 49 times the number of games plus $400 for the video player must be less than or equal to the saved $750, so $49n + 400 \leq 750$ or $750 \geq 400 + 49x$.

9. The number of samples saved for display, 50, plus the distribution at the rate of 25 per hour must be less than or equal to 250, so $50 + 25t \leq 250$.

Reteach

1. $3n$; $5 -$; $3n - 5$; $3n - 5 > -8$

2. $5n$; $+ 13$; $5n + 13$; $5n + 13 \leq 30$

Reading Strategies

1. $\frac{1}{2}(a + 6) \geq 20$

2. $12 + 3b \leq -11$

3. $2c - 8 < 5$

Success for English Learners

1. Sample answer: Five minus two times a number is greater than the opposite of four.

2. $3n - 7 \leq -10$

LESSON 7-3

Practice and Problem Solving: A/B

1. 5, 5; 24; 3, 24, 3; 8

2. 12, 12; −16; −2, −16, −2; 8

3. Because you are dividing by a positive number.

4. Because you are dividing by a negative number.

5. $-7d + 8 > 29$

$-7d + 8 - 8 > 29 - 8$

$-7d > 21$

$d < -3$

6. $12 - 3b < 9$

$12 - 12 - 3b < 9 - 12$

$-3b < -3$

$b > 1$

7. $\frac{z}{7} - 6 \geq -5$

$\frac{z}{7} - 6 + 6 \geq -5 + 6$

$\frac{z}{7} \geq 1$

$z \geq 7$

8. $50x + 1{,}250 \geq 12{,}500$ or $x \geq \$225$

9. $2n + 3.50 \leq 10$

$2n \leq 6.50$

$n \leq 3.25$

She can buy no more than 3.25 lb.

Practice and Problem Solving: C

1. $-5a > 15$; $-5a + 2 > 15 + 2$

2. $3b \leq 3$; $3b + 4 \geq 3 + 4$; $3b \geq 7$

3. $3x + 7 > 12$; $3x + 12 > 7$; $7 + 12 > 3x$

4. $x > \frac{5}{3}$; $x > -\frac{5}{3}$; $x < \frac{19}{3}$

5. All three solutions overlap at $\frac{5}{3} < x < \frac{19}{3}$, which gives the common solution for all three inequalities.

6. Answers will vary. Sample answer:

"The opposite of three is no less than a third of the difference of 6 and a number." $x \geq 15$

7. Answers will vary. Sample answer:

"Four times the sum of one and twice a number is less than the opposite of one half." $x < -\frac{9}{16}$.

Practice and Problem Solving: D

1. $y > 2$

2. $d \leq -4$

3. $r > -12$

4. Answers will vary. Accept any answer greater than 2.

5. Answers will vary. Accept any answer less than or equal to −135.

6. Answers will vary. Sample answer: 1, 2, 3

7. 32 bottles

8. 20 chairs

Reteach

1. $h \geq 5.5$, or 6 whole hours; 5 hours would not be enough to reach the 75-kilometer goal.

2. $b \leq 9.29$ bags, so 9 bags would be the greatest number that could be sold and still leave $10 worth of bird seed left over.

Reading Strategies

1. $12n \leq (750 - 50)\,10$

   $12n \leq 7000$

   $n \leq 583.3$

   $n \leq 583.3$, so 583 people can be given meals in 10 hours

2. $24h > 2{,}500 - 1{,}400$

   $24h > 1{,}100$

   $h > 45.8$

   $h > 45.8$, so it will take about 46 hours to recycle what is left of 2,500 liters of used oil.

Success for English Learners

1. No, x is less than 125, not less than or equal to 125.

2. There was no multiplication or division by a negative number.

3. Answers will vary. Accept any answer less than 40.

4. Answers will vary. Accept any answer less than or equal to −4.

MODULE 7 Challenge

1. $2(20 + x) \leq 100$; $x \leq 30$

2. $20x > 400$; $x > 20$

3. $0.5(20x) \leq 350$; $x \leq 35$

4. $0.15(20x) \geq 45$; $x \geq 15$

5. Accept any scale drawing that shows a garden with a width of 20 feet (10 units) and a length greater than 20 feet (10 units) and less than or equal to 30 feet (15 units).

MODULE 8 Modeling Geometric Figures

LESSON 8-1

Practice and Problem Solving: A/B

1. 15 ft; 6 ft; 90 ft^2
2. 16 m; 12 m; 192 m^2
3. The scale drawing is 10 units by 8 units.
4. a. 1 ft = 125 m
   b. 84 sheets of plywood tall
5. a. 40 bottle caps tall
   b. approximately 3 popsicle sticks tall

Practice and Problem Solving: C

1. 25.5 ft; 23.8 ft; 606.9 ft^2
2. Because the scale is 8 mm: 1 cm, and because 1 cm is longer than 8 mm, the actual object will be larger.
3. a. 42 cm by 126 cm
   b. 5,292 cm^2
   c. approximately 1.386 ft by 4.158 ft
   d. approximately 5.763 ft^2
4. 64 in.
5. 35.2 ft

Practice and Problem Solving: D

1.

Blueprint length (in.)	5	10	15	20	25	30
Actual Length (ft)	8	16	24	32	40	48

   a. 48 ft
   b. 2.5 in.

2.

Blueprint length (in.)	2	4	6	8	10	12
Actual Length (ft)	1	2	3	4	5	6

   a. 6 ft
   b. 16 in.

3. 24 ft; 12 ft; 288 ft^2
4. 10 units by 8 units

Reteach

1. 3 in.; 24 in.; $\frac{1}{8}$
2. 4 cm; 20 cm; $\frac{1}{5}$
3. 84 in.
4. 75 mi

Reading Strategies

1. 3 cm
2. Sample answer: $\frac{1}{10} = \frac{3}{x}$
3. 5 cm
4. Sample answer: $\frac{1}{10} = \frac{5}{x}$

Success for English Learners

1. Sample answer: The car would not be in proportion.
2. Sample answer: If the photo does not have the same proportions as the painting, the face will be stretched tall or stretched wide.

LESSON 8-2

Practice and Problem Solving: A/B

1.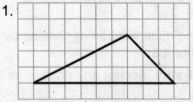

2.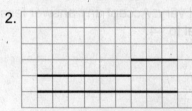

No triangle can be formed because the sum of the measures of the two shorter sides has the same measure as the longest side.

3. Yes, because the sum of the measures of the two shorter sides is greater than the measure of the longest side, e.g., $\frac{1}{3} + \frac{1}{4} > \frac{1}{2}$.

4. No, because the sum of the measures of the two shorter sides is less than the measure of the longest side, e.g., $0.02 + 0.01 < 0.205$.

5. Unique; since the sum of the angles is less than 180° and a side is included.

6. Many, since the sum of the measures of the angles is less than 180° but no side is included.

Practice and Problem Solving: C

1. They are angles *ACB* and *ADB*, formed by Earth's radii and the tangent lines running to the planet.

2. Both are Earth's radii.

3. *AC* is much less than *BC*.

4. *AB* and *BC* are approximately equal.

5. *AB* > *BC*

6. Isosceles triangle, since *AB* and *BC* are approximately equal.

7. The astronomer knows that *ACB* is a right angle and the angle *CAB* could be measured. This is enough information to compute *AB* using similar triangles or trigonometry.

Practice and Problem Solving: D

1. 3 and 4 units; less than 7 units, but greater than 1 unit; Diagrams will vary.

2. 3 and 7 units; less than 10 units, but greater than 4 units; Diagrams will vary.

3. 101°; 79°

4. 129°; 51°

Reteach

1. Yes; if *x* is the length of each side, then $x + x > x$ or $2x > x$, so the condition for a triangle to be formed is met.

2. No. The sum of the measures of the three angles is greater than 180°.

Reading Strategies

1. Diagrams may vary, but students should realize that the two 4-foot boards add up

to 8 feet, which is less than the 10-foot board, so no triangle can be formed with the boards.

2. Diagrams and calculations may vary, but students should first find the hypotenuse of the right triangle formed by the 5 and 6-inch sides, which is $\sqrt{61}$ inches. Then, they should find the length of the hypotenuse formed by the 25-inch side and $\sqrt{61}$ inches, which is $\sqrt{686}$ inches, or about 26 inches. A 30-inch bat would not fit in the box.

Success for English Learners

1. The compass could be used to make two arcs of radii equal in length to the shorter segments from each end of the longer segment. The point of intersection of the arcs would be where the shorter sides of the triangle intersect.

2. Yes, the sum of the measures of the angles given is 90°, so the third angle has to be 90 degrees for the sum of the three angle measures to be 180°.

LESSON 8-3

Practice and Problem Solving: A/B

1. cross section; The circle is a plane figure intersecting a three-dimensional curved surface. The figure formed is a curved line on the surface of the cone.

2. intersection; The edge of a square is a straight line and the base of the pyramid is a plane figure. A straight line is formed.

3. cross section; A square is formed.

4. cross section; The circle is a plane figure. A polygon results that is similar to the polygon that forms the base.

5. trapezoid

6. triangle

7. circle

8. ellipse or oval

Practice and Problem Solving: C

1. It is a square. The length of each of its sides is the same as the length of the side of the square.

2. An equilateral triangle; Since each of the segments from the vertex of the cube to the midpoint of the side is equal and the

angles at the vertex are 90°, the third sides of each triangle are equal and form the cross section.

3. A: circle; B and C: ellipses or ovals; D: a plane of length, h, the cylinder's height, and width, d, the cylinder's diameter

4. Area A < Area B < Area C < Area D

Practice and Problem Solving: D

1. a triangle that is similar to the base

2. a rectangle or a square

3. a trapezoid

4. a circle

5. Drawings will vary, but the cross section should be a regular octagon that is congruent to the bases of the prism.

6. Drawings will vary, but the cross section should be a regular pentagon that is similar to the base of the pyramid.

Reteach

1. Drawings will vary. Sample answers: a triangular cross section formed by a plane that is perpendicular to the base of the pyramid and including its apex point; a rectangular cross section formed by a plane that is parallel to the base of the pyramid

2. Drawings will vary, Sample answers: a triangular cross section formed by a plane that is parallel to the prism's bases and congruent to them; a rectangular cross section formed by a plane that is perpendicular to the bases and having a length that is equal to the height of the prism

Reading Strategies

1. Diagrams will vary but should show a rectangular cross section that is parallel to the base and similar to it.

2. rectangle

3. Diagrams will vary but should show a pentagonal cross section that is congruent to the bases.

4. parallel to the bases

5. congruent to bases

6. Diagrams will vary but should show a circular cross section of radius less than the radius of the sphere.

7. circle

8. similar to a circle that is the circumference of the sphere but smaller than that circle

9. Diagrams will vary but should show a plane passing through the cone's vertex, its lateral surface in two lines, and bisecting its base.

10. isosceles triangle

11. The two sides of the triangle that are equal length are the same length as the slant height of the cone. The third, shorter side is equal to the diameter of the cone's base.

Success for English Learners

1. It is a trapezoid; the edge of the cross section in the base is longer than and parallel to the edge of the cross section in the face of the pyramid.

2. Both cross sections are parallel to the bases. Each cross section is similar to the figure's base.

LESSON 8-4

Practice and Problem Solving: A/B

1. $\angle AEB$ and $\angle DEF$

2. $\angle AEB$ and $\angle BEC$

3. Sample answer: $\angle AEF$ and $\angle DEF$

4. 120°

5. 13°

6. 70°

7. 115°

8. 28

9. 18

10. 22

11. 15

Practice and Problem Solving: C

1. 66°

2. 125°

3. 114°

4. 156°

5. 39

6. 43

7. 24

8. 19

9. 41.25°

10. 33°

Practice and Problem Solving: D

1. $\angle MSN$ and $\angle PSQ$

2. $\angle PSQ$ and $\angle QSR$

3. Sample answer: $\angle MSN$ and $\angle NSP$

4. 60°

5. 100°

6. 130°

7. 55°

8. 30

9. 40

10. 35

11. 135

Reteach

1. vertical angles;

2. 90°; complementary angles

3. 180°; supplementary angles

4. 80

5. 20

6. 6

7. 25

Reading Strategies

1. 30°

2. 60°

3. 150°

4. 90°

Success for English Learners

1. 90°; 180°

2. 180°

Module 8 Challenge

1. A rectangular solid; $V_A = 4x(6x)x = 24x^3$

2. A trapezoid; $A_B = \frac{1}{2}h(b_1 + b_2) =$

   $\frac{1}{2}4x(4x + 8x) = 24x^2$

3. $V_{B\ part\ 1} = A_B(x) = (24x^2)x = 24x^3$

4. $V_{B\ part\ 2} = \frac{1}{2}A_B(3x) = \frac{1}{2}(24x^2)(3x) = 36x^3$

5. $V_{B\ total} = 24x^3 + 36x^3 = 60x^3$

6. A sphere; one fourth of a sphere;

   $V_C = \frac{1}{4}\left(\frac{4}{3}\pi(4x)^3\right) = \frac{64}{3}\pi x^3$

7. $V_{total} = V_A + V_{B\ total} + V_C = 24x^3 + 60x^3 +$

   $\frac{64}{3}\pi x^3 = 4x^3\left(21 + \frac{16}{3}\pi\right)$ or approx.

   $151x^3$.

8. Divide 33,000 by 151 to get about 218. Take the cube root; x is about 6 feet.

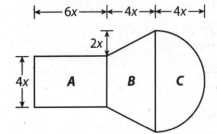

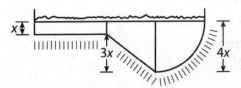

MODULE 9 Circumference, Area, and Volume

LESSON 9-1

Practice and Problem Solving: A/B

1. 18.84 in.
2. 56.52 cm
3. 4.71 ft
4. 25.12 m
5. 37.68 ft
6. 12.56 yd
7. 43.96 in.
8. 26.26 cm
9. 7.85 m
10. 66 ft
11. 132 mm
12. 88 cm

Practice and Problem Solving: C

1. 3.93 in.
2. 11.30 yd
3. 13.19 mm
4. 2.36 cm
5. 4.19 ft
6. 3.14 in.
7. 3.5 in.
8. 18 yd
9. 9.55 in.
10. 16

Practice and Problem Solving: D

1. 50.2 m
2. 62.8 in.
3. 9.4 ft
4. 22.0 mm
5. 18.8 cm

6. 12.6 yd
7. 110 yd
8. 28.3 in.
9. 125.7 cm

Reteach

1. 9; 28.26; 28.3
2. 13; 26; 81.64; 81.6
3. 40.8 cm
4. 31.4 ft
5. 9.4 in.

Reading Strategies

1. $C = 2\pi r$
2. $C = \pi d$
3. It is twice as long.
4. Sample answer: 3.14 or $\dfrac{22}{7}$
5. The circumference of a circle is the distance around a circle. It is given in units. The perimeter of a polygon is the distance around a polygon. It is given in units.

Success for English Learners

1. the length of the diameter.
2. 18 cm
3. Take half of the diameter, 17 ft, and substitute that value into the formula for r.
4. $d = 10$ so $r = 5$

$C = 2\pi r$	$C = \pi d$
$= 2 \cdot 3.14 \cdot 5$	$= 3.14 \cdot 10$
$= 31.4$	$= 31.4$

LESSON 9-2

Practice and Problem Solving: A/B

1. A
2. B
3. 50.2 in.^{2}
4. 153.9 m^2
5. 254.3 yd^2
6. π cm^2
7. 54.76π cm^2
8. 25π in.^{2}
9. 121π mm^2
10. 6.25π ft^2
11. 9π m^2

Practice and Problem Solving: C

1. 1.2544π cm^2; 3.9 cm^2
2. 0.0625π in.^{2}; 0.2 in^2
3. 0.16π in.^{2}; 0.5 in^2
4. 54.76π cm^2; 171.9 cm^2
5. 36,864π yd^2; 115,753 yd^2
6. 0.49π m^2; 1.5 m^2
7. $A = \pi$
8. $A = 6.25\pi$
9. $A = 16\pi$
10. The area of the 10-inch chocolate cake is 28.26 in^2 larger than the area of the vanilla cake.
11. The square's area is 1.935 m^2 larger than the circle's area.

Practice and Problem Solving: D

1. 19.6 cm^2
2. 379.9 in.^{2}
3. 28.3 mm^2
4. 78.5 in^2
5. 132.7 cm^2
6. 162.8 yd^2

7. 36π cm^2
8. 90.25π in^2
9. 12.25π yd^2
10. 121π yd^2
11. 9π m^2
12. 36π ft^2

Reteach

1. 64π in^2
2. 3600π m^2
3. 56.7 in.^{2}
4. 314 yd^2
5. 452.2 m^2
6. 66.4 cm^2

Reading Strategies

1. 49π cm^2; 153.86 cm^2
2. 6.25π yd^2; 19.625 yd^2

Success for English Learners

1. 10.24π mm^2; 32.2 mm^2
2. 90.25π yd^2; 283.4 yd^2

LESSON 9-3

Practice and Problem Solving: A/B

Answers may vary for Exercises 1 and 2.

1. 21 ft^2
2. 24 ft^2
3. 90 ft^2
4. 208 m^2
5. 140 ft^2
6. 23.13 m^2
7. 100 ft^2
8. 33.28 m^2
9. 57.12 m^2

Practice and Problem Solving: C

Answers may vary for Exercises 1 and 2.

1. 22 ft^2

2. 30 ft^2

3. 104 ft^2

4. 223.4 m^2

5. 60.75 m^2

6. 258.39 m^2

7. $A = 52 \text{ units}^2$; $P = 36$ units

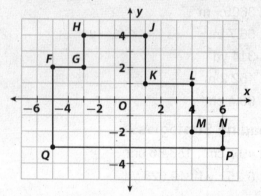

Practice and Problem Solving: D

1. C

2. B

3. 17 ft^2

4. 30.28 m^2

5. 174 ft^2

6. 84 m^2

7. 158.13 ft^2

8. 288 m^2

9. 189.25 ft^2

Reteach

1. $9, 1\frac{1}{2}, \frac{1}{2}, 1, 9, 1\frac{1}{2}, \frac{1}{2}, 1, 12$

2. 32, 6, 32, 6, 38

Reading Strategies

1. 63 m^2

2. 76 m^2

3. 30.28 m^2

Success for English Learners

1. Separate the figures into simpler figures whose areas you can find.

LESSON 9-4

Practice and Problem Solving: A/B

1. 142 in^2

2. 190 cm^2

3. $1,236 \text{ cm}^2$

4. $3,380 \text{ ft}^2$

5. Possible answer: I would find the total surface area of each cube and then subtract the area of the sides that are not painted, including the square underneath the small cube.

6. 384 in^2

Practice and Problem Solving: C

1. 101.4 in^2

2. 797.4 m^2

3. Check students' guesses.

4. B; 384 in^2

5. C; 340 in^2

6. A; 338.8 in^2

7. Discuss students' guesses and whether they were correct or not.

Practice and Problem Solving: D

1. 286 ft^2

2. $1,160 \text{ ft}^2$

3. 80 in^2

4. 124 in^2

5. 96 in^2

6. 384 in^2

7. 480 in^2

Reteach

1. $5 \cdot 8 = 40$ in^2; $2 \cdot 40 = 80$ in^2
2. $5 \cdot 3 = 15$ in^2; $2 \cdot 15 = 30$ in^2
3. $3 \cdot 8 = 24$ in^2; $2 \cdot 24 = 48$ in^2
4. $80 + 30 + 48 = 158$ in^2
5. 158 in^2
6. 340 in^2
7. 592 cm^2

Reading Strategies

1. 756 square feet
2. 600 square inches

Success for English Learners

1. 32 cm^2
2. 32 cm^2
3. 8 cm^2
4. 8 cm^2
5. 16 cm^2
6. 16 cm^2
7. 112 cm^2
8. Sample answer: There are 3 pairs of surfaces with the same areas: the top and bottom, the left side and right side, the front and back.

LESSON 9-5

Practice and Problem Solving: A/B

1. 84 in^3
2. 180 cm^3
3. 600 ft^3
4. 360 cm^3
5. 312 cm^3
6. 15.6 kg
7. 1.95 kg

Practice and Problem Solving: C

1. 124.4 in^3
2. 477.8 cm^3
3. 120 m^3
4. 20.2 cm^3
5. 135 cm^3
6. Marsha got the units confused. The volume of one marble is 7,234.5 mm^3. Marsha needs to convert that volume to cm^3, which is about 7.2 cm^3.
7. Answers will vary. Sample answer: If you divide the volume of the container by the volume of 1 marble, you can find the number of marbles that will fit inside the container. However, the volume of all the marbles will not equal the volume of the container, because the marbles are round and there will be empty space.

Practice and Problem Solving: D

1. 12 cubes
2. 24 cubes
3. 105 in^3
4. 48 m^3
5. length: 10 mm; width: 10 mm; height: 10 mm
6. 1,000 mm^3
7. 6 cubes
8. 6,000 mm^3

Reteach

1. 80 m^3
2. 120 in^3
3. 72 cm^3

Reading Strategies

1. 60 m^3
2. 720 in^3
3. 108 cm^3

Success for English Learners

1. 216 in^3
2. 108 cm^3

MODULE 9 Challenge

1. $2(20 + x) \leq 100$; $x \leq 30$

2. $20x > 400$; $x > 20$

3. $0.5(20x) \leq 350$; $x \leq 35$

4. $0.15(20x) \geq 45$; $x \geq 15$

5. $w = 20$ feet and 30 feet $\geq l > 20$ feet

6. 5 ft $\leq r \leq 7$ ft

7. $31\frac{3}{7}$ ft $\leq C_p \leq 44$ ft

8. 44 ft $\leq C_w \leq 56\frac{1}{7}$ ft

9. $157\frac{1}{7}$ ft^3 $\leq V \leq 308$ ft^3

UNIT 5: Statistics

MODULE 10 Random Samples and Populations

LESSON 10-1

Practice and Problem Solving: A/B

1. Answers may vary, but students should realize that the number of road runners born within a 50-mile radius of Lubbock, Texas is a subset of the number of road runners born everywhere or in Texas.

2. Answers may vary, but students should realize that the cars traveling at 75 kilometers per hour between Beaumont and Lufkin, Texas is a subset of the cars traveling between Beaumont and Lufkin at all speeds.

3. Answers may vary, but Method B is probably more representative of the opinions of any student chosen at random from the entire school population.

4. Answers may vary, but Method C may be more representative of all voters than a sample that consists of 25-year town residents who may or may not be voters.

5. Biased; library patrons have a vested interest in seeing that the library is expanded.

6. Not biased, if the cable company samples customers, regardless of their history and experience with the company.

Practice and Problem Solving: C

1. Sample A is random *within* each precinct but not across the city as a whole. If the precincts have different populations, the sampling from one precinct might outweigh that of another, less-populous precinct. The precinct samples may be biased, depending on the content of the survey questions.

   Sample B is random across the city. The sample may be biased, depending on the content of the survey questions.

   Sample C is not random and is biased in concentrating on the precinct in which the factory would be located and where it would have the greatest impact on

infrastructure. It is not clear if this precinct would benefit from the new jobs, either.

2. Some streets may have more residents than others. Some residents may not have private telephones; they may use cell phones or public phones.

3. a. They are not random across all persons in the city center who might rent a scooter, but they could be random across the two clusters that the owner wants to sample, office workers and apartment residents.

   b. The questionnaire with the lower weekend rates is biased against the weekday office workers and in favor of possible weekend rentals by apartment residents.

Practice and Problem Solving: D

1. Home runs hit in 2014–2015; Home runs hit one week in July

2. All of the sugar maples in the 12-acre forest; the six sugar maples

3. Sample C is the best method of getting a random sample.

4. Sample Z is the best method of getting a random sample.

5. The question shows bias because it only mentions the benefits of having a professional sports stadium and teams.

Reteach

1. The sample is biased. The passengers on one on-time flight are likely to feel differently about their flight than passengers on delayed flights.

2. The sample is not biased. It is a random sample.

3. The sample is not biased. It is a random sample.

4. The sample is biased. The people who go to movies are more likely to spend money on movies than on other entertainment.

Reading Strategies

1. When you collect information from a population, the entire group is surveyed. When you collect information from a sample, only part of the group is surveyed.

2. An unbiased sample represents the population and a biased sample does not.

3. biased sample

4. unbiased sample

5. biased sample

Success for English Learners

1. The population is all athletes on the track team.

2. Athletes who specialize in certain events could be sampled, e.g. athletes who are in field events, track events, or in both events. In any case, the samples would be small and biased in favor of the training needs of the events in which the athletes participate.

3. Answers will vary, e.g. the restaurant could sample families who come into its restaurant and ask if they go to cafeterias out of town but in south Texas, and if so how large their families are.

LESSON 10-2

Practice and Problem Solving: A/B

1. Answers will vary, but student responses should mention the median and mode, both of which are 11 concerts attended. Since all but one of the data points indicate that from 10 to 13 concerts were attended, the data point corresponding to 8 concerts should be considered an outlier and not used in computing average concert attendance.

2. Answers will vary, but students should observe that the median is 6 miles jogged daily. The number of miles jogged daily is anywhere from 3 miles to 8.5 miles, but the number falls somewhere from 5.5 miles to 7.5 miles about 50% of the time.

3. The high score was 32 and the low score was 25.

4. 26.5 and 29.5

5. No; three quarters of the test scores are less than or equal to 29.5; the median, 27.5, is a typical test score.

6. Yes; $\frac{7}{50} = \frac{56}{400}$, and 56 > 50.

7. $\frac{400}{3} = \frac{150,000}{x}$; $400x = 450,000$; $x = 1,125$; there will be 1,125 tokens with stamping errors.

Practice and Problem Solving: C

1. Answers will vary, but students should observe that the data is skewed to the left with median of 37.5 (or 38 in whole deliveries) and a mode of 35 deliveries. There is an outlier at 70, too.

2.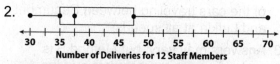
Number of Deliveries for 12 Staff Members

3. Answers will vary, but students should notice that the data wanted by the company is symmetric about a median of 50, with a low value of not less than 45 and a high value of no more than 55. Twelve sample data points could be the whole numbers 45, 46, 47, 48, 49, 50, 50, 51, 52, 53, 54, 55.

4. The hourly delivery rate of the typical delivery staff member will increase by 12.5, or about 13 whole deliveries per hour. The median of the collected data is 37.5 and the goal median is 50 deliveries per hour.

Practice and Problem Solving: D

1. a. 104°F;

   b. 102 °F (twice), 104 °F (3 times), 105 °F (twice)

2. a. 7 porpoises

   b. 4 porpoises

   c. about 50%

   d. Sample answer: Most observers saw more than 6 porpoises.

Reteach

1. 750 chips would be defective.

2. about 1,563

Reading Strategies

1. Answers will vary, e.g. the data is skewed to the right.

2. 10 blooms per plant is an outlier.

3. Sample answer: With the outlier, the median is shown as 17 blooms per plant. If the outlier is removed, the median will shift to the right.
   The amount of the shift is unknown since no information is provided about the values of the data points in each quartile of the data.

4. Answers will vary. Sample answer: the greatest concentration of data is the 25 percent of the data points between the lower quartile and the median. Since there is less variation in this data, it provides the statistic of the sample that can be used with the most confidence to make an inference about the entire of population of plants.

Success for English Learners

1. There could be times when there would be more or fewer than nine cardinals at the birdbath. The nine cardinals may visit the birdbath several times each day, too, especially early and late in a day.

2. Answers will vary, but students should realize that there are limits to drawing conclusions from a limited sample like this one to a larger population. An observer could watch the feeder over a longer period of time, e.g. several days or hours. Observers could also record the number of sightings of birds that visit the bird bath infrequently, e.g. thrashers, to see if their numbers change.

LESSON 10-3

Practice and Problem Solving: A/B

1. The sample is representative of the expected number of integers from 1 to 25 in a sample of 5 integers, which would be none or zero

2. A sample of 80 integers would be expected to have two integers from 1 to 25.

3. Three numbers from 1 to 25 is higher than expected since a sample of 40 numbers would be expected to have one number from 1 to 25, and a sample of 80 numbers would be expected to have two numbers from 1 to 25.

4. 25 out of 36 collars (shown in boldface below), or 69.4% are acceptable to ship, so about 500 out of a production run of 720 would be expected to be acceptable to ship.

   17, **14, 14, 16, 14, 15, 15, 15, 16, 14, 16, 14, 15, 15, 15, 16,** 13, 13, 13, 13, 13, **14, 14,** 13, 17, **14, 15,** 13, **14, 15, 16,** 17, **14, 17, 14, 15**

5. 4 out of 36 collars (shown in boldface below), or 11% have too much biocide, so about 79 out of a production run of 720 would be expected to have too much biocide.

   17, 14, 14, 16, 14, 15, 15, 15, 16, 14, 16, 14, 15, 15, 15, 16, 13, 13, 13, 13, 13, 14, 14, 13, **17,** 14, 15, 13, 14, 15, 16, **17,** 14, **17,** 14, 15

Practice and Problem Solving: C

1. A sample of 240 individuals would have to have 20 endangered species to meet the grant requirement of 1,000 endangered species in a population of 12,000 fish.

2. None of the samples have 20 endangered individuals, even though one of Hatchery A's samples had 19.

3. Answers will vary. Student solutions might include averaging the number of endangered in each sample, using the largest number of endangered as an indicator of the population etc.

4. Answers will vary, but students should notice that the extreme values of the number of galaxies are 1 and 30. Students might use groups of 10 for a range, e.g. 11 to 20, 21 to 30 etc. in which case students might observe that there are 12 samples between 1 and 10, 9 samples between 11 and 20, and 15 samples between 21 and 30, inclusive.

Practice and Problem Solving: D

1. a. Answers will vary. Sample answer: There could be as few as one or as many as 9 cattle grazing on an acre, or an average of about 5 cattle grazing per acre.

   b. If 250 cattle are divided by 40 acres, an average of about 6 cows should be grazing on each acre.

   c. Answers will vary. Sample answer: some of the pasture might not have enough food for the cattle, or there might be parts of the pasture that provide food, such as bare ground, creeks, or other such features.

2. a. mean: 20.5 errors; median: 17.5 errors

   b. mean: 23.5 errors; median; 25 errors; The mean for all 12 samples was 3 errors more than the mean for the first 6 samples. The median for all 12 samples was 7.5 errors more than the median for the first 6 samples.

Reteach

1. Answers will vary, but students should observe that in both outcomes, there are more 6's than most of the other numbers.

2. Answers will vary, but students may infer that the random sample outcomes will become more like the predicted results as the number of random samples increases.

Reading Strategies

1. Answers will vary. Sample answer: These results are close to what the farmer wants, even if they are a percent less.

2. Answers will vary. Sample answer: The numbers 1, 3, and 5 are representative of the number of females in all 18 litters. One female occurs four times, 3 females occurs three times, and 5 females occurs two times.

Success for English Learners

1. 7 teams

2. 2 teams

3. 9 goals; 8 times

4. 3, 8, and 10 goals; 2 times each

MODULE 10 Challenge

1. Population: all of the school's teachers; Sample: every third teacher from an alphabetical list. Within this population, the sample is a random sample only if every teacher on the list has an equal chance of being selected, which would be a function of the number of teachers in the school and its correlation to the 26 letters of the alphabet.

2. Population: all schools in the system; Sample: 5 randomly-selected schools in the system. The schools are selected randomly.

3. Population: all math-science classes in the school; or the ten math-science classes. Sample: The sample is described as 3 math and 3 science teachers. There is no stated randomness in any of these choices. For example, how did the director select the principal, how did the principal select the math-science classes, and why only math-science classes, and not classes of other subject areas?

4. Population: broken into two parts: teachers with 12 or more years of experience and teachers with less than 12 years of experience; Sample: 10 teachers in each of the population categories. Splitting the teacher population decreases the randomness of the sampling process. Also, it is not stated why "12 years" is used to break the population into two parts.

5. Population: all schools in the system; Sample: 4 randomly-selected schools. The sample is described as random.

6. Population: all schools in the system; Sample: different numbers of schools in each of three categories. It is not stated why the system's schools are separated into these categories, even though it is sensible. It is not stated why 10, 5, and 5 schools in each category were selected, or if they were randomly selected.

MODULE 11 Analyzing and Comparing Data

LESSON 11-1

Practice and Problem Solving: A/B

1. 7; 25; 25
2. 0.07; 0.15; 0.15 and 0.16 (bi-modal distribution)
3. Both are 3.
4. Plot A has 7 dots; plot B has 9 dots.
5. Plot A's mode is 21; plot B's mode is 23 and 24 (bi-modal).
6. Plot A's median is 21; plot B's median is 23.
7. Plot A is skewed to the left so its central measures are shifted toward the lower values. Plot B is skewed to the right so its central measures are shifted toward the higher values.

Practice and Problem Solving: C

1. The median is 21 pounds, the mode is 22 pounds, and the range is 9 pounds.
2. By both central measures median and mode, each shearing does not produce the 25 pounds he needs.
3. The median is 25 pounds, but the mode is 24 pounds. The range is 9 pounds.
4. The distribution is "almost" bi-modal with 24 and 27 pounds. Because of this and the fact that the median is 25 pounds, the rancher should feel confident that he is very close to the 25 pound target. If he needs more data, he could sample a larger population to see how its measures compare to the 50-animal sample.

Practice and Problem Solving: D

1. 15
2. 15

3. 15
4. Plot Y; Plot X range is 13 − 11 = 2. Plot Y range is 42 − 6 = 36
5. Plot X; 4 values of 11
6. 11
7. 30

Reteach

1. Answers will vary. The data are not symmetric about the center. The distribution is skewed slightly to the right. The mode is 6, the median is 6, and the range is 10.

Reading Strategies

1. Mean: 6.9; median: 7; mode: 7
2. Mean: 7.3; median: 7; mode: 7

Success for English Learners

1. If there are 12 dots, the median is the average of the 6th and 7th dots' values.
2. There would be two modes, "1" and "3."

LESSON 11-2

Practice and Problem Solving: A/B

1.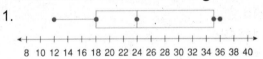
2. Amy
3. Ed
4. Ed
5. Amy; The range and interquartile range are smaller for Amy than for Ed, so Amy's test scores are more predictable.
6. Port Eagle
7. Port Eagle
8. Surfside; The interquartile range is smaller for Surfside for than for Port Eagle, so Surfside's room prices are more predictable.

Practice and Problem Solving: C

1.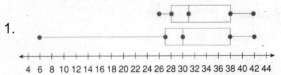
2. It increases the interquartile range by 1.
3. The range is more affected since the difference is 16.

4. If the farmer is concerned about "average" production, either box plot will do, since the medians are similar.

5. Answers may vary, but students should observe that the IQR for the top box plot is symmetric about the median, implying no skewing. The 3rd quartile of the bottom box plot is larger than its 1st quartile, which implies some skew to the right.

6. The range of the top plot is 1 unit greater than the range of the bottom plot. The IQR of the bottom plot is greater than the IQR of the top plot.

Practice and Problem Solving: D

1. The smallest data point value is 12; the largest data point value is 24.

2. 18

3. 12; 23

4. 50%

5.

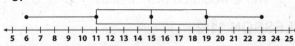

6. 17

7. 15

8. 11; 19

9. 8

10. The distribution is almost symmetrical.

Reteach

1. 20, 24, 25, 27, 31, 35, 38

2. 20, 38, and 27

3. 24, 35

4.

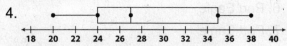

5. 61, 63, 65, 68, 69, 70, 72, 74, 78

6. 61, 78, 69, 64, and 73

7.

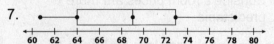

Reading Strategies

1. Class B; 8

2. Class B

3. Class A

4. 25%

Success for English Learners

1. Answers may vary, but students should understand that the quartiles divide the data set into four fourths: 25% below the lower quartile, 50% below the median, 25% above the upper quartile, and any other combination that reflects the definition of quartiles.

2. The only measure of "average" on this page is the median, so the team with the median of 54 fish had the greater average measure.

LESSON 11-3

Practice and Problem Solving: A/B

1. mean: 14.9; MAD: 1.9

2. mean: 14.6; MAD: 1.92

3. 0.3

4. The means of the two data sets differ by about 6.3 times the variability of the two data sets.

5. Sample answer: The median of the mean incomes for the samples from City A is higher than for City B. According to these samples it appears that adults in City A earn a higher average income than adults in City B. Also, there is a greater range of mean incomes in City A and a greater interquartile range.

Practice and Problem Solving: C

1. mean: 69.7; MAD: 18.3

2. mean: 73.4; MAD: 16

3. 3.7

4. 2.3

5. The means of the two data sets differ by about 1.6 times the variability of the two data sets.

6. Sample answer: The median of the mean incomes for the samples from City C is higher than for City D. However, they are close and there is a lot of overlap, so it is difficult to make a convincing comparison.

Practice and Problem Solving: D

1. mean: 65; MAD: 6.4

2. mean: 60.5; MAD: 6.4

3. 4.5

4. The difference of the means is about 0.7 times the mean absolute deviations.

5. Sample answer: Adults in City P clearly have higher incomes than adults in City Q.

Reteach

1. The difference of the means is 4.8. This is 0.3 times the range of the first group, and 1.2 times the range of the second group.

2. Based on the means, the people in the town Raul surveyed seem to receive fewer phone calls.

Reading Strategies

1. Survey more samples of students.

Success for English Learners

1. No, this is not enough information. You need the difference of two means.

2. Sample answer: Track the customers for more hours for a longer period of time and then analyze the data.

MODULE 11 Challenge

1. Sample answer: 8, 10, 11, 11, 12, 14
2. 10, 12, 12, 16, 17, 18, 20
3. 8, 9, 9, 10, 14, 14, 15, 17
4. 14
5. 8
6. 33

UNIT 6: Probability

MODULE 12 Experimental Probability

LESSON 12-1

Practice and Problem Solving: A/B

1. certain; 1

2. as likely as not; $\frac{1}{2}$

3. impossible; 0

4. $\frac{2}{3}$

5. $\frac{4}{5}$

6. $\frac{1}{2}$

7. No, 6 of the 9 cards involve forward moves. The probability of moving backward is $\frac{1}{3}$.

8. No; Only two cards will let him win. The probability that he will not win on his next turn is $\frac{7}{9}$.

Practice and Problem Solving: C

1. $\frac{4}{5}$

2. $\frac{4}{11}$

3. $\frac{3}{8}$

4. $\frac{2}{3}$

5. $\frac{1}{2}$

6. There were 8 cans in the cabinet, including 1 chicken noodle. Mother added 2 cans of chicken noodle soup and 5 cans of vegetable soup. So, there are 15 cans of soup, 3 of which are chicken noodle.

7. Answers will vary. Sample answer: The spinner is marked with numbers 1, 2, 3, 3, 4, 5, 5, 5. What is the probability that the spinner will not land on 5? $\left(\frac{5}{8}\right)$.

Practice and Problem Solving: D

1. A

2. C

3. B

4. E

5. D

6. $\frac{7}{9}$

7. $\frac{5}{6}$

8. as likely as not; Since he gets up by 7:15 about half the time, he will ride his bicycle about half the time. The probability is about $\frac{1}{2}$, or as likely as not.

9. likely; The probability of choosing a short-sleeved shirt is $\frac{4}{5}$, or likely.

Reteach

1. unlikely; $\frac{1}{24}$

2. as likely as not; $\frac{1}{2}$

3. impossible; 0

Reading Strategies

1. unlikely

2. impossible

3. certain

4.

Possible Outcomes	Desired Outcomes		
	6	Factor of 4	Greater than 0
0	no	no	no
1	no	yes	yes
2	no	yes	yes
3	no	no	yes
4	no	yes	yes
5	no	no	yes
Results	0 out of 6	3 out of 6	5 out of 6
Probability	impossible	as likely as not	likely

Success for English Learners

1. as likely as not; Sample answer: because there are 3 even numbers and 3 numbers that are not even

2. impossible; There are no purple marbles in the bag.

LESSON 12-2

Practice and Problem Solving: A/B

1. $\frac{11}{15}$

2. $\frac{7}{20}$

3. $\frac{2}{7}$

4. a. $\frac{99}{130}$

   b. $\frac{31}{130}$

5. a. $\frac{5}{8}$, 0.625, 62.5%

   b. $\frac{3}{8}$, 0.375, 37.5%

Practice and Problem Solving: C

1. a. $\frac{1}{150}$

   b. 14

2. a. $\frac{9}{200}$

   b. 270

3. a. $\frac{24}{25}$

   b. 400

4. a. $\frac{13}{8000}$

   b. Yes. The percent of defective spark plugs is 0.1625%, which is less than 2%.

5. a. $\frac{23}{300}$

   b. No. The percent of defective switches is 7.67%, which is greater than 1.5%.

Practice and Problem Solving: D

1. a. 9

   b. 15

   c. $\frac{9}{15} = \frac{3}{5}$

2. a. 40

   b. 48

   c. $\frac{40}{48} = \frac{5}{6}$

3. a. 36

   b. 132

   c. $\frac{36}{132} = \frac{3}{11}$

   d. $\frac{96}{132} = \frac{8}{11}$

Reteach

1. a. 12

   b. 15

   c. $\frac{12}{15} = \frac{4}{5}$

2. a. 9

   b. 14

   c. $\frac{9}{14}$

3. $P(\text{catch}) = \frac{4}{5}$; $P(\text{no catch}) = 1 - \frac{4}{5} = \frac{1}{5}$

Reading Strategies

1. 3; Sample: There are more 3's than any other number, so the probability that you will land on 3 is would be greater than the probability for the other numbers.

2. 1; Sample: There is only one 1, so the probability that you will on 1 is lower than the probability you will land on the other numbers.

3. Sample: No, I predicted the cube would land on 1 the least number of times.

4. Sample: No, I predicted the cube would land on 3 most often.

Success for English Learners

1. a. 28

   b. 40

   c. $\frac{28}{40} = \frac{7}{10}$

2. $\frac{18}{52} = \frac{9}{26}$; $1 - \frac{9}{26} = \frac{17}{26}$

3. Sample answer: Elena tossed a coin 30 times. It landed on heads 18 times. What is the experimental probability the coin will land on heads on the next toss? $\left(\frac{18}{30} = \frac{3}{5}\right)$

LESSON 12-3

Practice and Problem Solving: A/B

1. $\frac{62}{354} = \frac{31}{177}$

2. $\frac{39}{160}$

3. $\frac{23}{137}$

4. $\frac{170}{190} = \frac{17}{19}$

Practice and Problem Solving: C

1. a. 50;

   b. $\frac{182}{250} = \frac{91}{125}$

2. Sample answer: You could use a spinner with 3 equal sections for the individual, pair, and team. You could use notecards for the artistry points, and a number cube for the precision points.

3. Sample answer: Tossing two number cubes to advance around a board game.

4. Sample answer: Boys and girls being assigned to either a science class or a reading class when the number of boys and girls is not equal.

Practice and Problem Solving: D

1. a. 32

   b. 100

   c. $\frac{32}{100} = \frac{8}{25}$

2. $\frac{8}{50} = \frac{4}{25}$

3. $\frac{45}{200} = \frac{9}{40}$

Reteach

1. 200

2. $\frac{19}{200}$

3. $\frac{85}{200} = \frac{17}{40}$

4. $\frac{136}{200} = \frac{17}{25}$

Reading Strategies

1.

Section	Heads	Tails
1	3	4
2	2	3
3	5	3

2. $\frac{3}{20}$

3. $\frac{1}{10}$

4. $\frac{9}{10}$

5. $\frac{1}{2}$

Success for English Learners

1. a. 5

   b. $\frac{5}{50} = \frac{1}{10}$

2. a. $4 + 3 + 6 + 4 + 4 + 5 = 26$

   b. $\dfrac{26}{50} = \dfrac{13}{25}$

   c. $1 - \dfrac{13}{25} = \dfrac{12}{25}$

LESSON 12-4

Practice and Problem Solving: A/B

1. 140 times
2. 135 serves
3. 64 days
4. 330 people
5. 298 times
6. 49 shots
7. in Classes 1 and 3, because the percents preferring digital were 80% and 81%

Practice and Problem Solving: C

1. Yes, they should keep their plans. The location is likely to provide over 9 days without rain.
2. The train is more reliable. The bus is on-time 87.5% of the time, while the train is on-time 90% of the time.
3. No. It is likely to snow heavily more than two of the days.
4. a. DEF provides more reliable service. They are late only 13% of the time, while ABC is late more than 14% of the time.

   b. DEF did better than its average on Thursday and Friday, with delays of 9% and 10%.

Practice and Problem Solving: D

1. 40; 40
2. 570; 570
3. 15.675; 16
4. a. Math: 45 h; Science: 20 h; Social Studies: 18 h; Language Arts: 17 h

   b. Math: 33.8 h; Science: 15 h; Social Studies: 13.5 h; Language Arts: 12.8 h

Reteach

1. $\dfrac{25}{100} = \dfrac{x}{120}$; 30; 30

2. 495; 495

Reading Strategies

1. 4;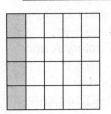

2. 9
3. Yes. The subway has been on time about 90% of the time. The elevated train is on time about 96% of the time.

Success for English Learners

1. No; $\dfrac{32}{91} = \dfrac{x}{14}$; $x = 4.9$, or about 5 days;

   $14 - 5 = 9$ days

2. Yes; $\dfrac{10}{62} = \dfrac{x}{14}$; $x = 2.3$, or about 2 days;

   $14 - 2 = 12$ days

MODULE 12 Challenge

1. The expected daily number of defective toys produced in each factory is calculated by multiplying the probability of producing a defective toy by the total production in each factory.

   Factory A: $\dfrac{2}{49} \times 3{,}000 \approx 122$

   Factory B: $\dfrac{17}{99} \times 3{,}300 \approx 567$

   Factory C: $\dfrac{13}{70} \times 2{,}900 \approx 539$

   Factory D: $\dfrac{11}{83} \times 3{,}200 \approx 424$

   Factory A produces the least defective toys.

2. Shlomo can select Factory A or Factory D. Factory A produces $3{,}000 - 122 = 2{,}878$ toys that can be sold. Factory D produces $3{,}200 - 424 = 2{,}776$ toys that can be sold.

3. Factory A produces $3{,}000 - 122 = 2{,}878$ toys that can be sold. Factory C produces $2{,}900 - 539 = 2{,}361$ toys that can be sold. The two factories produce $2{,}878 + 2{,}361 = 5{,}239$ toys that can be sold in one day. The total revenue produced by the factory

is 5,239 × $29.99 = $157,117.61.
Each day Factory A spends 3,000 ×
$2.39 = $7,170 to produce toys.
Each day Factory C spends 2,900 ×
$1.89 = $5,481 to produce toys.
The total expenses in Factory A and
Factory C are $7,170 + $5,481 = $12,651.
The profit earned in one day is
$157,117.61 − $12,651 = $144,466.61.

MODULE 13 Theoretical Probability and Simulations

LESSON 13-1

Practice and Problem Solving: A/B

1. $\frac{1}{2}$

2. $\frac{1}{3}$

3. 0.3

4. $\frac{7}{9}$

5. D

6. C

7. E

8. B

9. A

10. $\frac{4}{23}$

11. $\frac{18}{23}$

12. $1 - \frac{4}{23} = \frac{19}{23}$

13. 0

Practice and Problem Solving: C

1. $\frac{9}{14}$

2. $\frac{4}{13}$

3. $\frac{3}{4}$

4. 20

5. 250

6. 10 cats

7. $\frac{4}{17}$

8. $\frac{9}{34}$

9. $\frac{34}{34}$ or 1. Since there are no goldfish in the show, it is certain that one will not be picked.

Practice and Problem Solving: D

1. $\frac{7}{25}$

2. $\frac{1}{5}$

3. $\frac{1}{4}; \frac{3}{4}$

4. $\frac{3}{40}; \frac{37}{40}$

5. $\frac{3}{10}$; 0.3; 30%

6. $\frac{1}{10}$; 0.1; 10%

7. $\frac{6}{10}$ or $\frac{3}{5}$; 0.6; 60%

Reteach

1. $\frac{8}{15}$

2. 12 bottles of orange juice and cranberry juice

3. a. $\frac{7}{20}$

   b. $\frac{13}{20}$

4. 0.75

5. 0.05

Reading Strategies

1. a. heads or tails

   b. heads

   c. 0.5 or $\frac{1}{2}$

2. a. any of the 9 players

b. an outfielder

c. $\frac{3}{9}$ or $\frac{1}{3}$

3. a. outcomes

  b. event

  c. theoretical probability

Success for English Learners

1. $\frac{6}{18}$ or $\frac{1}{3}$

2. $\frac{5}{13}$

LESSON 13-2

Practice and Problem Solving: A/B

1. (Taco, Cheese), (Taco, Salsa), (Taco, Veggie)

2. (Burrito, Cheese), (Taco, Cheese), (Wrap, Cheese)

3. P(Burrito/Cheese) $= \frac{1}{9}$; P(Taco or Wrap with salsa) $= \frac{2}{9}$;

   P(Burrito/Cheese and Taco or Wrap with Salsa) $= \frac{1}{9} \times \frac{2}{9} = \frac{2}{81}$, since these are independent events.

4. $\frac{1}{8}$

5. $1 - \frac{3}{20} = \frac{17}{20}$

6. $P = \frac{1}{8} \times \frac{17}{20} = \frac{17}{160}$, since these are independent events.

7. $P = 0$. There are no pliers in the second basket.

Practice and Problem Solving: C

1. P(blue) $+ P$(white) $= P$(blue or white) $= 1$

2. Let $B =$ blue and $W =$ white. $P(X) \bullet P(B) = 0.18$; $P(X) \bullet P(W) = 0.12$; $0.18 \bullet P(W) = 0.12 \bullet P(B)$ and from Ex. 1, $P(B) + P(W) = 1$, which gives $P(B) = 0.6$ and $P(W) = 0.4$.

3. The values of P(B) and P(W) can be used with either row of brands X, Y, and Z to find those values by a process of elimination:

   $P(X) = 0.3$; $P(Y) = 0.2$; $P(Z) = 0.5$

4. $P(B) \bullet P(Y) = 0.6 \bullet 0.2 = 0.12$

5. $P(W) \bullet P(Z) = 0.4 \bullet 0.5 = 0.2$

6. a. P(metamorphic) $\bullet P$(pebbles) $= 0.6 \bullet 0.6 = 0.36$

   b. P(igneous) $= 0.25$, so pebbles: $(0.25)(0.6) = 0.15$; small rocks: $(0.25)(0.2) = 0.05$; medium rocks: $(0.25)(0.15) = 0.0375$; boulders: $(0.25)(0.05) = 0.0125$

Practice and Problem Solving: D

1. calculator: $\frac{1}{4}$; $\frac{1}{4}$; $\frac{1}{4}$; $\frac{1}{4}$; ruler:

   $\frac{1}{3}$; $\frac{1}{3}$; $\frac{1}{3}$; $\frac{1}{3}$; $\frac{1}{3}$; $\frac{1}{3}$; $\frac{1}{3}$; $\frac{1}{3}$; $\frac{1}{3}$; $\frac{1}{3}$; $\frac{1}{3}$; $\frac{1}{3}$

   each combination of calculator and ruler: $\frac{1}{12}$; $\frac{1}{12}$; $\frac{1}{12}$; $\frac{1}{12}$; $\frac{1}{12}$; $\frac{1}{12}$; $\frac{1}{12}$; $\frac{1}{12}$; $\frac{1}{12}$;

   $\frac{1}{12}$; $\frac{1}{12}$; $\frac{1}{12}$

2. $\frac{1}{4}$

3. $\frac{1}{3}$

4. $\frac{1}{3} \times \frac{1}{4} = \frac{1}{12}$

5. a. two: (heads, tails)

   b. six: (1, 2, 3, 4, 5, 6)

   c. twelve: (H1, H2, H3, H4, H5, H6, T1, T2, T3, T4, T5, T6)

Reteach

1–2.

		Ellen				
		M	P	R	S	W
Sam	M	O	⊗	⊗	O	O
	P		×	×		
	R		×	×		
	S	O	⊗	⊗	O	O
	W		×	×		

3. 4 possibilities

4. $P = \dfrac{4}{25}$

Reading Strategies

1. There are 3 events: picking pants, shirts, and scarves; 2 pants × 2 shirts × 2 scarves give 8 choices. Answers will vary. Sample answer: Use a tree diagram.

2. There are two events: person, movie genre; 2 people × 2 movie genres give 4 choices. Answers will vary. Sample answer: Use a list.

3. There are more than three events: 36 products and 36 sums. For an even product, there are 27 choices; for an even sum, there are 18 choices. Use a table.

Success for English Learners

1. They are duplicates.

2. Sample answer: The "doubles" such as C-C ad GO-GO form a diagonal from upper left to lower right.

3. Sample answer: tree diagram

LESSON 13-3

Practice and Problem Solving: A/B

1. $\dfrac{1}{2}$

2. 32

3. $\dfrac{1}{5}$

4. 12

5. $\dfrac{1}{3}$

6. 13

7. $\dfrac{5}{8}$

8. 125

9. 26

10. about 26

11. about 153

12. 4

Practice and Problem Solving: C

1. a. 36

  b. $\dfrac{5}{36}$

  c. 25

  d. 25

2. a. 36

  b. 20

  c. 30

  d. 85

3. a. 16

  b. 36

  c. 24

Practice and Problem Solving: D

1. $\dfrac{1}{2}$

2. $\dfrac{1}{3}$

3. $\dfrac{1}{5}$

4. $\dfrac{2}{5}$

5. $\dfrac{1}{2} \times 4 = \dfrac{1}{2} \times \dfrac{4}{1} = \dfrac{4}{2} = 2$

6. $\dfrac{1}{4} \times 16 = \dfrac{1}{4} \times \dfrac{16}{1} = \dfrac{16}{4} = 4$

7. $\dfrac{1}{6} \times 12 = \dfrac{1}{6} \times \dfrac{12}{1} = \dfrac{12}{6} = 2$

8. $\dfrac{1}{3} \times 15 = \dfrac{1}{3} \times \dfrac{15}{1} = \dfrac{15}{3} = 5$

Reteach

1. $\dfrac{1}{2}$

2. 10

3. $\dfrac{1}{4}$

4. 20

Reading Strategies

1. 4
2. 5
3. 8
4. 8

Success for English Learners

1. Theoretical probability is based on what should happen. Experimental probability is based on what has already happened.

2. To make a prediction, multiply the theoretical probability times the number of trials.

3. Answers may vary. Sample answer: Max rolls a number cube labeled 1–6 a total of 60 times. How many times can he expect the cube to land on 6? (10)

LESSON 13-4

Practice and Problem Solving: A/B

1. a. He or she runs multiple trials with 5 random numbers between 1 and 10 in each.

   b.

Trial	Numbers Generated	Shrimp Caught	Trial	Numbers Generated	Shrimp Caught
1	7, 3, 2, 7, 10	1	6	8, 4, 7, 6, 5	0
2	2, 4, 5, 3, 10	1	7	6, 10, 1, 7, 6	1
3	9, 9, 7, 6, 6	0	8	7, 9, 8, 3, 8	0
4	7, 9, 6, 6, 4	0	9	1, 4, 4, 8, 9	1
5	10, 6, 4, 6, 4	0	10	7, 8, 9, 5, 3	0

2. $\frac{4}{10}$ or 0.4

3. a. Let "1" represent seats with a prize and numbers 2 – 10 seats without a prize. Run multiple trials with the numbers 1 – 10 until a "1" appears. Record the number of seats reserved with each trial until the "1" appears.

   b. Answers will vary, but a "1" has to appear in the list.

Practice and Problem Solving: C

1. Results will vary, but model should use randomly generated numbers 1–10. Since the chance of making more than 4 goals is 30%, the chance of making 4 goals or less is 70% or 7 out of 10, so generate

7 numbers for each trial. Count the number of trials in which 4 appears, and divide it by the number of trials (5) to find the experimental probability. Sample answer:

Trial	Numbers Generated	Result
1	5, 9, 2, 1, 1, 5, 7	0
2	1, 8, 5, 10, 5, 8, 3	0
3	4, 6, 6, 8, 8, 7, 6	1
4	5, 7, 9, 3, 9, 10, 6	0
5	6, 7, 9, 9, 2, 4, 3	1

2. The experimental probability for 5 trials of a trial containing a 4 is $\frac{2}{5}$, or 0.4.

3. Answers will vary. Sample answer: It will be the same because the chance of getting a 4 is the same.

4. Results will vary. Sample answer:

Trial	Numbers Generated	Result
6	8, 9, 10, 9, 1, 6, 3	0
7	6, 5, 5, 8, 5, 7, 10	0
8	5, 7, 8, 10, 6, 4, 9	1
9	7, 7, 6, 1, 9, 1, 9	0
10	6, 8, 7, 7, 2, 4, 9	1

5. The experimental probability for 10 trials of a trial containing a 4 is $\frac{4}{10}$, or 0.4.

Practice and Problem Solving: D

1. a. $\frac{1}{4}$

   b. Answers will vary. Sample answer: 1

   c. Answers will vary. Sample answer: 2, 3, and 4

2. Results will vary. Sample answer:

Trial	Numbers Generated	Pizzas Bought	Trial	Numbers Generated	Pizzas Bought
1	3, 1, 1, 3	4	6	4, 2, 4, 3	4
2	3, 2, 4, 2	4	7	1, 1, 1, 2	4
3	2, 4, 3, 3	4	8	3, 4, 1, 4	4
4	3, 4, 2, 1	4	9	3, 2, 3, 4	4
5	2, 3, 1, 2	4	10	2, 3, 2, 2	4

Trial 1 is a winner since it has at least one 1. Trial 2 is not a winner, because it does not have a 1.

3. 5; 0.5 or $\frac{1}{2}$

Reteach

1. Results will vary. Sample answer:

Trial	Numbers Generated	Result	Trial	Numbers Generated	Result
1	1, 1, 1, 1, 1	5	6	1, 0, 1, 0, 0	2
2	0, 0, 1, 1, 1	3	7	1, 1, 0, 1, 1	4
3	1, 0, 1, 0, 1	3	8	1, 1, 0, 0, 1	3
4	0, 0, 1, 0, 0	1	9	0, 1, 1, 0, 0	2
5	1, 0, 0, 0, 0	1	10	0, 1, 0, 0, 1	2

The experimental probability is 5 out 10, 0.5, 50 percent, or one half or more that an outcome has a 50–50 chance or greater of occurring.

2. Results will vary. Sample answer: Let 1 and 2 represent the probability that an event occurs; let 3–5 be the probability that it does not occur.

Trial	Numbers Generated	Result	Trial	Numbers Generated	Result
1	4, 4, 3, 4, 4	0	6	3, 2, 1, 5, 3	2
2	3, 5, 2, 4, 2	1	7	2, 1, 3, 4, 2	3
3	2, 5, 5, 4, 3	1	8	2, 2, 1, 5, 3	3
4	3, 3, 4, 4, 1	1	9	2, 3, 2, 4, 1	3
5	2, 2, 1, 4, 1	4	10	2, 5, 5, 1, 3	1

The experimental probability is 3 out of 10, 0.3, 30 percent, or three tenths that an outcome has a 3 in 5 chance of occurring.

Reading Strategies

1. 1 out of 4; use the numbers 1–4 for randomization with 1 being the favorable outcome. Experimental probability results will vary, but only the outcome of 1 will be counted as a favorable result when it occurs exactly twice out of 10 randomizations of the numbers 1–4, e.g. **1**, 2, 4, 2, **1**, 3, 4, 2, 2, 4

2. 7 out of 8; use the numbers 1–8 for randomization with 1–7 being favorable outcomes. Experimental probability results will vary, but only one of the outcomes 1–7 will be counted as a favorable result out of 10 randomizations of the numbers 1–8, e.g. **6, 5, 4, 6, 3**, 8, **1, 5, 3, 7**

Success for English Learners

1. Answers will vary. Results or outcomes of 5 should be counted. Experimental probability should be near 17%.

2. Answers will vary. Results or outcomes of 1, 3, and 5 should be counted. Experimental probability should be near 50%.

3. Choices will vary. Some possibilities include the number 3, numbers less than 4, and numbers divisible by 3.

MODULE 13 Challenge

1. The probability that the arrow will land inside the circle is equal to the area of the circle divided by the area of the square. Let the side of the square have length x. The area of the square is then $x(x) = x^2$. The diameter of the circle is x, since the circle is inscribed in the square. The radius of the circle is half the length of the diameter, or $\frac{x}{2}$.

The area of the circle is given by the formula $A = \pi r^2$; $\pi \left(\frac{x}{2}\right)^2 = \frac{\pi x^2}{4}$.

The probability of the arrow landing inside the circle equals $\frac{\frac{\pi x^2}{4}}{x^2} = \frac{\pi}{4} \approx 0.785$.

2. a. Tobias is not correct. According to the simulation the probability of two or more days of rain per week equals 0.3 (Trials 1, 8, and 10 are weeks in which there were two or more rainy days). The probability of no rainy days in a week is 0.3 (Trials 4, 6, and 7 produced no rainy days). The probability of no rainy days is the same as the probability of two or more rainy days.

b. The probability of 0 rainy days is 0.3 (Trials 4, 6, 7).
The probability of 1 rainy day is 0.4 (Trials 2, 3, 5 and 9).
The probability of 2 rainy days is 0.
The probability of 3 rainy days is 0.2 (Trials 1 and 8).
The probability of 4 rainy days is 0.1 (Trial 10).
The probability of 5, 6 or 7 rainy days is 0.
One rainy day per week is most likely.